Strategic management applied to international construction

R. Howes and J. H. M. Tah

 ThomasTelford

Published by Thomas Telford Publishing, 1 Heron Quay, London E14 4JD.
www.thomastelford.com

Distributors for Thomas Telford books are
USA: ASCE Press, 1801 Alexander Bell Drive, Reston, VA 20191-4400, USA
Japan: Maruzen Co. Ltd, Book Department, 3–10 Nihonbashi 2-chome, Chuo-ku, Tokyo 103
Australia: DA Books and Journals, 648 Whitehorse Road, Mitcham 3132, Victoria

First published 2003

Front cover: International Finance Centre, Hong Kong.

A catalogue record for this book is available from the British Library

ISBN: 0 7277 3211 0

Printed and bound by CPI Group (UK) Ltd, Croydon, CR0 4YY

Foreword

Given the increasing pace of globalization, the commencement of the twenty-first century is a good time to write a book about the strategies to be adopted for the international management of all aspects relating to construction. Our investigation of the topic has indicated that there was a need for a book to provide a broad coverage of the knowledge required to address strategic issues related to the business of construction on a global scale.

Over the past 50 years there has been a steady increase in the number of construction businesses operating on a global basis and these have typically included design consultancies, contractors, property managers, material suppliers, equipment manufacturers and other specialists who provided services and products. Many companies have, in addition to their core business, diversified into specialisms by setting up or acquiring subsidiaries to operate nationally, regionally or globally. In recent years, three key developments have transformed the international business market into an integrated holistic global community. The first and most dramatic has been the development and improvement of communication systems, including satellite technology and the step function development of computer information technology. This has led to widespread use of the Internet and the development of e-commerce. In effect, the Internet has provided for instant global interactivity on a 24-hour basis where the relationship between time and distance has been revolutionized, thus presenting possibilities not dreamt of 25 years ago. The second is the manner in which international trade has developed since the end of the Second World War. The establishment of the United Nations and associated bodies such as the World Health Organisation and the United Nations Educational, Scientific and Cultural Organisation was a first step in encouraging nations to work together to solve world problems. Since then, governments have set up a number of organizations to help develop and regulate the world economy and international trade. The most prominent of these include the International Monetary Fund, World Trade Organisation and the General Agreement on Trade and Tariffs. There has also been the development and integration of countries into regional trading blocks and communities such as the European Union (EU), North Atlantic Free Trade Area (NAFTA) and the Association of South East-Asian Nations (ASEAN). Another body that acts in the interest of its membership is the Organisation for

Economic and Cultural Development (OECD). The establishment of the World Bank by the world's strongest economies to assist poorer nations with funding and loans, followed by the establishment of regional development banks and aid agencies have done much to support the reduction in poverty and improvement in living standards in the world's poorest countries. The third and most recent development has been the realization that most of the world's resources are finite and will not support current rates of economic and industrial growth indefinitely. Linked to this has been the discovery of strong evidence that the world's climate is being dramatically affected by atmospheric pollution caused by carbon and other pollution agents such as ozone. Hence, emphasis is being placed on reducing greenhouse gases, the development of sustainable solutions and the conservation of non-replaceable resources.

The impact of these factors is currently having a significant effect on global construction and will continue to do so in the foreseeable future. Governments and businesses are now working in an integrated manner, since the realization that the world economy and the environment cannot be divided up and treated separately. The primary investigation necessary to write this book has shown the dramatic growth in business alliances and networks where construction organizations are striving to offer clients more holistic and better quality solutions to meet their needs created by the increasingly complex demands of the global market-place.

This book has been written to appeal to a worldwide readership. Unlike previous texts in this category, it is not biased towards practice in any particular country. Instead, it provides knowledge that is universally applicable and the case studies provide important demonstrations of current best practice by American, Japanese and European organizations.

The book contains essential information and knowledge for postgraduate students studying construction management and it will also be a reference tool for undergraduates who are studying specialist options, or who have selected subjects related to international construction as a final year dissertation topic. The book will also be of interest to practitioners across all related construction disciplines who are seeking to supplement their strategic business and supportive knowledge and expertise in the broad spectrum of international construction. Profiles and case studies involving the world's leading consultants, contractors and suppliers of products, materials and construction equipment are included at the end of each chapter. Numerous illustrations support the text. Further reading references have been provided for readers who wish to expand their knowledge in a particular area covered by the book.

Rod Howes and Joe Tah
July 2002

Contents

List of profiles and case studies

List of figures

Chapter 1

Introduction

Preamble

The development of strategies for international construction demands knowledge and expertise beyond that required for domestic construction. Socio, economic, political and cultural factors come into play and these must be recognized and understood. This book covers the broad range of areas that comprise the subject of strategic management as it relates to the business of international construction. It is therefore not intended to be a definitive text in any specialist topic, but it does provide the reader with a solid foundation of knowledge and understanding that will enable development in the light of experience and further study. The theories, processes and practices described are supplemented by company profiles and case studies that provide examples of application and further insight into practice. Reading references are provided at the end of each chapter to give direction for further study and investigation of selected topics.

The book focuses on bringing together and interrelating the broad range of knowledge required by the subject and care has been taken to ensure international applicability. Detailed consideration has not been given to legal and contractual requirements and other matters, which relate to any particular country or state. Instead, broad principles and paradigms have been described which are generically applicable across national boundaries and provide the foundation for internationally accepted practice. The strength of the book lies in its neutrality, which makes it easier to identify the core knowledge required to address strategies applicable to international construction that are capable of transcending the differences in national culture, society and practice. This aspect is especially important given that the global construction industry is now a reality, rather than a theoretical view based on exemplars provided by individual companies that have transformed themselves into multinational enterprises.

Reference has been made in the text to the international construction company, which should be interpreted as a multinational organization offering a complete range of construction services from project inception to final completion. These services include design consultancy, construction management and other specialist functions, including facility management. Design consultants and specialists are referred to in their own right and contractors are concerned with the construction process only. Global construction companies are those organizations that operate throughout the world and are recognized for their activities in the global market, rather than maintaining a national identity associated with their home country base.

Material, product and equipment suppliers who share the same international and global distinction may be involved with industries other than construction and, under normal circumstances, they will not be directly involved with the construction process. The strategic management of manufacturing is not covered, but reference is made to the major role that manufacturing plays in the construction supply chain. Manufacturers are subject to similar environmental and marketing conditions to those in construction and the text recognizes the importance of supply chain management and the development of partnering and strategic alliances between members from both industries.

Profiles and case studies have been included at the end of each chapter to reinforce the points made in the text and to illustrate the practical application of principles and accepted paradigms concerning the development of corporate strategy suitable for the business of international construction. Care has been taken to select cases that provide exemplars of best practice and present a novel illustration that will be of interest to the reader. The reading references provided are for readers who wish to extend their knowledge in a particular area beyond the limitations of this text. The Internet is now a valuable source of current relevant information and key site addresses have also been included.

Preparation for entry into international construction

The decision to enter the international construction market requires a considerable amount of effort aimed at collecting sufficient information to provide a sound basis on which to develop a business strategy. The purpose of Chapter 2 is to introduce the subject from its inception by providing a framework, which identifies the factors that should be considered and evaluated to test the strategy for entry into a new international market. The approach is introductory and it provides the context necessary to link the key elements of the subject.

The magnitude of foreign market entry is emphasized since there is a major difference between a relatively small-scale operation concerning just one project and the decision to acquire full ownership of a foreign company. The tendency at the outset is to manage and control operations from a home base, and this is highlighted in relation to the degree of risk involved. This approach enables knowledge and experience to be acquired and, in the event that the venture is not successful, then withdrawal can be achieved quickly without substantial financial loss. Recognition has been given to the different strategic approaches necessary to be taken by consultants, contractors and suppliers and the distinction has been made between project-based construction activities and manufacturing that forms part of the construction supply chain. The degree of ownership is recognized as a key factor in the development of a strategy. Reference has been made to the appointment of agents, local partners and the establishment of joint ventures. These aspects will be developed later in the book alongside strategic alliances, franchises, mergers, acquisitions and divestitures.

International trade and the nature of international construction

An overview of world economic performance and trade is provided in Chapter 3. The intention is to profile and locate the world's economic wealth and to measure relative national economic performance. The principles of international trade are outlined and these are related to the activities of world trade bodies such as the World Trade Organisation (WTO), General Agreement on Tariffs and Trade (GATT) and the Organisation for Economic Development and Co-operation (OECD). Trade barriers and tariffs are matters that concern companies that trade across international boundaries and the reasons for national governments implementing these measures are described. Case studies are provided concerning the activities of WTO and GATT.

Countries have been classified as advanced industrialized (AIC), newly industrialized (NIC) and least developed (LDC). From the analysis provided it is obvious that the majority of construction activity occurs in AICs and the NICs provide data that may offer clues as to how the construction market is likely to change in future (Bon and Crosswaite, 2000). LDCs have been shown to have least economic activity and the majority of construction work is funded through the World Bank, regional development banks and aid agencies. A picture is given of the global construction market and its relationship with world trends in wealth and major political and social developments. Attention is drawn to the opportunities presented for business on a global scale since the end of the 'cold war' and the opening up of markets in the former USSR and the so-called 'eastern block' states. Reference is made to the growth of the Chinese construction market and the potential that may be represented by China's phased entry into the World Trade Organisation.

The contribution made to globalization by developments in communication, technology, transportation and shipping has been recognized. These developments have facilitated growth by supporting international business activity between companies leading to mergers and acquisitions. This classification is then used to examine the scale and nature of the construction market. Bon and Crosswaite (2000) provide a useful analysis of the international spend on construction according to a percentage of GDP of each country and region. This research has been used in conjunction with GDP statistics published by the IMF (2001) and the OECD (2002) to determine the overall scale dispersion of the global construction market. An overview is given of the main providers in the international construction market. The top 20 international construction consultants and the top 20 international contractors between 1994 and 2001 have been identified to establish the nations which are currently providing the expertise and the changes that have taken place over the past seven years, notably the decline in influence of the Japanese construction industry on the global construction market. The country profile of China as an international construction market and the company profile of the Caterpillar Corporation provide a more detailed insight into operating on a global scale.

Corporate strategy

The development of a sound and robust corporate strategy is essential to success in the international construction market. Chapter 4 examines the factors that contribute to the success of a strategy aimed at profitability and growth derived from operating internationally and globally. Porter's seminal work concerning industrial and national competitiveness is explained and applied. The Boston Consulting Group model is described as an alternative approach to the determination of the business portfolio.

Different approaches to global strategy are explained and the importance of periodic review, taking into account internal strengths and weaknesses, is stressed. Opportunities and threats are presented by the dynamics of the market and environmental changes and it is proposed that these should be kept under constant surveillance and review. Risk is categorized as political, financial, business and climatic and the methods of risk assessment are described.

Questions are posed concerning the formulation of a competitive corporate strategy. Possible outcomes are considered in the form of internal restructuring or by corporate mergers, acquisitions or divestments. Given the importance of merger and acquisition activity to international and global growth, more detailed consideration is given to the processes involved, including the importance of due diligence and an accurate valuation of the benefits to be derived. Joint ventures and strategic alliances are described as alternative approaches that are geared to specific projects or to agreements and understandings regarding how and where goods and services are marketed and sold. The chapter concludes with company profiles of two global organizations operating very different but successful policies and strategies in support of their corporate objectives. These provide the reader with a view of the importance of strategic implementation through the corporate organization structure and the business portfolio, supported by systems and processes geared to producing the outputs of the business.

Marketing, competitive advantage and procurement

Chapter 5 sets out to provide a framework for the development of a sound marketing strategy that will exploit corporate strengths in the face of competition, while minimizing risk. The functions of marketing are described and these are related to construction services, products, materials and equipment supplied to global, regional and national markets. Market research is explained, together with the role that it plays in providing the necessary intelligence and information on which business judgements and decisions will be taken. The survival and continuing success of an organisation depends on its ability to keep up to speed with technological development and its ability to innovate and develop new competitive services and products. The relationship between innovation and research is explained and new product development is described.

The processes by which clients procure construction projects are a major element in the strategy adopted by consultants, construction companies and contractors. These have been collectively described as traditional and non-traditional. The prime procurement routes have been described and their advantages and disadvantages have been identified. Risk associated with procurement route selection is also covered. The growing importance of public/private partnerships involving the use of private money to finance public projects has been highlighted alongside changes to the construction business involving concessions to generate income through the operation of buildings over predetermined periods of time.

International construction finance

The finance of construction activity on an international scale is more complicated than for the domestic market and requires specialist knowledge of the global financial market and prior knowledge of national, regional and global economic prospects. The strength of national economies, exchange rates and currency controls are important factors that need to be understood and taken into account in strategic decision-making. Chapter 6 opens with a description of the sources of finance for international construction and an explanation is given of the cost of capital. The international financial system is outlined and the method of calculating the key economic indicator of gross national product (GNP) is described.

Financial aid and assistance for developing countries is normally provided by means of the World Bank, regional development banks and aid agencies. Criteria for the approval and distribution of financial resources are provided and the processes of application and approval are explained.

A section is devoted to the financial evaluation of mergers and acquisitions and the importance of the realistic assessment of the intangible as well as the tangible factors that comprise a valuation is highlighted. Strategies for the financial management of multinational construction companies and consultancies are outlined and a key aspect is the degree of decentralization of control and financial autonomy. Risk is assessed in relation to foreign exchange and the influencing factors are identified. The chapter concludes with a brief account of the assistance available to exporters of goods and services by national governments.

International management culture

The prospects for intercultural management are examined in Chapter 7. The means of profiling and identifying the nature of cultures are explained and some conclusions are drawn. The chapter commences with the need to build a cultural map in order to increase understanding of the issues and elements that drive different cultures. Cross-cultural management factors are described and these are extended to include the dimensions of culture proposed by Hofstede (1980, 1991, 1993, 2001). The concepts of ethnocentralism, polycentralism and geocentralism are described and their effect in relation to local cultures is discussed. A further analysis by Triandis (1995) relating to individualism and collectivism is also described and evaluated. The chapter concludes with a brief appraisal of working cultures and the phases of cultural development appropriate to an international construction company.

International human resource management

International human resource management plays a fundamental role in the effective delivery of corporate objectives that are heavily dependent on human knowledge, expertise and commitment. Chapter 8 seeks to establish the importance of the interaction between the management of human resources and corporate strategies and management decision-making. Models of human resource management are proposed that have applicability to international construction related organizations and features presented by each of the models are evaluated. The basic functions of international human resources management are described and different national approaches to industrial relations are discussed. The chapter concludes with an outline of health and safety policies and how they should be applied according to corporate policies and national statutes and legislation.

Organization structure and management systems

Successfully conducting an international company whose business is concerned with construction depends on an efficient organization structure that provides the management and decision-making framework. This in itself will be insufficient without a closely integrated operational system determining the processes and procedures necessary to achieve the transformation of inputs into outputs in the form of desirable services and products. Chapter 9 explains the principles and influencing factors that determine the selection and evolution of organisation structures. Project organization structures are analysed and the advantages of matrix project management structures are explained.

The relationship between organization structures and systems is discussed and the principles of the systems approach are described. A methodology is proposed for the conduct of systems analysis that can be applied to an existing business to improve efficiency and productivity. Systems theory is then extended to soft systems methodology (SSM) and its application is described. Systems theory is then further developed to include an explanation of critical systems thinking that provides a universal approach to the consideration and integration of all relevant factors influencing the selection of corporate strategy.

Communications

The relevance, quality and interactive nature of communication are essential components in the effective management of an international business and there have been considerable recent developments in the means of achieving instant global communication. Chapter 10 presents the basic components of the communication process and discusses the implications on international and global organizations with respect to the influences of different languages and cultures. Reference is made to electronic communication and the use of the Internet. Intranets and extranets are defined and standards are described for the exchange of information. The case studies provided illustrate the successful use of web-based project collaborative systems involving multiple partners from different countries with different languages.

Project management strategies

International construction is primarily project based and many of the latest projects are concerned with new or improved infrastructure associated with power generation and distribution, water, sewerage treatment and transport systems and facilities. Other projects are associated with public, industrial and commercial buildings, together with housing and social facilities. Chapter 11 is concerned with the efficient management of the design and construction of construction projects and seeks to identify and describe the decisions, actions and arrangements that are required to realize projects within budget, on time and to the quality standards specified. Account is taken of location and the environment within which projects are to be completed. Importance is attached to the integration of design and construction in the task of complying with and, where possible, exceeding client needs. Emphasis is given to the creation of the project supply chain and its management, together with the need for comprehensive planning, monitoring and control of the process from inception to hand-over. Project management requires strong project leadership and the need for timely management decision-making to cope with dynamic situations caused by changes occurring outside the boundary control of the project. The need for teamwork is highlighted and the advantages gained by building understanding through longer-term partnerships are described. The case studies are from examples of successful projects involving client liaison, partnering, joint venture and an integrated team approach.

Future horizons

The final chapter attempts to address the prime movers for change and makes a prognostication about the future shape and development of the global construction industry. Global construction business strategies are extrapolated in the likelihood of more mergers and acquisitions and the further development of strategic alliances.

A futures view is taken of human resource management and its development, together with an evaluation of the impact that globalization has on local cultures. Developments in technology, industrialization and standardization are recognized as major factors that will affect employment within construction.

Sustainability and conservation are identified as being the key drivers that will determine future global strategies aimed at protecting the environment and conserving non-replaceable resources and sources of energy. An evaluation is made of the likely impact that such policies will have on international business strategy. Reference has been made to emerging issues and how they will be dealt with to effect improved futures performance. The chapter concludes with the recognition of the importance of investment in innovation and research in the development of new services and products that will create improved living standards and will conserve the environment and its resources for future generations.

Finally, this book has been constructed to eliminate noise and detail to expose the main body of knowledge that provides the basis for developing corporate strategies that can be applied to international construction. It will be essential for readers to build on this knowledge according to specific situations that arise from practice. Moreover, the book should be viewed as just one step in the quest for business success in the operational field of international construction.

Further reading

Bon R. (1994), 'Whither global construction?' 1992 and 1993 European construction economics research unit opinions surveys, *Building Research and Information*, **22**, No. 2, 109–126.

Bon R. (1997), 'The future of international construction: some survey results, 1993–1996', *Building Research and Information*, **25**, No. 2, 81–85.

Bon R. and Crosswaite D. (2000), *The future of international construction*, Thomas Telford, London.

Hofstede G. (1980), *Culture's consequences: international differences and related values*, Sage Publications, Beverley Hills, CA.

Hofstede G. (1991), *Cultures and organization: software of the mind*, McGraw Hill, Maidenhead, UK.

Hofstede G. (1993), *Cultural constraints on management theories*, Academy of Management Executive, Vol. 7, No. 1, 81–93.

Hofstede G. (2001), Culture's consequences: international differences and related values, 2nd edn, Sage Publications, Beverley Hills, CA.

Mawhinney M. (2001), *International construction*, Blackwell Science Ltd, London.

Langford D. and Male S. (2002), *Strategic management in construction*, 2nd edn, Blackwell Science Ltd, London.

Langford D. and Rowland V. R. (1995), *Managing overseas construction*, Thomas Telford, London.

Najjar G. R. (2002), Issues for the globalisation of the construction industry, *Proc. CIB W55 and W65, Cincinnati, USA*.

Triandis H. C. *et al.* (2001), 'Culture and deception in business negotiations: a multi-level analysis', *Int. J. of Cross-cultural Management*, Vol. 1(1), 73–90.

Chapter 2

Preparation for entry into international construction

Introduction

A firm wishing to explore the possibility of operating on an international scale must give careful consideration to all relevant factors. Although considerable knowledge and experience of operating in a domestic market will exist, this may not transfer in its entirety to foreign markets. It will therefore be necessary to make a full appraisal of the countries or regions to be targeted. Companies already operating internationally will have gained varying degrees of experience depending on the scale of operation and the type of involvement.

When entering new markets it will be necessary to undertake a full business appraisal and to make an assessment of the risks. Research will play a key part in collecting sufficient information about opportunities and threats, and to assist this process it will be prudent to acquire knowledge of local competition and trading conditions. The decision to seek contracts and assignments in foreign countries is a major step for any business and it should be taken based on the best possible information. The decision to extend business activities to other countries will invariably be brought about by a variety of diverse reasons, but the basic aim will always be to enhance profit by developing initiatives in new business locations where competitive advantage is perceived to be achievable at an acceptable level of risk.

This chapter provides a general framework intended to identify all the relevant factors that should be considered and evaluated to test the feasibility and viability of entering new international markets. The scope of the chapter is introductory in nature and reference has been made to later chapters, where appropriate, providing cross-references to more in depth coverage. The aim is to provide an overall context in which relevant subject matter covered by the remainder of the book will be located and linked together.

The construction stakeholders

Construction entrepreneurs wishing to enter a foreign market will be primarily interested in success and the ability to provide a good return on capital invested. Although small practices and businesses have been successful in operating internationally it is normally the larger organizations that are in a better position to operate more widely.

Design consultancies normally rely on reputation and the provision of specialist expertise to attract the interest of global clients and clients from other countries. The largest global consultancies expect to derive a significant proportion of their business from foreign sources and they will continue to develop their knowledge through experience gained from working at the forefront of design concept and technology in different global regions. By sustaining a reputation and position in the market-place such businesses are able to generate a steady flow of work. Evidence presented in Chapter 3 shows how consultants from the USA and Europe have increased their share of the world market in the past decade.

Many of the most successful international construction companies have developed their service to clients by providing them with a 'one stop shop' approach involving property development, design, construction and facility management. This is normally achieved using a multi-faceted organization comprising specialist group subsidiaries; an alternative would be the use of partnerships and alliances between consultants, contractors and specialists. Contractors who competitively tender for work on an international scale are dependent on their ability to acquire and deploy resources at the keenest possible price that conforms to specifications and quality standards. Key to this requirement is the capacity to employ adequately skilled labour alongside technical and managerial staff capable of providing the quality and efficiency required to increase the likelihood of an adequate return on capital invested.

The business strategies of construction product manufacturers and material supply companies will be different to those of consultants and contractors and these will be determined by the nature of their business. At the outset they will be concerned with setting up factories, or investing in quarries and processing plants. Both avenues usually require significant capital investment well in advance of the ability to generate income, hence the level of risk requires careful assessment. A common approach will be to acquire existing companies that fit harmoniously with corporate objectives and strategies as described in Chapter 4. The overriding intention will be to increase market share and, where possible, to dominate the market within the bounds of national legislation. Another strategy may be to enter into mergers or alliances where organizations agree to develop their business interests for mutual benefit. Sourcing raw materials, processing, manufacture and marketing are key elements that should be contained in the business plans of global suppliers. The subsidiary portfolio of a global company and its development are key to growth and success. Therefore, it will be necessary to acquire and dispose of subsidiary companies according to the manner in which the market changes. Success will depend on the appropriateness of the strategy adopted and how it is applied in practice. Mistakes are often expensive and care must be taken to ensure that all assets, liabilities, commitments and legal aspects are accounted for in fixing valuations for acquisition, merger or disposal. Equipment manufacturers and suppliers have similar strategies and market conditions. Emphasis will be placed on innovation, research and development to continually seek competitive advantage in support of maintaining and expanding markets, while at the same time looking for growth in new areas.

Construction is essentially a team process where all parties involved in projects are bound by the requirement to conform to specified quality standards and to operate within budget and according to the time schedule. Therefore all entities and persons concerned with the project have a stake in its successful completion. Most important is the client who will have made the ultimate commitment to invest in the project and who has the right to expect to receive good service and value for money. Similarly, design consultants and contractors will have an interest in providing a reputable product or service in accordance with their conditions of engagement.

Seeking work in the international market

There must be sufficient motivation to encourage a firm to seek work in a foreign market. This may be generated by occurrences experienced in the home domestic market or by factors relating to developments in the global economy, regional growth or by extraordinary events that require major construction work overseas. The ability to operate successfully on an international level has always carried a degree of kudos. Most governments actively encourage and support companies to seek work in foreign countries or within federations and groups of nations such as the European Union. The export of expertise, goods and services provides foreign income and improves the balance of payments that in turn contributes to national wealth.

Where companies have already developed strengths within their home markets there may be competitive advantage and good profits to be earned by expanding into foreign markets. Alternatively, where companies are experiencing adverse domestic market trading conditions, they might be tempted to look elsewhere to find markets that have less competition and higher potential demand for their products or services. There may be other reasons for entering foreign construction markets involving production costs, material shortages, disruption, taxation or legal restrictions.

The decision to move into a foreign market should be approached in a logical manner to ensure that the correct motives apply and that real market potential exists. Figure 2.1 provides the framework to enable such complex decisions to be taken.

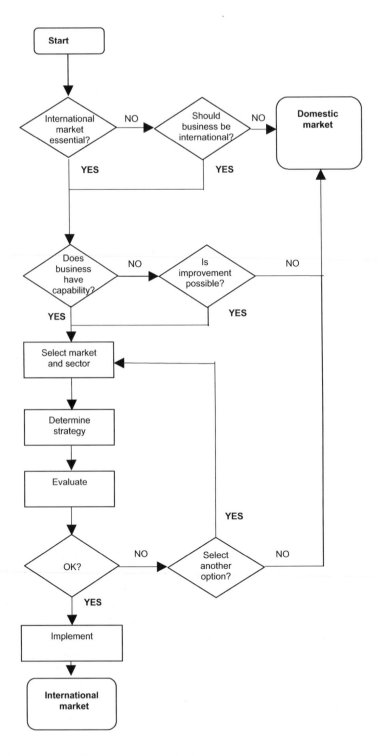

Figure 2.1: Foreign market entry decision process

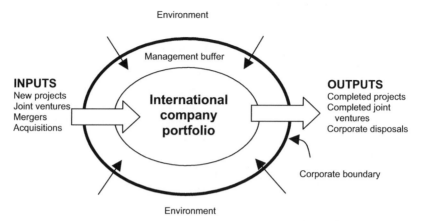

Figure 2.2: System conceptualization of the international company portfolio

The prime factors to be considered during the market evaluation will include:
- need and potential
- financial and economic considerations
- political and legal factors
- socio-cultural forces
- degree of competition
- freedom to trade
- codes and practices
- life cycles.

The conceptualization of an international organization

Before describing the structure and process of investigation and evaluation of an international market it is necessary to conceptualize an international construction organization. This can be achieved by viewing the venture as a company portfolio acting as a system that will require inputs to enable a transformation process resulting in outputs. Figure 2.2 shows the inputs as being new projects, joint ventures and corporate additions or changes to the portfolio.

Outputs are shown by completed projects and corporate disposals. The system will be open to influence from the environment and will therefore require continuous management to buffer adverse influences and to capitalize on beneficial circumstances. A prerequisite to survival is the need to change and develop business strategies according to the influence of the market. Success will be measured ultimately by the generation of growth and profitability, whereas the ability to continue the business will be threatened by losses and business failure.

Socio, economic and political environmental considerations

The decision to enter a foreign market will require evaluation of all aspects concerning the socio, economic and political environment that will affect corporate stability and the fairness of the trading environment. Investigation should include an analysis of past national and industry trends that have led to the current state of the economy and the political situation. Where possible, an attempt should be made to extrapolate likely future outcomes. In the case of entirely new ventures it is possible that there will be limited data on which to make detailed predictive judgements. Under these circumstances it will be unlikely that an analysis will be completely reliable and therefore the ability to cross-refer to other sources of information and to anticipate events intuitively will be helpful in assessing the likely success of the proposed venture.

The political situation should be assessed with regard to the type of regime and whether the system of government is currently stable and conforms to internationally accepted standards of moral and business ethics. Political systems and governments may be viewed with capitalism at one extreme and communism at the other, with various degrees of socialism existing in between. In a capitalist society companies normally have a higher degree of business freedom, but where a country's political system becomes closer to communism, less freedom will be enjoyed and constraints will be imposed by politicized rules intended to be in accord with a socialist market economy, as typified when undertaking business in China. It is worth noting that over recent years communism has been in decline and the centre of gravity has shifted towards a free market approach. Indications are that this situation, at least for the moment, seems likely to continue and prevail.

The state of individual national economies will be crucial to the likely potential of the market. The level of government spending on construction should be analysed in relation to key economic indicators such as GDP, national savings and balance of payments as described in Chapter 6. The status and strength of the national currency will be key to reducing financial risk and the ability to convert and move currency from one country to another.

Account must be taken of social values and the culture that determines the manner in which business and trading is conducted. This will also affect human behaviour in all its contexts and will influence relationships with clients, business associates and employees, as well as attitudes to change and the implementation of new ideas. Reference should be made to Chapter 7 (Hofstede, 1980, 1991, 1993, 2001).

An evaluation should be made to establish the state of the country's technology and the stage reached in the development of its social infrastructure.

The education system should also be appraised and the availability of an indigenous supply of adequately educated persons to undertake roles in the organization should be determined. It is expensive to deploy expatriate staff and ideally, apart from key appointments, local staff should be engaged. An assessment should be made of the availability of professional staff and skilled operatives and an appraisal should be made of the training necessary to achieve business objectives. A vital area will be the availability of skills necessary to operate sophisticated communication equipment to facilitate modern business systems using the latest technology. Policies relating to international human resource management as described in Chapter 8 will be key to the effective deployment of expatriates and the engagement of local employees.

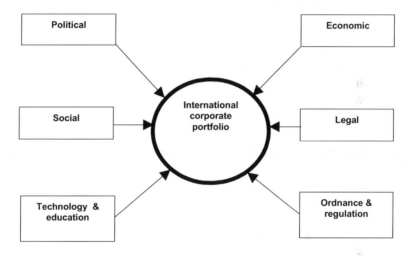

Figure 2.3: Social, economic and political factors

An investigation will be required of the legal system and its implementation, together with an assessment of codes and regulations. The extent to which international law and international contracts are acceptable should also be confirmed and the position regarding the acceptance of internationally recognised design codes and standards, i.e. BS, DIN and Eurocodes, should be established. This is particularly important where there is an absence of equivalent codes operated by the country in question.

A key action will be to identify the factors that recognize and classify social, economic and political influences. Figure 2.3 is a conceptual representation that shows the corporate portfolio within which the organization's international business activities will be undertaken and the influencing factors that will affect the company and its respective parts, including projects, subsidiaries and joint ventures.

The analysis will provide an understanding of the background and conditions under which construction-related activities will be performed. Areas of risk and uncertainty can be extracted from the data collected and these can then be classified according to the type of work to be undertaken. Strengths within the economy can be identified and opportunities can be derived from established market needs and what can be afforded.

Identification of construction clients

It will be necessary to establish a broad picture of the volume of construction work and how it is dispersed between infrastructure, commercial and housing development. The framework illustrated in Figure 2.4 shows the identification of the client structure and the split between public and private expenditure. The ratio between public and private expenditure on construction should be established and related to GDP. A breakdown will be required of expenditure on the various categories of building and infrastructure projects. Project expenditure plans should be sought for the public sector and an evaluation should be made of future private expenditure and development. The extent to which private funding is used to support the development of public projects should also be established. The state of the commercial sector must be assessed and a profile of expenditure should be built to indicate the size and type of projects that will be required. An appraisal should be made of the amount of foreign investment that either directly or indirectly generates construction work.

The marketing and procurement of work related to construction is explained further in Chapter 5.

An extrapolation of foreign investment trends will provide an indication of future construction expenditure emanating from this source. Where work is being considered in an LDC, it will be important to establish the extent of construction work that depends on aid and loans from agencies and banks.

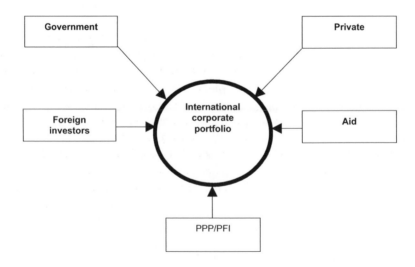

Figure 2.4: Identification of clients

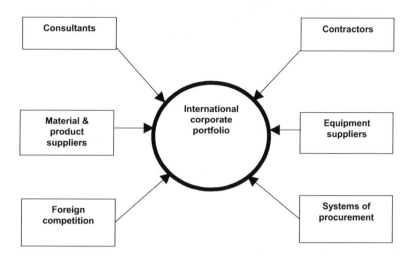

Figure 2.5: Supply side elements

Identification of nature and structure of construction and the extent of competition

The capacity of the indigenous construction industry should be broken down to identify the nature, size, capability and capacity of competitors as shown in Figure 2.5. Where possible an analysis of strengths, weaknesses, opportunities and threats (SWOT), should be undertaken to provide a comprehensive evaluation. Companies suitable for consideration as partners should be given particular attention and, where they appear to be candidates for acquisition or merger, further consideration should be given to future corporate strategy.

The extent and quality of the competition to be expected from other foreign companies participating in the construction process should be identified and an evaluation should be made of the strength of these companies as market competitors. An appraisal should also be made of established practice concerning the use of procurement methods to realize construction work and any peculiar aspects should be noted that might apply to these processes.

The outcome of this investigation will be a complete evaluation of market potential and the determination of areas where competitive advantage can be achieved (Porter, 1986). This information will provide a significant resource in helping to determine the viability of new ventures and will inform the decision to proceed.

The physical environment

An appraisal should be made of the natural environment of the country or region under consideration. This will take into account hazards such as earthquakes, landslips, tornadoes, flooding and droughts. Temperature ranges, rainfall, snowfall, wind strength and humidity are other important matters to be factored into the assessment of risk regarding the potential damage and disruption to construction work.

Physical geography, together with the provision and location of seaports, roads, railways, canals and airports will determine accessibility and these may have an important influence on the construction methods and the type of technology that can be economically adopted. Site access in remote areas should be subjected to a full assessment of the extent and quality of the transport infrastructure. Where delivery vehicles will be required to contend with difficult conditions such as narrow, unsealed roads traversing mountain passes and densely forested valleys, then limitations may need to be determined concerning the type of materials, components and equipment to be used for construction. In the event that goods need to be imported, an evaluation should be made of import restrictions and procedures. In certain countries, port congestion could impose considerable delays in the delivery of materials and components.

Services involving the supply of electricity, water, sewerage and telecommunications should be surveyed and appraised to establish any constraints that might be imposed on proposed business objectives and profitability. The mobilization and management of construction projects is covered in Chapter 11.

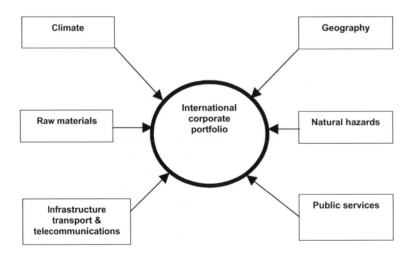

Figure 2.6: Factors for assessing the physical environment

Invariably, some countries will have an abundance of naturally occurring materials suitable for use in construction. The most common examples include aggregates, sand, gypsum, timber, steel and ceramic tiles. It is important to identify the source of indigenous materials as well as manufactured products and skills to avoid unnecessary import taxes and transportation costs. Where appropriate, suitable local materials and components may be accommodated within the design and construction methods selected. Figure 2.6 provides an illustration of an assessment framework.

The extent of ownership

International construction projects may be procured and supported from a head office situated in the home country. This will alleviate the need to set up and maintain a local office in the short term. Under these circumstances it may be advantageous to employ the services of a local agent or representative who has inside knowledge and contacts necessary to fulfil projects by the acquisition of good service from local companies. Agents are normally reimbursed in the form of a fee for services rendered. The advantage with this approach is that there is no long-term commitment and withdrawal can be achieved without incurring costs associated with discontinuation or disposal of the business infrastructure.

A construction organization wishing to take on a large project in a foreign market may seek a local partner who will be expected to share responsibility for the work and will usually provide expertise, local knowledge and a proportion of the finance to enable the effective employment of local resources. There is no universally accepted standard form of agreement for such a partnership; instead it is normal to treat each case on its merits before drawing up an agreement. In some countries it may be mandatory that a local partner be appointed in order to obtain a contract. Where there is a significant financial commitment from the local partner then it is legitimate that the organization should be considered as a bona fide stakeholder. Partnerships may be entered into on a corporate basis, usually in the form of mergers, especially where a greater degree of business convergence is seen to be an advantage. A more detailed coverage of this aspect is given in Chapter 4.

It is possible that the range of commitment required for any one project exceeds the expertise and resources of a single company. Under these circumstances it is necessary to consider the possibility of a joint venture where two or more organizations join together for the purpose of completing a specific project. Joint ventures are normally employed in the case of large, complex projects, but they can also be applied successfully to smaller projects. Local partners, as discussed above, can also be engaged on this basis.

A longer-term approach would be to investigate the desirability and feasibility of acquiring full ownership of a foreign construction company or consultancy through which business would be conducted in the country concerned. If this is the case, it will be vital to make an accurate valuation of assets and business prospects, together with an assessment of financial stability and reputation. Subject to the outcome being favourable, then approaches can be made to test whether there is a basis for acquisition to take place. The advantage of this option is that the company will enjoy the trading advantages associated with an indigenous company and will be more likely to be viewed as a national company rather than a foreign organization.

Company profile 2.1: Shimizu Corporation

Kisuke Shimizu founded the Shimizu Corporation as a construction company operating in the region of Tokyo in 1804. A long period of success resulted in the expansion of the company and in 1937 it was incorporated as Shimizu Gumi Ltd. After the Second World War the company was renamed the Shimizu Construction Company. By this time the company had expanded its area of domestic operation and the range of construction activities and services. The post-war reconstruction period provided the corporation with the opportunity to operate internationally within the Far East Asian region. Experience gained allowed the company to expand its interests to the vast markets of North America and Europe and subsequently to Africa and Central America.

Today, Shimizu operates a large domestic network controlled by its headquarters in Tokyo. Major branch offices operate in Yokohama, Chiba, Kanto, Osaka and Kobe. In all there are 19 branches, which incorporate an Institute of Technology, Tokyo Metropolitan Area Building Construction Headquarters and the Kansai Construction and Civil Engineering Headquarters in Osaka. The overseas network consists of Shimizu Europe incorporating offices in London, Paris and Eastern European States including Moscow. Shimizu North America has major offices in New York and Los Angeles, together with branches in Maine, North Carolina and Detroit. Shimizu Corporation de Mexico is based in Tijuana. The Asia division has branches and associate companies in Singapore, Kuala Lumpur, Jakarta, Manila, Bangkok and Hong Kong, together with interests in China, Bangladesh and Taiwan.

In 2001, the corporation employed 13,156 persons, of whom 2732 were architects and 2484 were engineers. Net sales have risen from 1304.7 billion yen in 1998 to 1418.2 billion yen in 2000.

The corporate aim of the corporation is to improve global standards of living while contributing to the advancement of society and development of the world. In order to achieve this, Shimizu recognizes the need to:

- refine its creativity and perceptions; then to call on accumulated technology and wisdom to add new value to the concept of space;
- expand the corporations' individuality and to respect human frailties; and
- stay in harmony with nature by blending with societies and genuinely recognizing the potential to create a more vibrant and richer culture.

Shimizu's overseas offices and subsidiaries are globally dispersed and the majority of them have a strong corporate identity, e.g. Shimizu Europe, Shimizu American Corporation. The company has expanded by devolving its own corporate structure and systems to overseas activities. In a minority of cases there are affiliated companies that do not carry the Shimizu name. The company has not used wide scale mergers and acquisitions to achieve diversity and growth.

Shimizu places great emphasis on the need to satisfy customer requirements by striving to keep ahead of the times and to discover ways of developing new demands. The Corporation intends to be a more vigorous and powerful entity, which can make a greater contribution to domestic and global societies. Particular importance is attached to environmental conservation and cultural activities and the commitment to the construction of high quality buildings.

Shimizu aims to maintain a spirit of innovation through its employees that contributes to company growth and development. Encouragement is given to the pursuit of new types of business development, sales activities, R&D and management. To achieve these ideals an atmosphere is generated by corporate policy that enables employees to gain pleasure from work and to generate enthusiasm.

Author's commentary

The Shimizu Corporation is an excellent example of corporate evolution that spans almost two hundred years. The opportunities presented by post Second World War reconstruction have been exploited and the success of domestic expansion has allowed entry into the international market, initially in the Asia Region and then on a global basis.

Shimizu recognizes the importance of satisfying the needs of clients and providing high quality buildings that represent good value and sustainability over their intended life cycles. To achieve this ideal the need to innovate and change with the times has been fully recognized in the quest for continued success and subsequent expansion. Due recognition is given to the respect and well-being deserved by the Corporation's employees, and the need to exploit the rich contributions that can be gained from recognizing and utilizing the best aspects of various cultures. Nevertheless, Shimizu's corporate culture is strongly Japanese and it appears reluctant to adopt host country cultures and practices, instead it seeks to harmonize Japanese culture and systems to suit local market requirements and conditions.

Company profile 2.2: The Bouygues Group

The Bouygues Group, founded by Francis Bouygues in 1952, has grown to become the largest construction contractor in the world with an annual turnover of 16.28 billion US$ in 2000 (*International Construction*, 2001). The company initially focused on the building sector in Paris but later extended its scope to include property development and industrial precasting, as well as broadening its area of operation through French regional subsidiaries.

Continuing success and expansion through the 1960s resulted in the organization being listed on the Paris Stock Exchange and in the 1970s the company was responsible for constructing the prestigious Parc des Princes Stadium, representing a breakthrough into the major works market. The creation of Bouygues Offshore and Maison Bouygues, specializing in catalogue homes, continued diversification and expansion.

Using the strong domestic business position the company had created as a national contractor, an ambitious strategy of diversification overseas and into service activities was put in place. During the 1980s, Bouygues successfully completed major projects abroad including the University of Riyadh, Saudi Arabia, Lagos thermal power plant and the Bubiyan Bridge in Kuwait. On the domestic front, Bouygues completed Charles de Gaulle Airport Terminal 2, the Orsay museum and the Ile de Re Bridge and the Grande Arche at La Défense.

In 1984, Bouygues had accumulated sufficient resources to acquire Saur, an established French water supply company and, in 1986, Bouygues became world leader in construction with the acquisition of Colas, Screg and Sacer who at the time were the largest roadworks group in France. Together, Bouygues and Saur acquired the Saint-Gobian subsidiary Cise in 1997, which was France's third largest utilities management group.

In 1987, Bouygues further extended its interests by becoming the operator of France's newly privatized leading thematic channel TF1. In December 1996, TF1 in association with major partners, launched the digital satellite platform TPS.

Bouygues Telecom, a company controlled by Bouygues, launched its services under the DCS 1800 standard in May 1996. It achieved coverage in record time and at the end of 2001 had 6.6. million customers.

The 1990s and 2000 witnessed successful expansion on the construction and international front with the construction sector redeploying its activities resulting in new contracts such as the French National Library, Stade de France and Normandy Bridge, Avignon viaducts, Coeur Defense.

Abroad, successfully completed projects include the Hassan II Great Mosque in Casablanca, Hong Kong Convention Centre, Sydney Metro, presidential complexes in Turkmenistan and Kazakhstan, motorways in Croatia, Hungary and the Beirut Seafront Redevelopment, Groene Hart

Tunnel in the Netherlands, Rostock Tunnel in Germany, various PFI contracts in the UK, the Girassol oil field in Angola and the CPC oil terminal and pipeline in Russia.

Colas, the world's leading roadworks group is pursuing development principally in North America through the acquisition of indigenous companies.

In 2001, Bouygues had become a diversified industrial group with strong corporate business activities as follows:

- telecom-media with Telecommunications (Bouygues Media TF1)
- services (Saur)
- construction, embracing building/civil engineering and electrical contracting (Bouygues Contracting)
- roads (Colas)
- utilities (Bouygues Immobilier).

The Bouygues Group is now established in 80 countries and has a workforce amounting to 125,000. Total sales amounted in 2001 to 20.5 billion euros, of which 7.6 billion were generated outside Bouygues. Market capitalization at 31 December 2001 amounted to 12.7 billion euros and the group is listed on the Paris Stock Exchange – prime market – and is include in the CAC 40 index.

Author's commentary

The Bouygues Group has grown quickly from its domestic Parisian founding roots in 1952. Having built a strong domestic business, the company sought to expand by acquiring French companies and at the same time initially developing an international business principally in the Middle East and Africa. With growing experience in construction, more prestigious worldwide contracts were completed such as the Hong Kong Convention Centre.

A feature of Bouygues expansion is by diversification into telecommunications and digital satellite media services, which have no direct links to construction. In fact, the rapid growth potential in these areas will undoubtedly have a dramatic effect on the future structure of the business. Concurrently, expansion has taken place domestically and internationally in the business areas of roads, services and utilities management, primarily by the acquisition of companies with strong business performance and expertise.

Although the strategy has been to acquire major French companies to achieve expansion and diversification it is interesting to note the policy now adopted by Colas to acquire North American companies to expand its business in the USA and Canada.

Company profile 3.3: Hochtief AG

Hochtief is now Germany's largest construction company, ranking 11th largest in the world with an annual turnover in 2000 of 8752 million US$ (*International Construction*, 2001). Hochtief's history began with the Helfmann brothers who initially owned a brick kiln, but later diversified into transport contractors and timber merchants. In 1872, the brothers registered their construction company as 'Fa. Gebr. Helfmann, Bauunternehmer' in Frankfurt am Main.

The Helfmann brothers began by specializing in building houses before diversifying into commercial construction by building Gieben University in 1878/79. Philipp Helfmann also became a respected real estate specialist and the business continued to prosper until Balthasar Helfmann died prematurely in 1896. To protect the interests of the company, Philipp Helfmann converted the partnership into a joint stock company named 'Aktiengesellschaft für Hoch- und Tiefbauten' later to be abbreviated to the present name Hochtief. The initial capital of the company was two million Deutschmarks and the conversion of the company attracted significant fresh capital.

Using the domestic strength of the business, Philipp Helfmann undertook the company's first foreign contract in 1899. The project involved the construction of a large reinforced concrete pneumatic conveyor equipped granary in Genoa based on a fixed price turnkey contract of 3.25 million Swiss francs.

After the death of Philipp Helfmann, Hugo Stinnes gained control of the company and moved Hochtief to the Ruhr region. After the First World War, Stinnes became its major shareholder and after his death in 1926 Hochtief was in serious danger of complete collapse. The company was only saved by the intervention of Rheinisch-Westfälische Elektrizitätswerk AG (RWE) which then became the main shareholder with 31% of the shares. This percentage remained about the same until after the Second World War when RWE gradually increased its shareholding until, in 1989, it had effective control of Hochtief with 56% of the shares.

In recent years, Hochtief has used its strong reputation and business performance in its core business, building construction in the domestic market, to position the company successfully in important international markets by means of subsidiaries and participating interests. The current structure of the company comes under the umbrella of HOCHTIEF AG.

HOCHTIEF Construction AG concentrates on core business activities, above all building construction in the domestic market, civil engineering and airport construction. In addition, it provides clients with the re-assurance of efficient solutions in all construction-related sectors. This service can incorporate, if required, everything from inception, design, planning, construction, marketing and facility management. The company's headquarters with the Executive Board and various service divisions is located in Essen and an outline of HOCHTIEF's organization structure is shown below:

Hochtief Airport		
Hochtief Construction AG		
Hochtief Development		
Hochtief N. America	**Turner Aecon**	**HOCHTIEF AG**
	Kitchell	
Hochtief Internat'l	**Ballast Nedam**	**CORPORATE HQ**
	Concor SA	
	HF Construcciones Arg'a	
	HF UK	
	HF Brazil	
	HF Poland	
	Leighton Holdings Aus	
	HF VSB Czech	
Hochtief Services		

HOCHTIEF Airport specializes in airport design and construction of airport facilities and the services of this company are typified by the successful completion of Athens International Airport as a turnkey project.

The whole basis of HOCHTIEF AG's corporate business and that of its subsidiary companies is cooperation in a spirit of true partnership with clients, investors, operators and business promotion organizations, with the goal of significantly reducing building and operating costs.

Author's commentary
HOCHTIEF provides another example of a long established company that started from a small inception and, having survived its formative years and two World Wars, was taken over by RWE under whose control the company has grown to be a truly global construction company in the past 13 years. Its core business is building construction and it has acquired sufficient expertise to offer clients a complete turnkey service from project inception to handover and commissioning building projects. Acquisitions

and the establishment of subsidiaries has enabled the company to operate effectively in North and South America as well as Europe and Australia.

Hochtief is an excellent example of a company that has fully diversified within the complete range of its core business without finding it necessary to diversify into unrelated business ventures.

Summary

This chapter has sought to outline the importance of undertaking a full investigation of all the relevant factors that may affect the decision to proceed with a new international construction business venture. A systemic conceptual view of international construction has been related to key factors that translate into all types of construction business activity. This provides a structure for the collection of data and information necessary for an adequate analysis to determine the feasibility and desirability of a corporate venture into the international construction market.

Stakeholder differences between consultants, contractors and suppliers have been identified and the potential for large and small organizations to operate on a global basis has been assessed. The degree of foreign corporate ownership has also been evaluated and basic advantages associated with the options available have been pointed out.

The company profiles provide an informative insight into the history of long established global companies that were initially successful in their domestic market before embarking on international work. Changes in ownership and difficulties brought about by conflict and the economics of the twentieth century are evident. The organizations cited have grasped opportunities as and when they occurred and today they are among the leading players in the global construction market. Progressive development and expansion has been achieved by diversification of business interest and geographic location. The increasing economic strength of the global economy over recent years has enabled faster growth by the use of joint ventures, mergers and acquisitions to gain entry to new markets.

The global construction organization is likely to consist of a group of companies that provide a range of interrelated products and services for the benefit of existing and new clients. All will strive for competitive advantage in the quest to develop long-term relationships with major clients by meeting and exceeding expectations and needs.

The knowledge provided by investigative framework will ensure that the most important aspects will be considered in preparation for a decision to enter into the international construction market for the first time, or to expand into new areas. It has not been possible to cover every eventuality in the text and the reader should be aware that it will be necessary to cover all relevant details that are likely to have an impact on decision making and business.

The next chapter aims to provide an outline of the theories associated with international trade and the nature of the international construction business.

Further reading

Bon R. (1994), Whither global construction? 1992 and 1993 European construction economics research unit opinions surveys, *Building Research and Information*, **22**, No. 2, 109–126.

Bouygues Group home page (on-line www.bouygues.fr).

Bon R. (1997), 'The future of international construction: some survey results, 1993–1996', *Building Research and Information*, **25**, No. 2, 81–85.

Bon R. & Crosswaite D. (2000), *The future of international construction*, Thomas Telford, London.

Drewer S. (1990), 'The international construction system', *Habitat International*, **5**, No. 4, 395–428.

Erramilli M. K. (1991), 'The experience factor in foreign market entry behaviour of service firms', *J. Int. Business Studies*, **22**, No. 3, 3rd Quarter, 479–502.

Fannin W. & Rodriques A. (1986), 'National or global? — control vs. flexibility', *Long Range Planning*, **19**, No. 5, 84–88.

Hochtief AG home page (on-line www.hochtief.com).

Langford D. & Rowland V. R. (1995), *Managing overseas construction*, Thomas Telford, London.

Mawhinney M. (2001), *International construction*, Blackwell Science Ltd.

Phatak A. V. (1982), *International dimensions of management* (3rd edn) Boston PWS-Kent Publishing.

Porter M. E. (1986), *Competition in global industries*, Harvard Business School.

Root F. R. (1994), *Entry strategies for international markets*, Lexington Books, New York.

Shimitzu Corporation home page (on-line www.shimz.co.jp/english).

Chapter 3

International trade and the nature of international construction

Introduction

Advances in communication technology, transportation and air travel have provided a global environment conducive to the rapid expansion of international business on a global scale. Companies operating successfully within domestic markets have been tempted by the prospect of access to foreign markets through better communication systems that facilitate easier corporate control and dynamic management. There is an increasing number of organizations seeking to expand their business into foreign markets by creating subsidiaries or by means of mergers, global alliances and acquisitions. Whatever solution is adopted, the intention is to gain competitive advantage in national, regional and global markets. These developments have brought increasing prosperity, especially for those countries that have experienced high levels of growth. The ability to attract direct inward investment from foreign investors is vital to the prospects of a nation and its ability to generate wealth. The amount of risk involved is a key investment consideration and the crux of this issue is national economic, social and political stability. Nations that cannot meet these basic requirements will find it extremely difficult to attract foreign investment and may be forced to rely on support from development banks and aid agencies.

Businesses from wealthy nations are constantly seeking to invest in overseas foreign businesses that can demonstrate competitive advantage and good prospects for future profitability. The inherent stability of wealthy industrialized countries makes it easy to attract attention from foreign entrepreneurs who wish to create safe investments. However, developing countries with low labour and infrastructure costs offer tempting targets, especially for multinational enterprises (MNEs).

The global construction industry is in a constant state of change, governed by the international need to procure construction work in support of sustained economic activity and growth. The collective dynamic nature of international construction activity is largely influenced by the location and distribution of projects. International consultants, contractors and suppliers therefore need to be organized and geared to manage in a dynamic and flexible manner such that the environmental and other factors associated with individual projects can be effectively controlled in order to achieve successful project outcomes.

The purpose of this chapter is to demonstrate the link between world economic activity and trade and the nature and distribution of construction activity. A world economic overview at the beginning of the twenty-first century is provided and the largest and most competitive construction markets are identified. Trading theories and international trade practices are outlined to provide the context within which international construction takes place. The extent and nature of the international construction industry is explained and the top global consultants and contractors are identified.

World economic overview

At the beginning of the twenty-first century, the United States, Japan and the remainder of the G8 countries attracted the majority of the world's direct investment and dominated world trade and commerce. Eastern Europe and emerging economies such as China are becoming more attractive, alongside some Asian, South American and African nations. The prime motivation for this situation is the continuing trend towards privatization and the fact that in some developing countries the opportunity exists to make high profits, given that risk aversion can be applied. Global networks created by alliances, mergers and acquisitions, joint ventures and licensing arrangements have also played a major part in promoting international trade. In 2000, World Trade accounted for 6,186 billion US$ and the dispersion is shown in Figure 3.1.

In 2001, China was the largest developing nation ranked in sixth position in the world league with Brazil, India, Mexico, Korea, Argentina, Russian Federation, Turkey and Poland in the world's 25 largest economies. Economically, China had a strong economy with a positive balance of exports over imports and her median savings rate was 42% of GDP. However, China's huge population reduces individual wealth to just 856 US$ GDP per capita indicating widespread poverty.

REGION	%
North America	17.7
Europe	37.7
Asia and Japan	16.2
Others	28.4
Total	100.0

Figure 3.1: Dispersion of world trade
Source: Adapted from OECD World Economic Outlook, April 2002

An even worse situation can be seen in India with just 471 US$ per capita. Figure 3.2 illustrates the disparity in per capita income caused by large populations and the inability to generate sufficient national GDP. These figures have important implications for world trade. Countries with low per capita GDPs, but which have an educated workforce and stability are prime targets for foreign inward investment by wealthy countries that are seeking to exploit world markets by means of technology transfer. The implications for construction are clear because new factories and production plants will need to be constructed and eventually the wealth they create will generate new infrastructure and other facilities.

India and China displayed strong GDP average annual growth rates at 6% and 10.7% between 1990 and 1999. During the 1990s, the fastest growing region was East Asia and the Pacific Rim countries with an annual growth in GDP of 7.5%, followed by South Asia at 5.6%. Europe and Central Asia fell by 2.3%, while Latin America, Middle East and North Africa grew by 3%. Since 1999, there has been a marked slow down in world economic growth, especially in Japan.

The wealthiest nations in North America, Europe and Asia will continue to look for opportunities to make foreign investments in advanced industrialized countries (AICs) and least developed countries (LDCs). Although the construction share of the GDP of AICs might be lower, the volume of GDP ensures that the prime construction markets remain in these countries. The implication is that global consultants and contractors must retain the expertise and ability to compete in the most demanding markets, while attempting to expand interests in newly industrialized countries (NICs) and LDCs. Material suppliers will have a different agenda because they will be sourcing the supply of raw materials, preferably in countries with abundant supplies and low labour costs. Lafarge is a good example of a large global organization that has exploited the opportunity to invest in NICs and LDCs with excellent sources of gypsum, timber and other basic construction materials. Equipment manufacturers have been quick to grasp opportunities to enter into joint ventures with regional manufacturers with specialist expertise. The company profile of the Caterpillar Corporation demonstrates how joint ventures and acquisition have helped the corporation to maintain its competitive position in the world market for almost half a century.

Indications are that the world's most wealthy nations will continue to dominate the world economy with the United States being the prime player. All AICs have recognized the need for investment in innovation and research to improve efficiency and competitiveness. Not all innovation and research is a success, but developed nations have accepted that sufficient activity needs to take place to ensure the generation of winning initiatives that, coupled with development, create increased wealth through greater efficiency. For those nations that do not generate enough wealth to be able to afford innovation and research the prospect is bleak. The efficiency gap between AICs and LDCs has a tendency to increase, thereby imposing wage reductions and creating more poverty in the poorest countries. This is a matter that the development and aid agencies are continuing to address, in some cases with less than convincing results.

The direction for those companies and corporations operating in construction is clear and they must be capable of competing in the toughest and most advanced markets, as typified by North America, Europe and Asia. Expertise in consultancy and contracting can be transferred to NICs and LDCs to compete for and win construction contracts and assignments, either alone or in partnership with others. Material manufacturers and component suppliers will be seeking to source materials from locations throughout the world. Global competitive advantage will also be sought by the availability of low labour and processing costs. Likewise, equipment suppliers will be looking for competent regional partners and the availability of locally based competent dealerships.

Country	GDP 2000 per billion US$	GDP 2000 US$ per capita
USA	9883	35,102
Japan	4677	36,894
Germany	1870	22,763
UK	1413	23,653
France	1286	21,852
China	1080	856
Italy	1069	18,534
Canada	690	22,450
Brazil	588	3,456
Mexico	575	5,869
Spain	555	14,068
India	479	471
Korea	457	9667
Australia	394	20,526
Netherlands	365	22,928
Argentina	285	7696
Russian Fed	251	1725
Switzerland	240	33,426
Belgium	231	22,532
Sweden	227	25,595
Turkey	200	3,062
Austria	191	23,586
Hong Kong	163	23,977
Denmark	161	30,150
Poland	159	4113

Figure 3.2: Top 25 countries ranked by GDP
Source: Adapted from World Bank 2001

Trading theories

International trade has become an increasingly important area of economics as countries have chosen to pursue principles associated with free market economies where market driven imperatives have taken over from state driven policies. It is now generally recognized that free trade between nations leads to greater efficiency and more prosperity. The more successful nations will, of course, enjoy stronger economies, the symptoms of which include a healthy balance of exports over imports, low inflation and low interest rates. Nevertheless, not all countries can be successful at the same time and as a consequence those nations that are not doing so well may be tempted into stifling imports through such means as tariff barriers and quotas. Inevitably, this sort of action leads to retaliation on the part of other trading nations.

It may also be concluded that generalized theories associated with international trade have a significant influence on the creation and development of project supply chains and partnering arrangements. Invariably, members of the supply chain will be required to operate across national boundaries and in so doing will need to accommodate requirements and rules applied by governments to regulate trade and to protect national interests. Trading theories establish broad principles, which identify and classify the rationale behind the need for nations to trade with each other in pursuit of mutual benefit. The following represent some of the most important theories that influence world trade:

Ricardo's theory of labour value
The oldest model of trade is associated with David Ricardo (1817). Ricardo is credited with establishing a model, which states that a country's prices must reflect the relative ratio of labour costs of different types of production, and hence the pattern of trade is determined by labour productivity among countries.

Today, the amount of labour required is influenced by technology and automation, together with developments in technology and management efficiency. This helps to explain why production utilizing cheap labour in LDCs is unable to compete with higher wages in AICs and NICs where a higher level of technological application and automation exists. The Ricardian model also explains some of the truths about world trade, but further explanation may also be required to reflect other theories and concepts.

Absolute advantage
The theory of absolute advantage maintains that a nation that specializes in certain areas and develops products more efficiently and better than elsewhere can increase its economic strength and prosperity. The rationale behind specializing in certain areas is based on many factors, which may include unique expertise, readily available materials, or environmental factors such as the climate.

By trading with other nations who have specialisms of their own and different natural advantages, it is possible for all to gain. This theory does not indicate ratios or volumes of trade between partners.

Comparative advantage

This theory maintains that countries do not necessarily trade purely in cash terms. Instead, goods are exchanged based on their relative values and as a consequence it is possible that both trading partners can gain advantage, which would not otherwise be the case if monetary values alone were to be taken into consideration.

The problem with the theory of comparative advantage is that it does not deal with the internal distribution of wealth. In other words, there could be winners and losers, hence a solution which does not stifle free trade may need to be found where losers have the opportunity to rectify their situation.

Hecksscher-Ohlin theory

Commonly known as Factor Endowment Theory, this theory contends that nations will concentrate on exporting products consisting of resources that they have in abundance. Conversely, they will import products consisting of resources that are scarce within the country. This theory does not take into account the relative quality of goods, nor does it explain the use of higher technology to improve the function and performance of the product. Generally, countries with low skill labour forces will concentrate on the low quality volume end of the market, e.g. China, whereas countries with more highly skilled labour forces such as the USA and Germany will concentrate on high performing innovative products which, although costing more, may well outperform the cheaper product in the long run.

Vernon's international product life cycle theory

Vernon's Theory describes a process, which commences with the development of an innovative product in the home country, normally an advanced industrialized nation. Assuming the product to be successful in the home market and that expansion subsequently continues, export begins to other countries of comparable wealth. With the continued success of the product, manufacturers in other nations will seek to produce competitive and improved alternatives. This leads to the advent of the maturing product, which eventually becomes the standard. The final phase is the drive to cut costs by expanding into less developed country markets. This will mean relocation of manufacture to less developed countries using home country 'know how'. Eventually the product is produced so cheaply, that it becomes an imported product to its country of origin; nevertheless, the manufacturer will attempt to differentiate the product in order to maintain the maximum possible selling price and in the process maximize profits.

This theory is helpful in explaining some of the rationale behind international trade. However, it is important to understand where products are at a given point in time during the life cycle.

Other factors

Theories often work in combination; moreover they are influenced by a variety of factors, which can be associated with the economic, social and political spectrum. Fashion and style, which may or may not be a product of marketing, will play a significant part in demand and the price that people are prepared to pay. Reputation and prestige are also powerful influencing factors.

Movements in currency exchange rates will also play a major part in a country's ability to trade internationally. When a currency is strong, imports become cheaper and exports are more expensive to customers, hence the positive balance of exports over import comes under pressure. Currency speculation can also influence movement in exchange rates, especially in the short term.

International construction is far more dynamic and fluid than its manufacturing counterpart due to the temporary nature of the projects that comprise by far the majority of its turnover. Each project must be properly designed, mobilized, executed and commissioned. This involves a dynamic time-constrained process during which a project team is put together, developed and disbanded on completion. A supply chain will need to be created to provide services, materials, products and equipment from a variety of sources, which will invariably involve companies and businesses from other countries. The theories applicable to international trade are therefore highly relevant in the creation of capable construction project supply chains. Goods and services procured outside national boundaries will automatically be classed as imports and will therefore be subject to controls and regulations designed to ensure national wellbeing and stability.

International construction requires a range of knowledge and experience beyond that required for domestic construction projects. The mobilization and execution of international projects demands the necessary expertise to cope with trading conditions and regulations imposed by national governments. These often involve exchange controls, tariffs and trade barriers, which need to be thoroughly understood and dealt with.

International trade

Foreign direct investment is vital to all national economies and it is therefore important to possess the ability to attract and maintain inward investment in business and real estate. Such investment takes the form of equity funds that are invested in other nations. Advanced industrialized countries (AICs) have invested heavily in other AICs, principally for the reasons stated previously, and smaller amounts have been invested in newly industrialized countries (NICs). As countries become more prosperous they tend to invest in other countries and geographic regions that have displayed economic growth potential and stability.

In particular, those sectors such as manufacturing, banking and insurance have been singled out for special attention.

International trade is in a state of continual development and it is important for national governments to gain and hold strong international trading positions and to have a profile capable of attracting sufficient inward investment. It is therefore essential that economic competitiveness is maintained and that adequate control is exerted over trading regulations to encourage a healthy relationship between the exportation and importation of goods and services. A nation's major business enterprises must also develop the capability to operate globally as MNEs. The key to operating competitively is through innovation and the development of new technologies; however, economies of scale, labour costs, interest rates and monetary exchange rates will be influential factors.

Economic competitiveness is continuously changing and it is therefore vital to understand the factors that govern international trade and, through this, the way that international construction is influenced in its dispersement and operation. The theories of international trade relate closely to the factor conditions that determine the nature and scale of a nation's competitiveness and the type of goods and products that it produces. In addition, a vitally important activity is the development of world-class specialist expertise backed by investment in innovation and research to keep ahead of competitors. The availability of natural resources, geographic location, human resource expertise and experience will be very influential in determining the mix of products and services that can be exploited in the international market. Successful nations will constantly strive to develop new products and services and to invest in innovation, research and associated knowledge and technologies. A strong home market that has a propensity to anticipate changes in international demand can be used as an indicator of what the global market is likely to require and thus helps to support the maintenance of competitive advantage.

Local supply chains can have a significant impact on international competitiveness, especially where they are encouraged to develop in a supportive and harmonious manner. National strengths associated with business culture should be continuously advanced and tested and local rivalry should be encouraged to establish international competitiveness. It will also be an advantage to maintain a vigilant watch for paradigm shifts in know-how and technology, which in the worse case scenario could render whole industries obsolete.

The extent to which governments should become involved in international trade is a very controversial matter. Many are of the opinion that their government should intervene and restrict importation of foreign goods in order to protect local jobs and businesses. A strong case for government intervention would be where goods are being dumped at prices less than cost because of gross surpluses, especially when this may have been brought about by foreign government subsidies. In most cases the erection of such trade barriers will cause retaliation from other countries.

Non-governmental organizations that promote international trade

Negotiations intended to encourage free trade and fair-trading practices are an ongoing activity. The General Agreement on Tariffs and Trade (GATT) is an organization that negotiates trade concessions among its member countries. The members of this organization meet on a periodic basis to broker agreements intended to increase international trade to their mutual benefit. The fundamental principle of GATT is non-discrimination amongst its members, but there are four important exceptions:

1.   developed countries can give tariff preference to developing countries;
2.   countries entering into regional trade agreements do not need to extend these to a Most Favoured Nation (MFN) basis;
3.   a country can impose a safeguard to protect its own industry on a temporary basis where it would otherwise sustain serious injury; and
4.   where a country experiences serious balance of payment problems it can invoke a temporary quantitative restriction.

The World Trade Organisation (WTO) is an umbrella body that has a significant influence on the international trading system. Its origin can be traced back to the Atlantic Charter of 1941 and it now stands alongside the World Bank and the International Monetary Fund (IMF) as a major part of the world economic system. The membership of WTO has grown considerably and it now consists of over 130 member countries, including China who has recently joined under transitional arrangements. WTO operates on the principle of non-discrimination amongst its members in that there should be equal application of barriers and other forms of trade regulation. It also applies the concept of most favoured nation status, which involves liberalization measures, which with some exceptions is granted to all members. Where disagreements occur, WTO has a dispute resolution mechanism intended to ensure fast and timely compliance with the principle of non-discrimination. The activities of the Trade Review Body, which has the task of monitoring the trade policies of members, are published regularly to assist transparency. Further information is provided by Case Study 3.1.

The Organisation for Economic Development and Co-operation (OECD) is based in Paris and it comprises 30 member countries that share a commitment to democratic government and the market economy. The OECD interacts widely on a global scale and it has active relationships with some 70 other countries, non-government organizations including GATT, WTO and civil society. It is widely recognized for its publications, statistics and work that covers economic and social issues from macroeconomics to trade, education, development, science and innovation.

The OECD promotes good governance in the public service and in corporate activity. It assists governments to ensure the responsiveness of key economic areas with sectoral monitoring. By identifying emerging issues and producing policies that work, it assists strategic policymaking. The OECD is well regarded for its individual country surveys and reviews.

The OECD produces internationally agreed instruments, decisions and recommendations to promote rules of the game in areas where multilateral agreement is necessary for individual countries to make progress in a globalized economy. Sharing the benefits of growth is also crucial and this can be demonstrated within emerging economies, sustainable development, territorial economy and aid. Communication, consensus and peer views form the core OECD. It is governed by a Council comprising representatives of member countries and it provides guidance on the work of OECD committees and decides the annual budget.

OECD countries account for 72.4% of all goods exported and 75% of all goods imported in the world. It may therefore be concluded that the members of this grouping dominate world trade. Confirmation of this notion can be made by a comparison of OECD and non-OECD export figures between 1997 and 2001, which show a high degree of correlation. Using 1995 as a base of 100, exports increased from 112 at the beginning of 1997 and steadily increased to 157 by the third quarter of 2000, before falling away to 150 by mid-2001. In 2000, OECD nations accounted for 88% of the world GDP.

During the past 30 years, advances have been made in the development of international trade against a backdrop of macro changes in the world economy and trade. The development and expansion of the European Union and the end of the 'cold war', linked to the development of newly industrialized countries (NICs) has created considerable interest in the potential further development of international trade. The fall of Europe's communist countries has served to broaden the free economy and the continuing economic growth of China has further emphasized the importance of globalization and the need to think in a more strategic manner.

Impediments to trade

Where countries come under pressure because they are importing too much it is common practice to restrict imports by the introduction of barriers of one form or another, according to the circumstances prevailing at the time. The main concern invariably is the protection of domestic industries and jobs. It may also be necessary to protect 'know-how' which may be lost if an industry dies as a result of other countries dumping their over-capacity, or simply applying a strategy to wipe out the competition.

The most commonly used barriers are detailed below.

1. Price barriers: these are applied in the form of additions to the cost of the import, usually as a percentage, but can also be a fixed or other amount. The purpose is to make imported goods more expensive than locally produced goods and to provide revenue for the country's exchequer.
2. Price fixing: this can be achieved by a number of countries collaborating as a cartel to achieve a monopoly in the international market.

3. Exchange controls can take a variety of forms, the most common being to limit the amount of foreign exchange for the purpose of purchasing imports and to distort the market exchange rate inside the country to the advantage of the national currency.
4. Control of foreign investment by giving local partners the majority share or by restricting the transfer or remittance of funds.

Non-tariff barriers include the following:
1. Quotas: this is where the maximum level of import is stated for a period of time, normally per annum. If the quota is set at zero then this is generally referred to as an embargo or sanction.
2. Technical requirements: imported products may be subjected to stringent regulations such as those associated with health and safety, or there may be standards or dimensional requirements. In cases where these are severe it may completely deter the importation of certain products or services.
3. Protection of domestic industries by the introduction of a combination of quotas linked to fixed and variable tariffs.
4. Anti-dumping legislation: these are regulations designed to protect domestic industry from the dumping of products where there is a gross surplus, which may have been brought about by foreign government subsidies. Such legislation may include heavy tariffs on such imported goods.

International consultants and contractors will always seek to optimize the creation and composition of the project supply chain in the interest of efficiency and quality. However, the ideal solution may not always be possible due to the circumstances described above.

Promotion of international trade

It should be remembered that despite trade barriers there is a need to encourage inward investment and the development of new technologies and industry. Hence, countries need to be careful in applying economic policy to encourage free trade and to promote trade which is of mutual benefit.

Where currency exchange difficulties occur, or there is a lack of foreign exchange in the country purchasing goods or services, then counter-trade arrangements may be best applied. Essentially, this is where payments are made by the equivalent value in goods, which are readily available. Once an equivalent barter exchange is agreed then the deal can be efficiently carried out subject to all the necessary safeguards.

Another possibility is to trade services internationally such as banking, insurance and transportation. Normally such services are highly regulated involving complex deals and safeguards, which protect national interests and identity.

Economic and enterprise zones are often used by governments to encourage commercial investment into regions where there is poverty or underemployment of available resources. Such zones provide exemption from the payment of taxes and duties and they may include free land and infrastructure provision. Free trade zones can provide the equivalent of an offshore assembly plant and therefore their strategic location is of vital importance. It is intended that such developments are mutually beneficial to all concerned and the favourable effects generate prosperity and growth.

International trade and its relationship with construction

A healthy construction market will always exist where international trade is promoted in the interest of industrial and business growth and the promotion of prosperity. This will be easier to achieve in countries that exhibit the ability to create wealth through the generation of high investment supported by innovation and technological development. These countries will also possess indigenous expertise capable of participating in projects under partnership and joint venture arrangements. AICs and NICs comprise the majority of countries in this category. Poorer countries, primarily classified as LDCs, often lack strong technological development and do not possess the necessary indigenous knowledge and skills required by the latest construction design and technology. Hence, they are forced to procure construction projects overseas as a total package. Such work is invariably supported and controlled by international funding agencies that provide soft loans and aid. These agencies also oversee the procurement and execution of the projects.

The international construction industry

The extent and nature of construction undertaken throughout the world is highly dependent on wealth creation by businesses that operate nationally and/or internationally. According to Langford and Rowland (1995), economic development progresses from LDCs to NICs and then eventually to AICs. Research has shown that the construction share of GDP increases during the transition from LDC to NIC and then declines as a country reaches AIC status (Bon and Crosswaite, 2000). The proportion of GDP associated with construction is generally in the region of 8–12% and therefore there is a direct relationship between the wealth of a nation and the proportion of construction that takes place.

The global construction industry is large, complex and diverse. There are five prime elements that comprise the process associated with construction on an international scale, namely design consultancy, contracting, equipment supply, products and materials and, more recently, facility management. The relationship between these elements depends on client requirements and the procurement method selected for the delivery of the projects. Whatever method is adopted, project management will play a key role in the efficient execution of construction projects. Therefore the selection of appropriate systems and organization structures is of crucial importance. The nature of large projects procured overseas using resources from different countries and continents requires, as a fundamental prerequisite, a high degree of coordination and communication.

Consultants who have specialist expertise in design and management have considerable potential to operate on a global scale and this has been made more possible by recent advances in information technology. Unprecedented immediate access is now available to all the expertise contained within major consultancy practices by means of the Internet and it is now possible to dynamically generate innovative solutions to problems collaboratively, irrespective of geographical location. Many consultants have set up a network of overseas offices to reflect the growth in construction activity and their particular specialisms. Moreover, it is now common practice to employ indigenous design professionals who have knowledge of local conditions. According to Figure 3.3. global contracting in 1994 was dominated by Japanese companies, but by 2001 contractors from the USA and Europe, who had advanced sufficiently to mount a successful challenge, had broken this domination. Construction companies from NICs have still to make a significant impact on the international construction scene, although it is clear that China State Construction Corporation is a fast growing international player which will potentially provide tough competition.

Figure 3.4 illustrates the nationality of the top twenty professional design consultancies in 1994 and 2001. It is significant that, with the exception of Egypt, all are from AICs, with the USA and European countries dominating the market.

Materials suppliers and component manufacturers have experienced major developments in technology and manufacturing processes. Efficiency gains have been made in the processing of raw materials and product design has been improved to provide greater efficiency and in-use performance. These advances and the developments referred to at the beginning of this chapter have opened up the potential to exploit global markets. The expansion of the global construction market has led to widespread mergers and acquisitions aimed at achieving national, regional and global market advantage. The largest and most successful organizations are currently seeking to create global networks for the exploitation of their materials and products. In suitable circumstances, locally occurring natural materials such as clay, chalk, gypsum and aggregates have been processed and exported to countries where the demand for construction is prevalent.

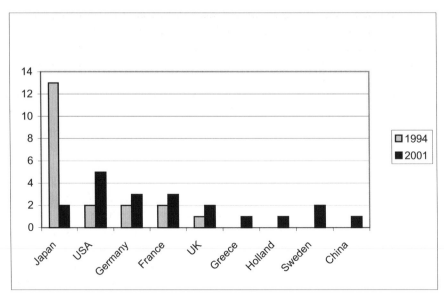

Figure 3.3: Top global contractors 1994 and 2001
Source: ENR 2001

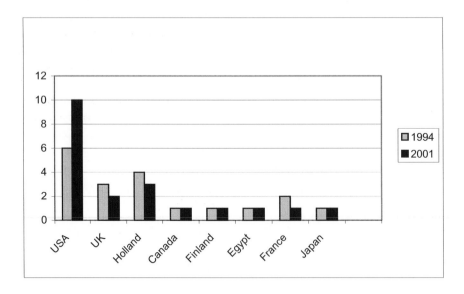

Figure 3.4: Top global consultants 1994 and 2001
Source: ENR 2001

Equipment manufacturers have a long track record of operating globally. Japanese manufacturers have joined the international trade in earthmoving equipment, once dominated by American corporations, e.g. Caterpillar has a joint venture with Mitsubishi Heavy Industries and Komatsu have built a worldwide reputation. European manufacturers such as Leibherr and Potain have been leaders in the manufacture of tower cranes, but now there is worldwide competition from USA, Scandinavia, China and the Russian Federation.

Property and facility management is still growing in prominence. The development of facility management has been made more significant by increasing demands emanating from environmental issues and the continuing trend in privatization. Industry has responded by embracing the growing practice of private public partnerships (PPP) and the use of private funds to support public projects. Such projects normally incorporate a concession to allow the potential for organizations delivering construction projects to extend their involvement by participating in the income generated from the completed building. Such arrangements take a number of different forms from Build Operate and Transfer to Private Finance Initiative where a concessionaire generates funds for the design and construction of the project, which will be set against operating income over a specified time period.

International trade in construction goods and services concerns a range of economic transactions, which occur across national boundaries between two or more organizations for mutual direct or indirect benefit. Orders are placed and contracts are awarded internationally when an organization in one country has gained competitive advantage over competitors in other countries, usually by exploiting expertise, low labour costs and indigenously occurring raw materials. However, the motivation to export and import goods and services will in some cases be subjected to moderation by national regulations that keep close control over the balance of exports and imports to ensure that national economies remain stable. Construction spending in 2000 represented a total of 2,722,980 million US$ and dispersion over world regions is shown in Figure 3.5.

Region	Million US$	%
North America	903,340	33.175
European Union	641,160	23.546
Asia and Japan	683,820	25.113
Russia & E. Eur.	80,790	2.967
South America	136,790	5.024
Middle East	49,400	1.814
The Rest	227,680	8.361
Total	2,722,980	100.00

Figure 3.5: Dispersion of construction spending
Source: Generated from World Development Indicators, World Bank 2001
        and Bon & Crosswaite 2000

Evidence from Figures 3.5 and 3.6 shows a correlation with world trade and that North America spends considerably more on construction when compared with Japan, Europe and the remainder of Asia.

The ranking of the top ten countries by construction spending in 2000 was dominated by AICs , however, there was a significant NIC presence from China, Brazil and the Republic of Korea. Consideration of the top 10 countries ranked by construction spending per capita provides an indication of individual prosperity, but this ranking is still dominated by AICs (Figure 3.6). Nevertheless, NIC nations with small populations and high GDP per capita are present, notably Singapore and Hong Kong.

In a survey conducted by ENR and reported by Bon and Crosswaite (2000), an attempt was made to establish the views of respondents concerning the fastest growing construction markets in the world for the period 1993–1998. The results showed overwhelming support for China, followed by Germany, Vietnam and Malaysia. It is clear from Figure 3.7 that NICs feature far more strongly, which provides an indication that some movement is taking place in the world's economic activity and hence the distribution of wealth.

Country	Rank by constr. spend 2000	Ratio of highest spender	Country	Ranked by highest spending per capita 2000	Ratio of highest spender
USA	1	1.0000	Luxembg	1	1.0000
Japan	2	0.4732	Japan	2	0.8544
Germany	3	0.1892	USA	3	0.8130
China	4	0.1638	Switzerland	4	0.7753
UK	5	0.1429	Norway	5	0.7684
France	6	0.1301	Iceland	6	0.7276
Italy	7	0.1081	Ireland	7	0.7180
Brazil	8	0.0891	Denmark	8	0.6983
Mexico	9	0.0727	Hong Kong	9	0.6934
Canada	10	0.0727	Singapore	10	0.6697

Figure 3.6. Top 10 countries ranked by total and per capita spending on construction in 2000
Source: Adapted World Development Indicators, World Bank 2001 and Bon & Crosswaite 2000

Rank	Country	Frequency
1	China	416
2	Germany	16
3	Vietnam	14
4	Malaysia	13
5	Indonesia	12
5=	Russia	12
6	South Korea	9
7	RSA	8
8	USA	6
9	Brazil	4
9=	India	4
9=	Poland	4
9=	Thailand	4
10	Croatia	3
10=	Mexico	3

Figure 3.7: Respondent predictions of the fastest growing
construction markets in the world 1993–98
Source: Bon and Crosswaite (2000)

In 2000, the Chinese construction market grew by 10%, which was approximately in line with the growth in GDP. It is predicted that China's construction industry will grow at approximately 8% per annum up to 2004. These figures make it clear that China will become a growing force in the global construction industry. This is confirmed by the activities of the international arm of China State Construction Corporation which now operates in all continents throughout the world. It is also worth noting that growth within China is expanding, especially in materials manufacturing industries that traditionally supply construction, particularly cement, steel, ceramic tiles and gypsum. Low costs in China ensure that any surpluses will be exported to earn hard currency in North America and Europe. A similar situation is occurring in India where wage structures and costs are at a similar level.

Bon and Crosswaite's study indicates that the more wealthy nations are likely to spend more on construction, but the per capita ranking in Figure 3.6 gives an indication of individual wealth which may provide some clues regarding the profile of construction work undertaken. It was further established that AICs are likely in future to require refurbishment and maintenance services in greater proportion compared with new work, but it should be remembered that the ability to generate wealth in itself promotes the need for construction work and in particular new projects.

Case study 3.1: Opportunities and benefits of the WTO rules-based system

At the fundamental core of the WTO is a rules based system intended to provide freedom for international trade to take place. The ideal involves negotiated commitments between members which promote progressive trade liberalization and guarantee fairness in commercial relations and safeguards against protectionist impulses. All the rules are negotiated and agreed by consensus between Member governments. Associated with this is a system of rights and benefits that adhere to the principle of good governance, which in turn will attract foreign direct investment.

Many countries throughout the world have stable and credible economies and governance, however, it is important to demonstrate their commitment to trade policy stability and good governance. One way of achieving this is through membership of the WTO. Moreover, it has been proved over the past 50 years that the WTO liberalization and trading system works. Trade within a free and peaceful environment generates foreign exchange earnings and mobilizes domestic resources for economic growth, which implies that capacity in terms of resources and infrastructure must be in place to support such development.

At the WTO Doha Ministerial Conference held in November 2001, members accepted an agenda to launch a comprehensive set of trade negotiations to be completed by 1 January 2005. An interim Ministerial Conference to be held in Mexico was set in place for September 2002 to check progress and to make further decisions as necessary. It was recognized that one of the keys to success would be technical assistance and capacity building intended to assist poorer members to integrate fully into the trading system and to participate fully in negotiations. In 2002, members approved a global trust fund of 30 million Swiss francs for technical assistance to support the Doha Agenda. The WTO is seeking to be innovative, using its Training Institute to provide courses for government and trade officials who will advise Ministers representing poorer members. In association with other agencies, WTO is also developing a new database intended to identify the gaps in trade-related technical assistance. WTO recognizes that developing countries and economies in transition for WTO require trade-related technical assistance that extends far beyond what WTO is able to provide, nevertheless much can be achieved by facilitation through membership alone.

It has been estimated that reducing barriers to trade in agriculture, manufacturing and services by 33% would increase the world economy by US$613 billion, and if trade barriers were eliminated altogether global income could be boosted by US$2.8 trillion and would have the effect of bringing 320 million people out of poverty by 2015.

Of most concern is the extent to which trade barriers and tariffs imposed by rich countries affect the world's poorest countries. In terms of development, the elimination of all trade and non-tariff barriers could result in developing countries gaining US$32 billion in agriculture, US$162 billion in manufacturing and US$182 billion in the services sector. The faster that these impediments can be removed, the quicker that returns to developing countries will take place.

For trade facilitation to work there must be transparency in government procurement, competition policy and trade facilitation at the highest political levels. This must be supported by public infrastructure able to promote domestic property rights and justice systems adequately — further domestic red-tape only serves to support bureaucracy and is costly and corrosive. It may therefore be concluded that the Doha tasks set for WTO in the interest of improved international trading relationships are increased technical assistance, improved transparency and accountability, facilitation of coherence with other world agencies and effective communication of benefits to all concerned. The accession to WTO membership is directly linked to a credible system of domestic reform intended to align internal economic and legal structures with international norms, of which the WTO Agreement is an expression.

Author's commentary
WTO Membership has served the interests of its initial membership, i.e. the world's most powerful nations, however, it has now embarked on broadening its membership to include less prosperous developing nations, as typified by the Doha Ministerial Conference. This presents an unprecedented challenge and it will be interesting to see if the objectives laid down can be achieved by 2005. The episodes of 2002 relating to squabbles about steel and agricultural tariffs between the United States of America and the European Union did not set a good example in the light of the requirements and promises made to third world ministers at Doha.

It is clear that there needs to be a unifying body that will act in the common interest of all member states and at the moment the WTO is appropriate to that need.

With the increasing scale of membership, countries that remain outside WTO will face increasing difficulty in pursuing international trade. It is therefore not surprising that the number of countries seeking membership has dramatically increased. The membership structure of WTO has the potential to create a new world order in the conduct of international trade.

Case study 3.2: General Agreement on Tariffs and Trade (GATT) and the Goods Council

The operation and implementation of the GATT agreement is the responsibility of the Council for Trade in Goods (Goods Council), which comprises representatives from all WTO member countries.

The positioning and relationships that the Council for Trade in Goods has within the WTO structure is shown in the diagram below:

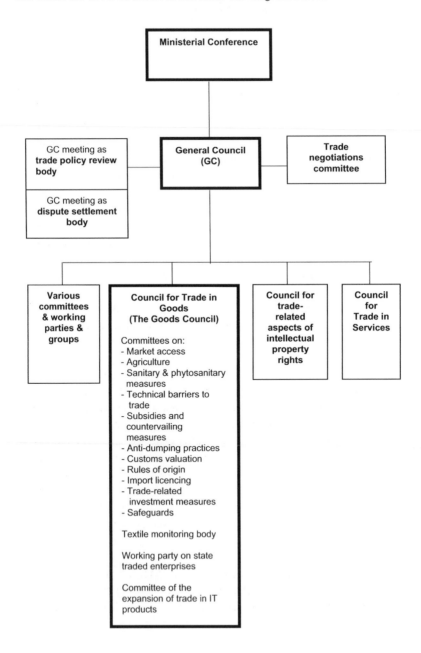

Some prime features of the work of the Goods Council are:

Anti-dumping actions
Dumping is when a company exports a product at a lower price than it normally charges on its home market. Governments will normally take action against dumping when indigenous industry is threatened. The Agreement does not pass judgement, instead it concentrates on how governments can or cannot react to dumping, therefore it could be said that the WTO disciplines anti-dumping actions. GATT Article 6 allows countries to take action against dumping.

Safeguards: emergency protection from imports
Under Article 19 a WTO member may take action to restrict imports of a product temporarily if domestic industry is seriously threatened. The WTO Agreement sets out the requirements for safeguard investigations by national authorities, which must include publically announced hearings where all interested parties can give evidence.

When a country restricts imports in order to safeguard domestic producers, in principle something must be given in return and if no agreement is reached then the exporting country will be entitled to retaliate by taking equivalent action. Developing countries are to some extent shielded from safeguard actions in that safeguarding measures cannot be taken if their imported market share in that country is less than 3%.

The WTO Safeguards Committee oversees the operation of the Agreement and is responsible for the surveillance of member commitments. The Committee also reviews reports from governments on each phase of safeguard investigations and related decision making.

Subsidies and countervailing measures
The agreement disciplines the use of subsidies and regulates the actions of countries in countering the effects of subsidies. A country can seek the withdrawal of a subsidy, or its adverse effects, through the WTO's dispute settlement procedure. Alternatively, a country can mount its own investigation which, if a measure is proven to cause serious harm to domestic producers, can lead to countervailing measures where extra duties are charged on the imported goods in question. There are three categories of subsidy namely, prohibited, actionable and non-actionable. Least developed countries with less than US$1000 per capita GNP are exempted from disciplines on prohibited export subsidies.

Trade facilitation
Trade facilitation may be described as the simplification and harmonization of international trade by the utilization of trade procedures, processes and formalities necessary for the movement of goods in international trade. This definition covers a wide range of activities including cross-border

procedures, customs licensing procedures, transport formalities, payments and insurance.

At the Doha Conference, members of WTO recognized the progress that had been made in this area over the past four years but agreed that there was a case for further expediting the movement, release and clearance of goods, including goods in transit. Steps have therefore been taken to clarify and improve relevant aspects of Articles V, VIII and X of the GATT 1994 and identify the trade facilitation needs and priorities of Members, in particular developing and least developed countries.

Author's commentary

GATT plays a fundamental role in the achievement of the ideals laid down by WTO.

Members are free to take their own actions relating to freedom of trade, however, GATT provides an agreed and identifiable framework within which members are expected to operate. Members who ignore and continue to breach articles contained within the Agreement will face sanctions from other members and ultimately expulsion.

The WTO has been criticized for retaining mass management of its members, which does not lend itself to operational efficiency or serious policy discussion. In contrast, the IMF and the World Bank have an executive board to direct the officers of their organizations. The converse argument is that a world trading order can only be achieved through consensus rather than dictate; hence the outcomes are more important than the process.

Country profile 3.3: Peoples' Republic of China

China's construction market is continuing to grow despite a downturn in the world economy. GDP in 2000 was 1076.9 billion US$ and the projected growth in GDP 2000–2004 is expected to be 7.4%. Exports in 2000 amounted to 249.4 billion US$, while imports were 225.1 billion US$ therefore producing a healthy balance of payments. Despite strong economic growth, GDP per capita (2000) remained low at 853US$ and the GDP per three-person household amounted to only 2559US$. World Trade Organisation membership is being phased in over a ten-year period but the yuan(RMB) remains a non-convertible international currency, although the final intention is that it should eventually be a freely traded currency.

Global construction consultants, contractors and suppliers already have business interests in China but there is only a small number of medium-sized companies, who are engaged solely for their specialist expertise.

The Chinese construction industry has been regarding as a 'pillar industry' and has therefore attracted considerable government investment in construction projects. The Government's current five-year plan is concentrating on developing the rural Western regions of China that have not attracted the same sort of investment as the eastern coastal region. This initiative is known as the 'Go West' programme.

Housing reform and the provision of improved housing standards is a major priority and annually China is producing approximately 300 million square metres of new housing every year. The development of the country's transport system has been a priority and the building of expressways, airports and railways linking the major cities has provided opportunities for foreign consultants. Power generation has been another priority area, the most important project being the construction of the Three Gorges Dam, which also is intended to improve water supply and irrigation as well as making the Yangtze River more navigable throughout the year.

Foreign construction engineering companies making enquiries about the potential of the market are in danger of being dazzled by the scale of development, but all is not what it appears. Unrestricted access to the construction and engineering market is not possible and it will be necessary to conform to restrictions imposed by the government. It is normally the case that competition will not be allowed from a wholly owned foreign enterprise and it will therefore be necessary to enter into a joint venture with a local partner or a collaborative agreement with a Chinese design institute, of which there are upwards of 12,000.

All construction design undertaken by foreign firms must be approved by a Chinese design institute, and the detailed design will invariably be undertaken locally. The domestic construction market is protected by the Ministry of Construction, which has issued a decree stating that foreign firms only have access to the following projects in China:

i.   projects that are entirely foreign-invested;
ii.   projects that are financed by international organizations that require an international tender or bidding process;
iii. Chinese–foreign joint venture projects where the domestic enterprise cannot cope by itself due to a lack of technology or experience; and
iv.   domestic projects where a suitable designer, engineer or architect cannot be found.

As a result of these restrictions foreign firms can only compete for a small percentage of China's numerous construction projects. While it is true that many foreign enterprises are winning new projects every year, the overwhelming majority of Chinese-funded infrastructure and housing projects are not open to foreign competition.

The Ministry of Construction licenses four classes of Chinese design institutes and construction enterprises. Firms with a 'Class A' licence are permitted to undertake design and construction of any size or complexity of project anywhere in China. The remaining classes, namely 'B', 'C', and 'D' licence holders can win contracts for progressively smaller projects at the provincial, city and county levels.

There are approaching 100,000 Chinese construction enterprises, over 2000 of which are large companies with in-house design teams, or who have close working relationships with the design institutes. While the quality of work may not be first class, there is nevertheless a plentiful supply of cheap design and construction capability over the broad range of construction work.

One of the most common market entry strategies is to win contracts through the international bidding process, which will mean establishing a joint venture, opening a representative office or entering into a cooperative agreement with a design institute. Another way would be to enter an international design competition.

Although the market is restricted, foreign companies have been successful in undertaking preliminary design work and project management for hotels, commercial developments, infrastructure and petrochemical plants. Clearly, the cost of entry into this potentially huge market will need to be offset against the ability to maintain income from a continuing ability to win work. Problems associated with culture, language and currency make the Chinese market especially difficult in the light of restrictions imposed by the socialist market economy. There would appear to be scope for global materials and component suppliers who can tap into the low cost production and raw materials with a view to exporting products to wealthy countries while at the same time making good profits.

Author's commentary

The next ten years will very probably bring major changes and advances in the Chinese market as phased WTO membership is introduced. However, there are considerable risks, which need to be appraised carefully before market entry, or before established companies initiative further investment and expansion.

Company profile 3.4: A global strategic player: Caterpillar Inc. Peoria, Illinois, USA

The Caterpillar organization was conceived in 1890 by Benjamin Holt ,together with Daniel Best who experimented with steam engines before pioneering gasoline powered tractor engines. The company diversified its product line over a fifty-year period, and in 1945 was producing a large range of heavy earthmoving and grading equipment. In 1950, the first venture was taken overseas with the establishment of Caterpillar Tractor (GB) Co. Ltd in the United Kingdom. This was the forerunner of many overseas operations   created to assist the management of foreign exchange shortages, tariffs, import controls and above all to serve customers around the world.

In 1963, Caterpillar and Mitsubishi Heavy Industries Limited formed one of the first joint ventures in Japan, which included partial US ownership. Caterpillar Mitsubishi Ltd started production in 1965 and has since been renamed Shin Caterpillar Mitsubishi Ltd, and is now the second largest manufacturer of construction and mining equipment in Japan.

In 1996, Caterpillar made a further acquisition with the takeover of Mak Motoren Germany and, by purchasing Perkins Engines, UK in 1997, the company became the world leader in commercial diesel engine manufacturing. Caterpillar is now the world's largest manufacturer of construction and mining equipment, diesel and natural gas engines and industrial gas turbines. Caterpillar has a Logistics Division that provides fully integrated logistics solutions for both internal and third party clients and it also offers a variety of financing options through its Financial Products Division.

The company's 2001 sales and revenues were $20.45 billion, $275 million higher than 2000 and 50% of sales were to overseas customers. This performance has maintained its position as a leading US exporter with US exports amounting to $4.8 billion in 2001. Caterpillar products and components are manufactured in 48 plants in the United States and 58 plants located in 20 overseas countries. To maintain itself as a world leader, Caterpillar has invested heavily over the past six years, which has resulted in more than 2800 patents being filed. In 2001, the company spent more than $700 million in research and technology.

A key part of Caterpillar corporate strategy has been the institutionalization of the 6 Sigma culture and philosophy. 6 Sigma is a relentless quest for perfection through the disciplined use of data based, fact driven, decision making methodology. It is the key to achieving growth and cost reduction targets that translate to improved shareholder value. 6 Sigma will complement and accelerate many efforts currently underway, such as Class A certification, cost reduction teams and quality improvement teams. Caterpillar seeks to achieve a competitive edge through its dealer network, which is tasked with providing superior customer service. The worldwide network consists of 220 dealers, 157 outside the United States. Caterpillar dealers operate more than 1840 branch locations around the world with 643 Cat Dealer Rental Stores.

Recently, Caterpillar Inc. and Mitsubishi Heavy Industries Ltd (MHI) have signed an agreement to expand and strengthen their long-standing joint venture, Shin Caterpillar Mitsubishi Ltd (SCM). Over the next few years, MHI will transfer its construction equipment production, excluding motor graders, to SCM's manufacturing facility in Sagamihara, Japan. This includes the production of compact wheel loaders, track-type tractors, mobile rock crushers, crawler carriers and articulated trucks. The transfer will provide additional manufacturing space for MHI's growing material handling and engine businesses, where MHI and Caterpillar also have alliances. Shin Caterpillar Mitsubishi Ltd is a 50/50 joint venture between Caterpillar Inc. of Peoria, Illinois (USA) and Mitsubishi Heavy Industries Ltd of Tokyo, Japan. The partnership, one of the oldest and most successful joint ventures involving a US company in Japan, will celebrate its 40th anniversary in 2003.

SCM has become a leading supplier of earthmoving and construction equipment in Japan. The joint venture manufactures construction equipment under the Caterpillar brand name for sale domestically and exports to Caterpillar marketing companies worldwide.

Mitsubishi Heavy Industries Ltd provides a broad range of products and services including shipbuilding, steel structures, machinery for industrial and general use, power systems, air conditioners and aerospace systems. MHI posted sales and revenues in 2000 of $24.58 billion.

Caterpillar is dedicated to sustaining the environment and improving the quality of life. In everything it does the company is guided by its 'Code of Worldwide Business Conduct'. The intention is to meet or exceed local environmental regulations, develop solutions to customers' environmental challenges, advocate free trade and take the lead in the business community on important issues. One such breakthrough technology is Advanced Combustion Emissions Reduction Technology (ACERT™ technology), which Caterpillar expects to make available to meet on-highway truck emissions regulations in the third quarter of 2003. ACERT technology dramatically reduces engine emissions without sacrificing the reliability and durability expected by customers. Caterpillar will offer ACERT technology as an environmentally responsible alternative to cooled-EGR technology offered by others in the industry.

Author's commentary

The historical development of Caterpillar Inc. provides a classic illustration of a company that created a strong home market because commencing its overseas operations in the 1950's. The rationale behind this development was to overcome difficulties created by foreign exchange shortages and import controls.

By the adoption of a consistent policy of acquisition, joint ventures and strategic alliances, the company has grown into a truly global organization whose product brand is known and respected throughout the world.

Successful business results over a number of years has made Caterpillar financially strong and this has provided funds for product programs to meet future customer needs, provide financing for dealers and customers, and reward its shareholders. The company expects to generate sales in excess of $30 billion by the middle of this decade and, based on past performance, this would appear to be a reasonable prediction.

Summary

This chapter draws attention to the growing globalization of the world's construction industries assisted by developments in communication technology and international transportation systems. A study of the international construction industry indicates that the top consultants, construction companies and suppliers are in a constant state of change brought about by the need to expand and diversify their activities according to corporate aims and objectives. Such change is compounded by the continuous requirement to take on projects in order to maintain turnover and profitability.

There is a link between the strongest trading nations and the strength of their respective economies, which generate growth and prosperity. It may therefore by concluded that the prime regions for construction activity are North America, Europe and the Far East (including Japan). The world's strongest economies are the prime strategic markets to be targeted by most global consultants and contractors. Newly industrialized countries will also be targeted and performance will be appraised regarding future prospects for investment and growth. There will also be a market in LDCs for infrastructure projects funded by the World Bank and other regional development banks.

As a general rule, NICs and LDCs actively encourage direct foreign investment since it provides new technology, creates jobs and makes a significant contribution to the economy and balance of payments. South American countries at first glance look to be attractive because of plentiful supplies of raw materials and low labour costs, however, these economies have a reputation for being volatile and in some cases politically unstable and therefore extreme caution is necessary when considering investment. African states are notoriously unstable and in the main have weak economies and a relatively poorly educated workforce, hence they experience great difficulty in attracting sufficient foreign direct investment. Instead they rely on aid and soft loans to survive. The unfortunate consequence is that the relative development of their economies is slower and as a result the economic gap with NICs and AICs is continually widening with adverse affects on national economies and jobs.

The largest global players have recognized the need expand their interests where market demand is high and to accommodate the need to adapt to the specific needs of regional and local markets. Hence, joint ventures, mergers and the acquisition of compatible businesses are accepted as being the normal means to expand and undertake further work that otherwise would have been impossible. Joint ventures are more likely to be concerned with individual projects, whereas mergers and acquisitions are of a more strategic and long-term nature. It is therefore very difficult to assess the extent and size of the largest global organizations in construction because their business portfolios are in a continual state of change.

The relationship between national prosperity, international trade and the incidence of construction work on a global scale has been demonstrated. North America, Europe and Japan dominate world trade, and as a consequence the global construction market, but it is important to look at newly industrialized nations and their recent growth rates. China is a leading player with the potential to change the future nature of the global construction industry in the next 50 years. India also has demonstrated impressive growth, but the prosperity of individuals, as indicated by GDP per capita, is low due primarily to population size. Other countries with potential include Brazil, Korea and Mexico. African countries continue to make progress, but they are held back by a lack of foreign direct investment and instead rely on assistance in the form of aid and soft loans made by international agencies such as the World Bank.

The ability to attract direct foreign investment is an important aspect of wealth generation and this is a vital prerequisite for the generation of construction work. Countries with poor economic, social and political stability will be unlikely to attract the attention of foreign investors who will be looking at only the best markets to generate a good return. An important prerequisite is for governments, especially those of LDCs, to create the necessary environmental and trading conditions where investment risk is perceived to be acceptable. Inward foreign investment creates jobs and contributes hard currency to strengthen local economies.

Non-governmental institutions such as the WTO, GATT and the OECD play an important role in promoting fair trade and harmonizing trading practices. The growing gap between the most prosperous nations and the poorest nations is a matter of concern and positive steps are being taken by these organizations to eliminate unfair trade barriers and provide greater opportunities for LDCs. The IMF is an important global body that seeks to support countries in financial difficulty by means of loans that carry heavy conditions regarding the regulation of national expenditure. The World Bank and the various regional development banks provide vital support for LDCs, the prime objectives being poverty reduction and the improvement of living standards. The international bodies mentioned are key to world economic and social stability and they have a crucial role in promoting and supporting global business.

Innovation and technological development play an important role in sustaining the global construction industry and as a consequence AICs will continue to dominate the international construction market. Reference has been made to the change in nature of the construction industries associated with AICs in the sense that the emphasis changes from new work to maintenance and refurbishment. As a general rule, the proportion of GDP spent by AICs on construction drops when compared to NICs.

The following chapters will cover essential topics that contribute to the overall understanding of the execution of construction related activities across national boundaries and cultures. The complexities and causality of world trade in general and the specific markets concerned with construction have a strong and distinctive relationship. The key drivers are the creation of prosperity and stability that translate into the need to procure construction work necessary to support the business and living environments.

Further reading

Arthur K. *et al.* (1998), *Global project business and the dynamics of change*, Global Project Business.

Bon R. & Crosswaite D. (2000), *The future of international construction*, Thomas Telford, London.

Buckley P. J., Purton F. N. & Mizza H. (1998), *The strategy and organization of international business*, Macmillan.

Caves R. E., Frankel J. A. & Jones R. W. (1999), *World trade and payments: an introduction*, 8th edition, Addison Wesley.

Chinowsky P. S. (2001), 'Strategic management in engineering organisations', *J. Management in Engineering*, **17**, Issue 2, 60–68.

Costa L. A. (1999), 'Steeling for a trade war', *Fortune*, **139**, No. 1.

ENR (1995), Top global contractors, ENR 28-08-95, pp. 99–100.

ENR (1995), Top 200 international design firms, ENR 24-07-95 pp. 41–42.

ENR (1998), 'World market overview', *Engineering Record*, Nov. 30, 35–38, McGraw-Hill, New York.

ENR (1999), Top 225 International contractors, ENR 16-08-99, pp. 66–77.

ENR (2001), Top 200 International design firms. (on-line: www.enr.com)

ENR (2001), Top 200 International contractors. (on-line: www.enr.com)

General Agreement on Trade and Tariffs (2002), GATT (on-line www.gatt.org).

Hecksscher E. (1991), *The effect of foreign trade on the distribution of income*, MIT Press.

International Monetary Fund (1997), *Statistics Year Book*.

Langford D. & Rowland V. R. (1995), *Managing overseas construction*, Thomas Telford, London.

Mawhinney M. (2001), *International construction*, Blackwell Science Ltd, London.

Mendenhall M., Punnett B. J. & Ricks D. (1995), *Global management*, Blackwell Publishers.

OECD (2001), *Basic structural statistics* (on-line www.oecd.org).

OECD (2002), *Main economic indicators* (on-line www.oecd.org_).

OECD (2002), *Main trade statistics* (on-line www.oecd.org).

Ricardo D. (1981), *The principles of political economy and taxation*, Chapter 7, Cambridge University Press.

Schmitt N. (1991), *New international trade theories and europe*, Simon Fraser University, Burnaby, Canada.

US Department of Commerce (on-line www.itaiep.doc.gov).

World Bank (2001), World development indicators database (on-line www.worldbank.org).

World Bank (2002), *Overview and mission statement* (on-line www.worldbank.org).

World Bank (2002), *International development association* (on-line www.worldbank.org).

World Trade Organisation (2002), *A system for change*, (on-line www.gatt.org/docsystem.html).

Worrell H., Norman G. & Flanagan R. (2001), 'Intervention analysis and overseas trade in UK construction related materials and components', **13**, Issue 6, *Construction Management & Economics*, E. & F. N. Spon, London.

Chapter 4

Corporate strategy

Introduction

The international construction market is in a constant state of change and it is important that those companies already participating in other foreign countries should keep their corporate strategy under periodic review. This requires a conscious effort to gather market intelligence and to keep ahead of events, thus mitigating adverse circumstances before they have a chance to make a full impact. Construction companies that already operate internationally can be classified by those who operate globally, regionally or in a limited number of countries where they have gained previous experience and competitive advantage. There will also be companies whose previous interests relate exclusively in the domestic market but who are seeking to enter the international market for the first time.

The majority of international construction companies will have commenced with a limited operation, normally involving one country. Those who experience initial success will be more likely to expand their businesses, eventually leading to growth by investing in other countries. Conversely, a lack of success is likely to encourage withdrawal back into the domestic market.

This chapter examines the factors that contribute towards developing a robust corporate strategy applicable to companies who operate internationally. The objective will be to enhance the likelihood of success and to reduce the risk associated with international construction.

The decision to seek international work and the foreign entry choice

The reasons for seeking business in other countries are diverse, however the overriding driver is the perceived opportunity to achieve an improved rate of return on investment. When there is plenty of work in the domestic market and the potential to make profit is good then it is more difficult to establish valid reasons to seek work in other countries. Where there is recession in the home market, or where there is excessive competition that drives profits down, firms may be tempted to look elsewhere to find more favourable market conditions. If the home market has reached saturation then growth will be difficult to achieve and new markets must be found to achieve expansion. Under these circumstances it is reasonable to investigate foreign markets where there is a demand for the company's services and products.

The prime task will be to gather information in a structured manner so that it can be objectively assessed. A model useful for this purpose is Porter's model, which describes five forces that determine industry competitiveness (see Figure 4.1).

Porter's model is commonly used to evaluate the balance and competitive state of a country's construction industry by examining the degree of rivalry between the market players. Where growth exists and profits are high it is likely that new entrants will be attracted to enter the market. In order to do this they will need to be more competitive and attractive to potential clients. This will cause retaliation from existing players who will try to hold on to their customers by keeping costs to a minimum and by calling on client loyalty. They might also lobby government to place restrictions on new foreign competition entering the market.

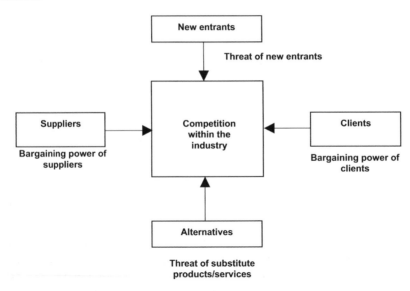

Figure 4.1. Porter's five forces model of industrial competitiveness
Source: Adapted from Michael Porter, *Competitive strategy*
(New York Free Press, 1980), p. 4

Informed clients will be well aware of the degree of competition and will be keen to obtain the best possible deal. Hence, industrial competitors will each have their own strategy to retain existing customers and to attract new clients, thereby increasing their market share at the expense of the competition. One way of staying competitive will be to improve the performance of the supply chain by quality improvement and cost reduction. Competitiveness can also be increased by acquiring control of key suppliers to the industry. In this manner more control can be exerted over the prices that can be charged for services, products and goods.

There will always be the threat from services and products that have been developed through innovation and research or the progressive improvement of existing products. It must also be recognized that from time to time major leaps forward in technology are likely to render existing services and products obsolete. Therefore market intelligence is vital to anticipate such changes well in advance.

The model seeks to evaluate the relative attractiveness of the five forces and this will form a sound basis for developing the company's corporate strategy. A typical application of the model is shown in Figure 4.2.

Other approaches have been proposed, including the Boston Consulting Group (BCG), who historically emphasized concepts relating to:

1. experience curve: as the volume of output increases unit costs fall at a geometric rate due to standardization, specialization , learning and scale effects;

2. product life cycle: a line of business develops through four phases: development, growth, maturity and decline. Life cycle growth is represented by a bell-shaped curve that in its cumulative form translates into an s-curve;

3. unsuccessful firms in the decline stage will either merge or exit from the industry; and

4. portfolio balance: seeks to combine attractive investment segment (stars) with cash generating segments (cash cows). Question marks are raised over segments with low market share in high growth markets, while segments with unattractive prospects (dogs) should be considered for disposal or closure Figure 4.3.

It is argued by critics of this approach that volume cost relationships and product life are mainly applicable to product manufacturing and are less relevant in project situations and that judging the portfolio balance on growth does not take into account such factors as innovation, quality and choice. Given that there are limitations on growth and if competitors adopt the same strategy, then there must be winners and losers and hence in the case of the losers the strategy will fail.

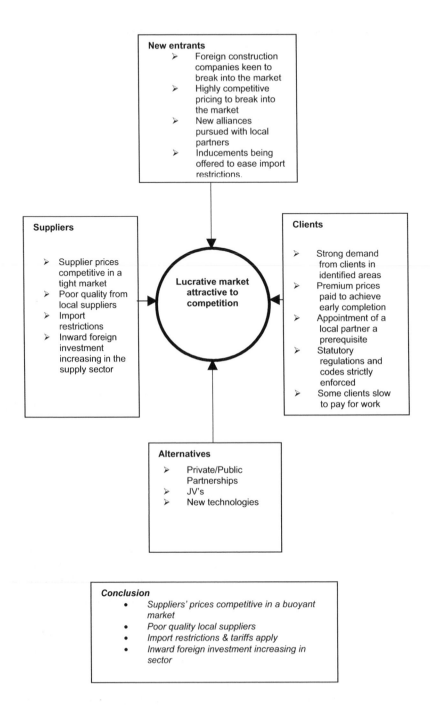

Figure 4.2: Environmental analysis utilizing Porter's model of international
        competitiveness

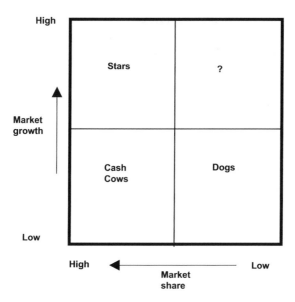

Figure 4.3: BCG portfolio matrix

Other writers stress the uniqueness of the organization and emphasize the importance of matching resources to investment opportunities under environmental uncertainty, compounded by uncertain competitors actions and reactions (Ansoff and McDonnell, 1990; Mintzberg, Quinn and Ghogal, 1995). Unstructured problem situations of this nature require adaptive processes whereby solutions are determined in an iterative manner, as opposed to all-embracing solutions, normally involving mathematical models.

National competitiveness

An important part of national competitiveness is the ability of a nation to continually innovate. Some nations have acquired the knowledge and culture to effect continuous improvement across a broad range of their output, whereas others have not. Porter (1990) maintains that there are four attributes that collectively and individually contribute to and determine national competitive advantage. These are factor conditions, demand conditions, related and supporting industries and the structure of firms and their rivalry which are assembled diagrammatically in the form of a 'diamond' as shown in Figure 4.4.

Factor conditions are those resources in the form of skills, raw materials, know-how, financial and infrastructure. The abundance of such resources will considerably influence the international trading status of a nation.

Demand conditions concern the make-up of demand in the domestic market and its nature and sophistication relative to that of other markets. For example, an unsophisticated product is unlikely to be an attractive item to export.

Related and supporting industries will be internationally competitive and will contribute to their domestic supply chains. Such industries will also play an important part in adding value and competitiveness to products and services capable of being exported.

Firm structure and rivalry concern the corporate goals and quality of management within individual companies and the degree of competition that exists resulting in a continuous drive for competitive advantage.

Environmental variables will also play a role in this model and will need to be taken into account. Government influence and policy will have a significant bearing alongside the occurrence of the unexpected.

Porter's diamond framework can be extended to undertake an evaluation of a combination of company and national advantages. It is therefore possible to create a competitive advantage loop where company-specific advantages (CSA) and national-specific advantages (NSA) are periodically reviewed to establish whether changes to corporate strategy are necessary (Figure 4.5).

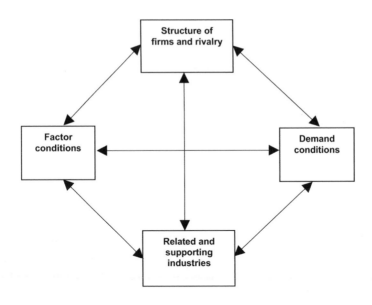

Figure 4.4: Porter's diamond framework
Source: Adapted from M. E. Porter (1990)

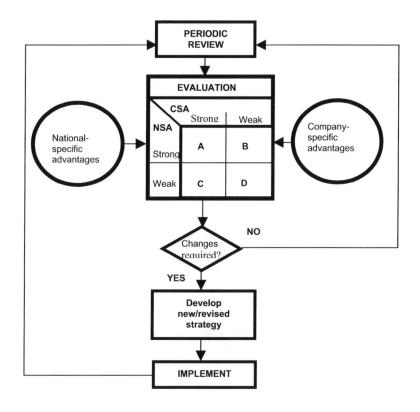

Figure 4.5: Methodology for review of corporate strategy

Companies in position A will be at the greatest advantage. Companies in B and C are in positions with potential for improvement by moving to A. The solution for companies in position C may be to move the business to a nation with strong advantages, whereas companies in position B will be looking inwardly at how to improve. A company in position D is in danger of going out of business altogether.

Macro-global strategies

The simplest global strategy is to operate as far as possible from the home base and to standardize procedures and systems involved in infrastructure support for projects.

Figure 4.6 shows that there are many different kinds of strategy depending on the configuration of the global company and the way in which it manages its value and supply.

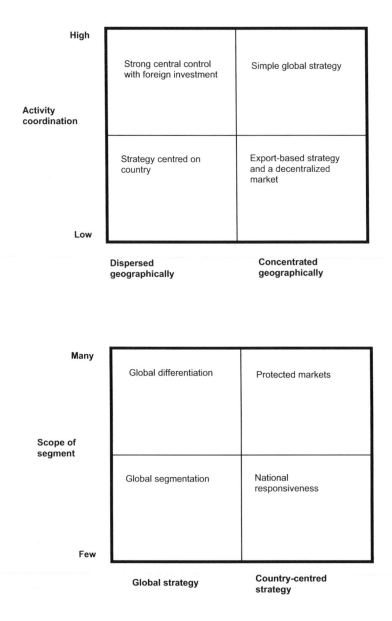

Figure 4.6: Different types of global strategy

It may therefore be stated that a company's global strategy seeks to gain competitive advantage from its international presence, through either a concentrated configuration or by coordinating many dispersed activities, or a combination of both. The ability to coordinate the geographical dispersion of business activities and projects is a growing requirement where companies must seek out competitive advantage and then overcome organization and system barriers to exploit opportunities. This is likely to occur where the home country provides a good platform of relevant factor conditions for a business to operate competitively.

In order to operate globally it will be necessary to take advantage of relevant factor conditions that occur in more than one country, hence the need for a more diversified strategy requiring higher coordination and stronger central control.

Internal capability assessment

Further analysis will be required to examine a firm's strengths and weaknesses in the light of the market identified and the extent and competence of the competition. The GE-McKinsey matrix shown in Figure 4.7 develops the BCG matrix of Figure 4.3 by including strategic decisions that determine the fundamental business direction of the whole or individual parts of the business.

Critics argue that both the GE-McKinsey and BCG models are too simple and that they do not represent the reality of business decision making. As a consequence, firms like Shell have accepted more complex matrices comprising three or more dimensions. Figure 4.8 illustrates the Shell model.

The physical resources available to enable the firm to support entry into a new construction market will need to be fully assessed to establish how they can be effectively utilized. Location and disposition must be judged according to the cost of delivering services and products to various projects within the country in question. Those construction companies that already have an established infrastructure, network and supply chain will have a considerable advantage over new entrants into the market who will need to incrementally build up their contacts and suppliers.

The manner in which an organization structure is built up will usually play a key role in the success of an international construction company. Cost effectiveness, unique competitiveness and the ability to focus on strengths to meet market demands are of vital importance. Some companies will be horizontally integrated where the prime components of the business are brought into play to satisfy market demand. In construction this may be typified by bringing together design specialisms, product and equipment supply, project management and facility management. Where such subsets of the business work entirely within its corporate boundary then there is always the danger of becoming inward-looking and uncompetitive with competitors operating in the free market. It may be a better proposition to adopt a federal corporate structure where the business has major components that are largely independent profit centres that compete in the market, but will be affiliated to the holding company.

It is essential that the needs of the market are compared with the capability and capacity of the firm as it exists to accommodate demand. Where shortfalls occur then it will be necessary to establish what internal measures are necessary, together with the cost involved and the developmental time-scale. This process is illustrated in Figure 4.9. It requires the adoption of a competitive posture that best fits the corporate aims and objectives.

High
Stars
Optimize
?
Upgrade or maintain
Market growth
Cash cows
Milk
Dogs
Divest
Low
High
Low
Market share

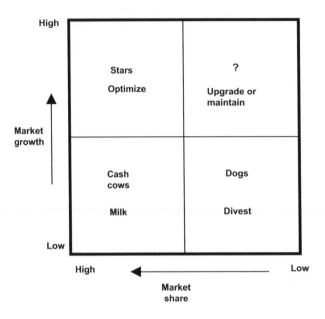

Figure 4.7: GE-McKinsey matrix

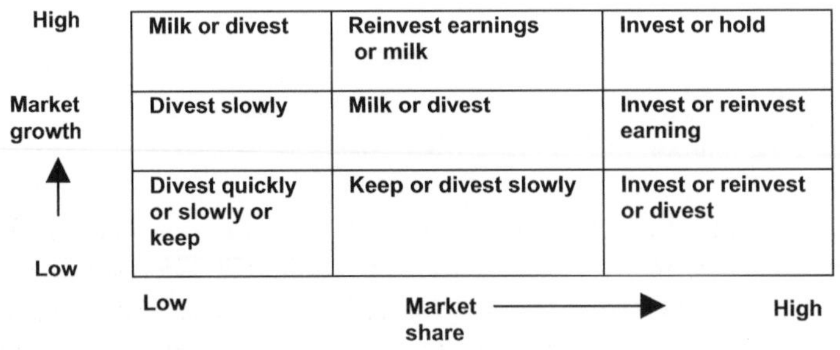

High
Milk or divest
Reinvest earnings or milk
Invest or hold
Market growth
Divest slowly
Milk or divest
Invest or reinvest earning
Divest quickly or slowly or keep
Keep or divest slowly
Invest or reinvest or divest
Low
Low
Market share
High

Figure 4.8: Shell matrix

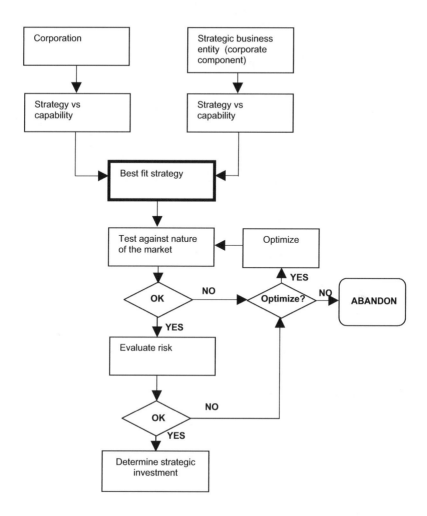

Figure 4.9: Strategic capability assessment

Consideration should also be given to the balance of the corporate portfolio and the degree of synergy created by the level of interaction between the different aspects of the business. The creation of unnecessary internal competition and adverse causal effects created by one part of the corporate business on other parts should be identified and avoided.

Developing the corporate value chain

The corporate value chain comprises all a firm's support functions that are brought together in a specific manner to carry out the business objectives necessary to achieve corporate goals. The schema shown in Figure 4.10. identifies the value chain which is initiated by the market from which a corporate strategy is developed.

Projects will be procured from clients who require construction work to be undertaken. In order to realize completed projects according to the budget, time-scale and quality standard required it will be necessary for support functions to deliver innovation, design and production according to a systemic methodology linked closely to an integrated organization structure. In this manner the resource requirements for projects are organized and managed to realize the transformation process necessary for the successful completion of projects.

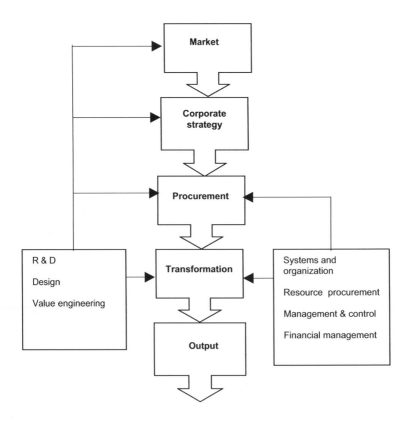

Figure 4.10: The corporate value chain

Working towards the formulation of a competitive corporate strategy

Strategic alternatives should be sought, from which will be selected the most suitable course of action that relates to the company's current situation. Account will need to be taken of the internal and external means available to the business to achieve desired objectives. The prime elements to be considered will be size, growth, stability, flexibility and technical breadth. The following questions will require robust answers.

- Can the goals of the business be achieved more quickly through external acquisition of business interests?
- Will the cost of developing the organization exceed the cost of acquisition or merger?
- Are there lower costs, fewer risks and a shorter time-scale associated with external solutions?
- Will the company find it easier to fund the purchase of other companies, rather than to fund internal development?
- Will the firms suitable for acquisition or merger gain by the adoption of the acquiring company's assets?
- Are there any tax advantages with external solutions?
- Are there any opportunities to add to the capabilities of other firms?

Where the answers to the above questions are minimal then internal solutions should be seriously considered. Because external solutions invariably involve large investment and significant risks, the advantages perceived need to be realistic, achievable and substantial. Normally, mergers and acquisitions will not make an ideal fit and the cost of making adjustments to align with business objectives will need to be taken into account. Joint ventures and strategic alliances usually involve less investment and risk; nevertheless they require substantial justification to improve the chance of a successful outcome.

Other possibilities to be considered include restructuring and divestment. Where parts of a business no longer fit comfortably into the company portfolio, or have poor profitability brought about by various factors, then they should be considered for disposal. Similarly, where the sale price is likely to be high and funds are required elsewhere, then a possible sell-off should not be overlooked. Restructuring will usually involve internal adjustments involving departmental closure and reductions in staffing and resources.

Ownership of foreign assets

The ownership of valuable foreign assets will invariably be crucial to the wealth and success of an international business and will have an influence on the degree of risk involved. Where trading conditions are favourable and a long-term involvement is envisaged then a company might be tempted to opt for total ownership. This will involve significant investment which will be exposed to risk that, under normal circumstances, should be judged to be as low as possible. In this instance, the company has complete control of operations. However, such an investment does imply the possession, or acquisition, of prior knowledge and experience of the country and the market under consideration.

An alternative approach is to seek alliances or partnerships where ownership is shared. There are three main reasons for this approach, the most common being that competitive advantage can be gained by combining expertise and resources using strategic alliances that operate across international borders. Secondly, where there is free selection of a competent and trustworthy partner, then advantages will be accruing from developing working practices and cultures, together with an established business network. The third reason is the requirement for a local partner imposed by host governments. However, there are disadvantages and risks posed by this arrangement, especially if there is a limited choice or no choice of partner.

Although many alternative variants exist, experienced international organizations commonly utilize the wholly owned subsidiary approach which is normally generated through mergers with suitable foreign companies or by means of corporate acquisition.

No ownership of foreign assets

The simplest solution in this case will be the wholesale export of products or services from the home country. This is normally considered as a safe first step, since if the venture is not successful it is easy to withdraw. Trading conditions will need to be viable and it may be possible to appoint local foreign agents to provide business assistance and advice in conjunction with an assigned project manager who will be responsible for setting up a local office and appointing local staff as required. Where single contracts are taken on it is likely that this approach will be the cheapest and most effective, since it may be possible to provide all the necessary temporary facilities within the boundary of the site.

In the case of product manufacturers, it may be possible to grant licenses to produce goods in exchange for royalty payments. In this manner, access is gained to a foreign market with low risk and investment. The main disadvantages associated with this approach are that revenue will be less and there is less control over quality. There may also be problems associated with patents and intellectual property rights.

Another solution would be to appoint a foreign company that could contribute capital and run the business to produce branded products and services. The prime advantage with this approach is that rapid expansion can be achieved with a minimum amount of capital and shared risk. Image and brand are of paramount importance and therefore the franchiser imposes strict quality control procedures.

Mergers and acquisitions

The consideration of mergers and acquisitions can form an important part in developing a robust corporate strategy for entering into new international markets or expansion within existing markets. Mergers involve the joining together of two or more organizations by mutual consent to form one economic unit. Horizontal mergers are where firms in the same line of business join together, whereas vertical mergers involve different stages of a business, e.g. design and construction. Conglomerate mergers involve companies in unrelated lines of business.

The company initiating the merger will be known as the acquiring company and the other will be the acquired company (target). Normally, target companies will have some sort of weakness, but this may not always be the case, especially where there is perceived to be a high degree of equality and mutual benefit. Acquisition may not always be by mutual consent and this is often referred to as a takeover. Where agreement cannot be reached with the managing board of the target company, then a direct approach can be made to the shareholders or stakeholders. In the event of a positive response to the bid, then the acquiring company will have the power to replace the directors of the acquired company. This is known as a hostile takeover.

The merger process involves a progressive sequence of activities, namely:
- strategic assessment of the possible transactions
    - identification of possible merger partners and confidentiality contacts to discuss transaction;
    - indication from the potential merger partner of interest in progressing by discussing to a more advanced stage
- negotiation and documentation
    - definitive merger and reorganization agreement
    - pro forma composition of board of directors and management
    - employment agreements
    - tax implications
    - preparation of legal documentation
- board of directors' approval
    - approval of transaction
    - independent financial advice
    - signing of definitive agreements
- shareholder disclosure and regulatory filing
    - statements to shareholders
    - regulatory consents
    - shareholders' meeting
    - preparation of integration plans
- shareholders' approval
- closure
    - close merger and implement reorganization
    - effect issue of new shares.

An important part of the merger and acquisition process is the intensive investigation of a company and, if appropriate, its subsidiaries, undertaken by venture capitalists, bankers, investors and others into the details of the potential investment. The following provides a list of the documentation that should be reviewed:

- corporate documentation
- stockholder information
- comprehensive financial information and audited accounts
- tax status
- contracts and agreements
- government regulations including permits, licenses and investigations into company activities
- any litigation
- product and service evaluation, market share, inventory and major suppliers
- marketing analysis and appraisal of competition
- management structure and systems
- appraisal of the potential of personnel
- identification and evaluation of property and equipment
- research and development benefits
- other information that is relevant.

The above represents the minimum requirement necessary to undertake a full analysis of the prospects of the target company. This process is known as 'due diligence' and it is essential to the proper valuation of the target company and where appropriate its subsidiaries. Valuation is a vital but difficult and complex activity that assesses the rate of return on the investment to be made. Previous company performance will have a considerable influence on what price should be paid for the merger or acquisition. There will also be many intangible factors that will come into play concerning the benefits to be gained, including the potential to improve efficiency and hence competitiveness in the market-place.

To be able to place a value on a company it is important to have a clear understanding of the motives for the merger or acquisition. The following are examples of the prime motivating drivers:

- to strengthen a position in a flourishing market by the continued full operation of the acquired company in its present form
- to achieve a stronger market position by restructuring to eliminate the weakest parts and enhancing those parts with potential to provide a stronger corporate portfolio
- to gain mutual and harmonious benefit by combining expertise and other strengths, while reducing weaknesses
- to increase market share
- to diversify the product range on offer
- to reduce the amount of competition
- to eliminate the company and sell off the assets.

Once the valuation has been determined and agreed by the parties involved, then a financial transaction will be arranged on the basis of a cash payment or an exchange of securities, or a combination of both.

In the invent of large mergers and acquisitions it will be important from an early stage to assess the impact that will be caused and the chance of attracting attention from national monopolies and merger watchdog bodies whose task is to operate in the national interest by recommending the imposition of restrictions. In the past, MNEs have used their global presence to mitigate such restrictions. However, with the growing strength of the EU and other trading blocks such as NAFTA and ASEAN extra care is required not to fall foul of federal and anti-trust legislation.

Joint ventures

There are many cases in construction where companies do not see any advantage in corporate fusion by means of mergers and acquisition. The predominance of project work supports the concept of the joint venture where participants continue to exist as separate organizations but come together for the express purpose of completing individual projects. Joint ventures can also be used to create a new business enterprise. It may therefore be stated that a joint venture can be organized as a partnership or a company or any other form of appropriate business organization. The characteristics of a joint venture are as follows:

- contribution of resources, knowledge, skills and other assets by partners
- mutual management and control
- joint property and intellectual interests
- expectation and right to share profit
- operations limited by objectives as a single undertaking.

It may therefore be stated that joint ventures are of limited scope and duration involving only a small part of the business activities of each participant. The rationale behind a joint venture requires that each partner have something positive to offer in the form of specialist expertise, assets or competitive advantage. The alliance between the partners will apply to the joint venture only and it will normally be the case that they will continue to remain competitors in other business areas.

More recently, joint ventures have been developed by the concept of 'strategic alliances' where networking strategies are operated in certain sectors of the market in a beneficial manner. This may involve agreements to combine assets to achieve specific objectives or to offer only limited services or products in a particular region in exchange for favours or less competition elsewhere. There are innumerable business reasons that can be used to justify the establishment of a strategic alliance. Joint ventures can also be used to reduce the risk of expanding into a foreign market and to meet legal requirements concerning the appointment of a local partner.

In conclusion, it may be stated that the rationale for joint ventures revolves around the sharing of knowledge, skills, assets and resources to achieve specific time-related objectives. Risk is shared and economies of scale will also be a factor. Benefits will be derived from the need to make a smaller investment while retaining corporate identity and control. There may also be advantages to be derived from favourable treatment by host governments where a local partner is appointed.

Restructuring and divestitures

A successful company will interact with the changing needs of its customers and the opportunities and threats presented by technological progress and the actions of competitors. An organization must therefore be dynamic and possess the ability to introduce strategic change by means of innovation and the creation of new services, products and solutions. Moreover, this will require knowledge and skill development, investment in people, equipment and business infrastructure. The creation of new services and products that meet with the need of clients will be judged against success factors and will be promoted and developed accordingly. Those parts of the business that are in decline or no longer make an effective contribution should be considered for disposal.

Internal restructuring is required to effect changes to the processes, systems and organization structure of a company. This may involve the creation, combination or disposal of subsidiaries, divisions, departments or sections. Assets that are no longer required should be valued and put up for sale. Normally these actions have a significant impact on people and the human aspect will be covered in Chapter 8.

External restructuring may concern the divestiture of distinct parts of the business. In the region of 35–45% of all merger and acquisition transactions represent divestitures by other firms. This implies that there is a variety of strategic reasons for selling off parts of the business; examples include:

- adjustments to the corporate portfolio to comply with changing strategic objectives
- raising capital to invest elsewhere, or to pay off debts
- selling off assets while the price is high
- poor profits
- loss of skill base
- inability to compete in the market.

In cases where companies cannot be sold as a going concern due to insolvency then voluntary liquidation may be the only option. In cases where creditors are involved then it is likely that creditors will institute bankruptcy proceedings and in this instance liquidation is said to be involuntary. Before entering into this course of action, creditors should establish that there is little hope of survival in the event that no bankruptcy action is taken. It is normal practice for an administrator to be appointed to oversee the disposal of assets and the payment of creditors in full or in part. Any residues remaining after all debts and commitments have been fulfilled will be returned to the stakeholders, less fees.

Risk assessment

A vital component in the determination of an international corporate business strategy is the assessment of risk. This process must be undertaken in a logical and structured manner so that a clear picture can be established of uncertainties, which must then be subjected to a rigorous evaluation. Risk assessment is not a precise art and it will involve a degree of subjective judgement, taking into account the best possible information available.

In order to identify specific types of risk it is advisable to classify risk into the following categories:

- political
- financial
- business
- climatic.

Political risk

Political risk is one of the most difficult areas to anticipate and predict. Political instability is normally associated with Third World and Developing Countries that are undergoing large changes, but this may not always be the case. There will invariably be trouble spots around the world caused by conflict and war and, unless there are very compelling reasons, these areas should be avoided. Notice should also be taken of stable countries, which for domestic reasons introduce restrictions on international trade and investment.

Major political risks could, at worst, involve the expropriation of company assets without compensation, or could involve trade sanctions. There may be risk introduced by laws, which require nationals to hold a controlling interest in all businesses. Minor political risk is generally associated with government intervention by the introduction of regulations imposing requirements and restrictions on international business for political ends. This could involve using local resources in preference to those available on the world market.

Political risk is not a static entity and regular monitoring will be necessary to detect changing political philosophies, social circumstances and priorities and the potential effect that these will have on the market.

Financial risk

The major financial risk is associated with foreign exchange rate fluctuations caused by adverse events or trends. In countries where high inflation exists in the local currency then all transactions may be required in a stable currency such as the US dollar. If this is not possible then this should be considered as a major risk, which if not mitigated by other arrangements could make investment impossible.

Transactions in foreign currency in the purchase of goods and services will subject a company to the risk of adverse currency exchange and therefore the need to top up the difference resulting in a real loss. To counteract this, a number of hedging strategies can be used which relate to payment for goods and services linked to stocks held according to whether trends are adverse or beneficial.

Forward exchange contracts can be entered into whereby a fixed exchange rate is agreed at some future date for the supply of goods. Alternatively, currency options can be taken where the purchaser has the right to buy or sell a currency within a specified future period at an agreed rate.

Business risk

Business risk is primarily associated with the market, which in turn will be influenced by the state of the economy of the nation involved. A prevalent danger is the bankruptcy of those directly involved, whether it be the client, business partners or debtors. Hence, a significant part of risk aversion is the requirement to check out the financial and business standing of business associates of all categories, especially those that are most heavily involved.

Developments in technology and the degree of competition from organizations in the same business will always be present. There is a need for good market intelligence to understand the dynamics of the market and to enable trends to be identified and potential developments anticipated. Trading standards and business ethics are other important considerations which, if improperly undertaken, can lead to legal action resulting in financial penalties and, in the worst cases, imprisonment of those responsible. Hence, it is important that these matters are resolved with local partners and associates. Health and safety issues need to be carefully evaluated, both in terms of employees and the public at large. There will invariably be conflict between the health and safety standards applied locally and those of the parent company. These issues need to be dealt with at an early stage and policy must be determined and implemented.

Climatic and geographic risk

The climatic and geographic risks associated with flood, drought, storm, earthquakes and other natural phenomena should be thoroughly checked out and, where necessary, reasonable precautions should be taken. Such risks may be ameliorated by taking out insurance policies or by insisting that the contract conditions provide for the client to share a proportion of the risk. The safety of personnel will also be a major consideration and adequate steps will need to be taken.

Methods of assessing risk

There are various techniques that can be employed to assess the likelihood of risk. These can be divided into the following approaches.

- *Risk management*: a formal process of balancing the risks against the advantage to be gained from a course of action. This will be achieved by the consideration of business objectives in relation to identified uncertainties, as in Figure 4.11.
- *Qualitative risk appraisal*: many business situations do not lend themselves to being analysed in a precise manner that produces a definitive answer. Invariably, the subject under consideration is too complex and hence this drives the analyst to rationalize the situation by

grouping or categorizing factors in an attempt to understand basic relationships and interactions. Such an understanding helps to reduce risk by seeing the global picture. Detail is then dealt with by experience and judgement.

- *Quantitative risk appraisal*: there are various techniques for appraising risk, given that the variables can be identified. Evaluation is undertaken by the application of probability theory, decision trees and statistical techniques related to measures of central tendency.
- *Predictive risk models*: it is now usual to employ models to predict outcomes in order to assess the extent of risk and thereby assist the process of decision making. The most widely used models now include:
  - sensitivity analysis: this technique is used to demonstrate the effect of each business or project variable. The results of the analysis are usually plotted graphically with one axis showing the percentage change in the variable and the other the percentage change in the project, normally in terms of net present value (NPV).
  - Monte Carlo simulation: utilizes random numbers to generate chance outcomes which are then built into a probability distribution

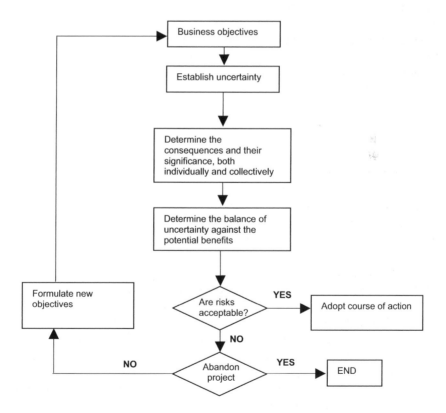

Figure 4.11: Business risk assessment model

to simulate risk. This technique has a wide range of applications from financial investment to project management.

— Earned value analysis: used for predicting project total project costs and completion times based on an extrapolation of project performance to date.

— Forecasting using S-curves: the shape of the s-curve is analysed from inception to current time and the future shape of the s curve is generated mathematically using one or more exponential or cubic equations.

Setting the business aims

To ensure the relevance of a corporate strategy it is necessary to continually re-assess the environment in which the organization operates. An industry analysis will enable a firm to recognize the key factors that contribute to industrial competitiveness and the opportunities and threats present. By establishing the relative strengths and weaknesses of competitors and their likely future strategies it is possible to establish the current state of competition facing the organization. The usual way of doing this is by using an analysis of strengths, weaknesses opportunities and threats (SWOT). The analysis will draw information from the results derived from the framework models previously described, the environmental analysis, the internal assessment and the evaluation of risk. These are then built into a single representation, usually in the form of a diagram as illustrated in Figure 4.12.

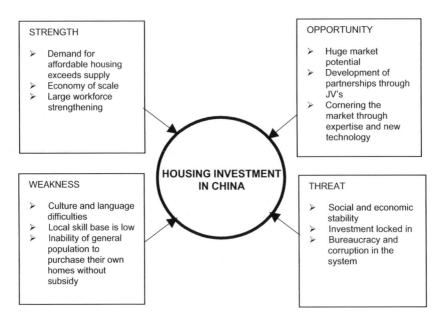

Figure 4.12: SWOT analysis

The next step is to identify desirable business aims, which should be impartially evaluated according to the degree of uncertainty present and the likely risk involved. As a general rule, there should be a relationship between profit potential and associated risk. Hence, it is reasonable to assume that high risk should be commensurate with high profit, therefore this a matter of business judgement with no guarantees. Such judgement should be based on an organized and rational approach utilizing all the information and facts available at the time. Tangible factors should be quantified and intangible factors should be separated for further consideration. Account should also be taken of how a new venture fits into the overall business aims and profile. In this manner the degree of uncertainty can be profiled which will then provide a valuable foundation on which to make a risk assessment.

Once the desirable aims have been determined the objectives need to be established and the appropriate strategies should be formulated.

Corporate interaction with host governments

The generation of goodwill and trust linked to a reputation for excellence and good business practice are key factors in how a foreign construction firm will be viewed by government officials and departments. Where there is perceived to be a genuine expression of interest in national goals and the welfare of the population, this is likely to be viewed favourably. A joint venture with a local partner who has a sound track record in winning public works contracts will be a positive factor and therefore the brokerage of such an arrangement should be given serious consideration. The acquisition and full ownership of a local company should accrue domestic benefits that might not be available to foreign companies, especially in the case of trade restrictions and exchange controls.

Some companies will employ local agents who have strong and influential contacts in government and society. Care is required to establish the credentials of potential agents to establish that they enjoy a sufficiently high profile in local affairs to ensure that favourable consideration should be given to a company's business interests. The performance of such agents should be closely monitored. In some countries there will be no choice but to appoint intermediaries. Where good relations can be developed with government by senior management, then this option should always be given priority. Usually the construction company's country of origin will promote trade through its embassies and trade consulates and will be able to put senior management in contact with relevant government officials responsible for procuring work from overseas companies.

Implementation of corporate strategy

Although it is not possible to draw a precise distinction between formulation and implementation of corporate strategy they do form two separate stages in the process of strategic management.

The implementation of strategy is facilitated through the corporate organization structure and the business portfolio, together with the integration of systems to support processes referred to in Chapter 9 which should be geared to producing output in the form of services, projects and products. Functional areas including marketing, finance, production, research and development and human resource management must contribute harmoniously to the achievement of the corporate strategic aims and each will be required to produce tactical strategies for this purpose. Theoretical concepts and practical steps in support of implementation are contained in the remainder of this book.

Company profile: 4.1. SNC-Lavalin Inc., Quebec, Canada

The SNC-Lavalin Group was founded in 1911 by Arthur Surveyor as a small engineering consulting office in Quebec, Canada. It is now one of the world's leading engineering and construction firms and a key performer in the ownership and management of infrastructures. The organization operates across Canada and globally with, typically, 100 projects in progress at any one time controlled through offices in 30 countries. SNC-Lavalin has adopted a policy of making its worldwide business units autonomous with the potential to draw on global resources needed to take responsibility for all aspects of a project, on a fee for services, turnkey or concession basis, on its own or in partnership. The financial divisions of the organization arrange funding for SNC-Lavalin projects and they are sufficiently developed to support the growing area of build-own-operate-transfer (BOOT) and public–private partnerships (PPP). The structure of the organization is shown below.

SNC-Lavalin's corporate strategy is for sustainable growth based on the development of its portfolio of world class products utilizing its extensive international network and on expanding its financial capabilities. This ideal is supported by the company's experience, culture, innovation and vision to develop new expertise and methods in order to respond to the changing market and client needs within the total field of its operation.

SNC-Lavalin's vision is that it will be an engineering, procurement and construction focused company including project management, project packaging, and related technical and financial services and solutions.

SNC-Lavalin's corporate objectives are outlined below.

- To be a company strongly established and diversified in Quebec, with a significant presence across Canada, with 2 to 3 major foreign operating bases constituting an efficient network of more than 40 permanent offices worldwide.
- The range of activities will be appropriately diversified to minimize the impact of the cyclical nature of its markets.
- Aiming to derive 50% of its revenues from outside Canada by maintaining a comprehensive worldwide international marketing network.

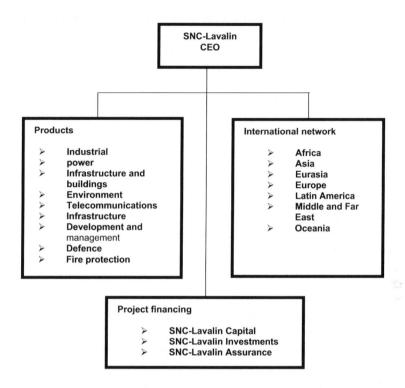

- To be a multicultural organization that excels in its ability to operate in many languages and cultures, but with special emphasis on its strong presence in Quebec to secure a significant volume of business in French-speaking countries.
- To establish alliances with financial partners for the purpose of development projects requiring equity participation, and in the privatization of government-owned facilities.
- Adopting a flexible and understanding approach on how best to meet client needs and to using the total range of its worldwide expertise, and remaining aware of emerging trends and potential technological breakthroughs.
- Ensuring that all clients benefit from access to its total worldwide knowledge base through networked information and communication systems.
- Developing a more stable client base through repeat business and developing closer and more value-added relationships with clients, partners and the supply chain.
- Investing in industry sectors with high returns that support the domestic and global thrust of the business.

- Generating sustainable long-term profit alongside optimal growth for the benefit of its shareholders.

The above objectives are founded on values that respond to SNC-Lavalin's code of ethics, the environment, quality and continuous improvement in service of the social and economic benefits for the communities and countries within which the firm operates. Prime attention is also paid to the motivation and well-being of employees and their participation in the company as stakeholders.

Emphasis is placed on the development of technical and managerial know-how and the maximization of marketing and financial skills to maintain competitive advantage in the market. This is supplemented by constant effort to achieve cost competitiveness through simplification of business processes and the optimization of human, physical and financial resources.

Author's comments

SNC-Lavalin is a successful global group that has been able to articulate its corporate policies clearly alongside a sound implementation strategy set within the context of firmly held values. The organization has recognized its strengths, which are clearly indicated in its marketing strategy.

The core business relates to its products, however to provide clients with a more comprehensive service, especially in BOOT and PPP projects a strong financial arm has been developed and this is supplemented by risk management and insurance services.

The Group has also recognized the importance of its prime asset and has sought to engage fully with 'its people' by means mutual development and well-being. Attention is also given to innovation and development by anticipating change and developing new ways of satisfying client needs.

Company profile 4.2: Lafarge

Lafarge is a French-based global company, which is world leader in the supply of building materials. Moreover, it holds top-ranking positions in each of its four divisions, namely cement, aggregates and concrete, roofing and gypsum.

Lafarge was created in 1833 and, more recently, has achieved spectacular growth through acquisitions and joint ventures. In 2001, annual sales rose to 13.7 billion euros, which represents an increase of 12% in the context of a strategy of sustainable development. The company has 83,000 employees, operates in 75 countries and has 210 individual shareholders.

The corporate aim of Lafarge is to develop and improve building materials by situating the customer at the very heart of its concerns. The company offers the construction industry and the general public innovative solutions that will bring more safety, comfort and well-being to their daily lives.

Lafarge has operations on every continent and it is committed to a strategy of international development. It aims to simultaneously:

- increase its business in the markets of countries that can demonstrate high growth potential; and
- further develop products enjoying growth in mature markets by capitalizing on opportunities offering synergy with existing businesses.

The company's international growth policy is by way of mergers and acquisitions in growth markets. This has resulted in each of its four divisions expanding rapidly, the following being the most recent acquisitions and joint ventures.

- *Cement*: the acquisition of Blue Circle UK has raised Lafarge to the largest cement manufacturer worldwide and joint ventures have seen moves into the South Korean and Japanese markets.
- *Aggregates and concrete*: the acquisition of Pine Hill Materials and American Ready Mix Concrete has provided Lafarge with eight new production sites in the eastern United States.
- *Roofing*: the acquisition of the Kloeber Plant in Germany and a clay tile plant in Brazil.
- *Gypsum*: the joint venture with Boral resulted in the acquisition of Siam Gypsum in Thailand and the acquisition of Continental Gypsum strengthens the presence of the group in New York. Lafarge has also entered into a joint venture with Arcom Gips to become the wallboard market leader in Romania.

A key ingredient of Lafarge's corporate strategy is the promotion of innovation and research in the development of its products and services. Examples include: the joint development in association with Bouygues and Rhodia of 'Ductal' an ultra-high performance concrete, currently licensed in Japan; a optimal self-placing concrete called 'Agilia'; the development and launch of 'BIG' in Germany which is a large roofing tile increasing laying efficiency; and a plasterboard partitioning system for multiplex cinemas. Other key elements include cost reduction, improved product value, creation of new market opportunities, strengthening Lafarge by the "management by values' approach and maintaining Lafarge's brand image.

The 'Lafarge way' involves participatory management where its divisions are autonomous, thus promoting the decentralization of responsibilities, personal initiative and the involvement of all staff in the strategic aims of the company. In this manner, those staff who are near to the ground are able to solve problems by the adoption of solutions that are rooted in the local business.

The Group is divided into business units controlled by a manager that comprise one business in one country or a geographical zone. The business unit is responsible for its own performance, which is continuously monitored by an Economic Value Added (EVA) indicator that is incorporated into the Group's management system. EVA allows for the determination of all costs associated with operations and sheds light on the return on capital invested. This system is progressively being used to determine the bonuses of managers.

The devolution of responsibility brought about by the policy of decentralization is set within a common corporate business framework entitled 'Principles of Action' which sets down group ambitions and responsibilities. A full version can be found on www.lafarge.com.

There are areas such as research and development and environmental protection, which are vital to the group's future performance, but cannot be quantified by EVA in the short term, instead this is done by means of 'key performance indicators'.

Author's commentary

Underlying Lafarge's corporate strategy is sustainable rapid growth by mergers and acquisitions on a global scale within its four divisions of business. At the same time the group is very conscious of the need to satisfy and provide good value to its customers. It also seeks to improve and develop its products to maintain competitive advantage in the market by means of investment in research and development, while at the same time encouraging its employees to make improvements through innovation and good local management.

The group operates a decentralized organisation structure by means of autonomous divisions, however, these are closely monitored and controlled through the EVA system. Clearly, areas of business not generating value added will be subjected to investigation and action.

Lafarge, by means of its 'Principles for Action' lays down a common direction for the whole group, which also includes social and environmental responsibilities. This is a clever management solution that allows for local diversity and scope for local managers to improve their performance and hence their bonuses. There are, of course, risks associated with this approach, however the group is so diversified that it is unlikely that all aspects of the business will perform badly at the same time.

Summary

A prerequisite to a successful business is the development and implementation of a sound and well-balanced corporate strategy. Construction firms are no exception to this requirement, irrespective of their nature and size.

Entry into a new foreign market represents an important action that must have been properly analysed and evaluated to reduce risk and improve the chance of success. The adoption of strategic corporate models establishes a framework that provides the facility to examine the strengths, weaknesses, opportunities and threats with a view to establishing areas where competitive advantage can be achieved.

The global construction market is dynamic and it is in a constant state of change brought about by factors that drive social, economic, business and political activity. Change is also brought about by innovation, technological advancement and improvement by continuous development. It is therefore essential that international construction organizations, including the largest global players, keep their corporate strategies under constant review according to perceived and anticipated change. This should be associated with internal capability assessment to determine gaps in expertise, knowledge and financial and physical resources. International competitiveness should also be kept under review to determine the current state of competitive advantage and areas that are identified as deteriorating or weak. Steps should be taken, where necessary, to reverse adverse trends.

The corporate aims of the business should be reviewed and continually tested to establish their relevance. Where necessary, changes should be made and the impact on the corporate strategy should be assessed. Reformulation of corporate strategy is a continuing process involving periodic and ad hoc review according to extraordinary events. Evolving from this process will be internal actions associated with reorganization, new systems, innovation, research and development and divestiture. External actions will include mergers, acquisitions, joint ventures and strategic alliances.

This chapter has identified the basic steps necessary to establish the information required to enable an adequate analysis in support of the development of a robust corporate strategy. The strategy should also be in line with the outcome of an internal assessment of a company's capability to enter a new venture successfully or to continue to participate in the international market. The following chapters are concerned with the implementation of the effective strategy.

Further reading

Ansoff I. & McDonnell E. (1990), *Implementing strategic management*, 2nd edn, Prentice Hall.

Beamish P. W., Killing J. P. & Crookell H. (1991), *International management*, Homewood, IL, USA, Irwin.

Doz Y. (1980), 'Strategic management in multinational companies', *Sloane Management Review*, Winter, 27–45.

Garland J., Farmer R. N. & Taylor M. (1990), *International dimensions of business policy and strategy* (2nd edn) Boston PWS Kent Publishing.

Ghosal S. (1987), 'Global strategy: an organizational framework', *Strategic Management Journal*, **8**, No. 6, 425–440.

Kim W. C. & Mauborgne R. A. (1993), 'Effectively conceiving and expanding multi-nationals' worldwide strategies', *J. International Studies*, **24**, Issue 3, 3rd quarter, 419–448.

Lafarge (2002), Home page (on-line www.lafarge.com).

Loraine R. K. (1992), *Construction management in developing countries*, Thomas Telford, London.

Merrifield D.B. (1992), 'Global strategic alliances among firms', *Int. J. Technology Management*, **17**, Issue 1, 77–83.

Mintzberg H., Quinn J. B. and Ghogal S. (1995), *The strategy process*, European edn., Prentice Hall Europe.

Morrison A. & Roth K. (1992), 'A taxonomy of business-level strategies in global industries', *Strategic Management Journal*, **13**, No. 6, 399–417.

Pietroforte R. (1996) *Building international construction alliances*, E. & F. N. Spon.

Porter M. E. (1986), 'Changing patterns of international competition', *California Management Review*, **28**, Winter, 9–40.

Porter M. E. (1980), *Competitive strategy*, Free Press, USA.

Porter M. E. (1986), *Competition in global industries*, Harvard Business School.

Porter M. E. (1990), *The competitive advantage of nations*, Macmillan.

SNC-Lavalin (2002), Home page, (on-line at www.snc-lavalin.com).

Weston J. F., Chung K. S and Hoag S. E. (1990), *Mergers, restructuring and corporate control*, Prentice Hall International Editions.

Woodward D. & Woodward T. (2001), 'The efficacy of action at a distance as a control mechanism in the construction industry when a trust relationship breaks down: an illustrative study', *British J. Management*, **12**, Issue 4, 355–384.

Chapter 5

Marketing, competitive advantage and procurement

Introduction

The strategic role of international marketing relates to the configuration and coordination of marketing activities and integration with the company's value chain. The marketing effort creates and provides the important link between potential clients and promotes company know-how and the quality of company services and products.

International marketing forms an important part of a company's overall corporate strategy. From the outset, it is necessary to distinguish between companies that operate in one or more foreign countries on a local or regional basis and those organizations that operate globally. In the former case, marketing policies should be geared to local needs and the characteristics of each country. Global organizations will have the additional task of integrating local and regional marketing actions that are linked to global corporate strategy in order to improve competitive advantage. It is argued that concentrating activities in selected locations in order to serve a world market can help to simplify the business and produce economies of scale and the standardization of procedures. The relationship between global strategy and international marketing is therefore complex and each instance must be considered on its merits.

This chapter sets out to provide a logically developed framework for the development of a sound market strategy that will ensure that the organization is able to exploit its strengths in the face of competition, while minimizing risk.

Seeking work in the international market

There must be sufficient motivation to encourage a construction company to seek work in a foreign market. This may be generated by occurrences experienced in the home domestic market or by factors relating to developments in the global economy, regional growth or by extraordinary events that require major construction work overseas.

The ability to operate successfully internationally has always carried a degree of kudos. Most governments actively encourage and support companies to seek work in foreign countries or within federations and groups of nations such as the European Union. The export of expertise, goods and services provides foreign income and improves the balance of payments that, in turn, contributes to national wealth.

Where companies have developed strengths within their home markets there may be competitive advantage and good profits to be earned by expanding into foreign markets. Alternatively, where companies are experiencing adverse domestic market trading conditions, they might be tempted to look elsewhere to find markets that have less competition and higher potential demand for the products or services on offer. There may be other reasons for entering foreign construction markets involving production costs, material shortages, disruption, taxation or legal restrictions.

The decision to move into a foreign market should be approached in a logical manner to ensure that the correct motives apply and that real market potential exists. Figure 5.1 provides the framework to enable such complex decisions to be taken.

The prime factors to be considered during the market evaluation will include:

- need and potential
- financial and economic considerations
- political and legal factors
- socio-cultural forces
- degree of competition
- freedom to trade
- codes and practices
- life cycles.
-

International marketing

International marketing strategy should be evaluated according to the required levels of dispersion, coordination and integration required. Where individual countries are concerned, then the strategy should reflect specific national needs and cultures. Regional marketing will have the additional task of establishing common requirements that provide the opportunity for strategic convergence where services and products can be offered to a number of countries, with or without adaptation to meet national requirements. The strategy applicable to global operation will require the strategic deployment of the value chain to gain competitive advantage.

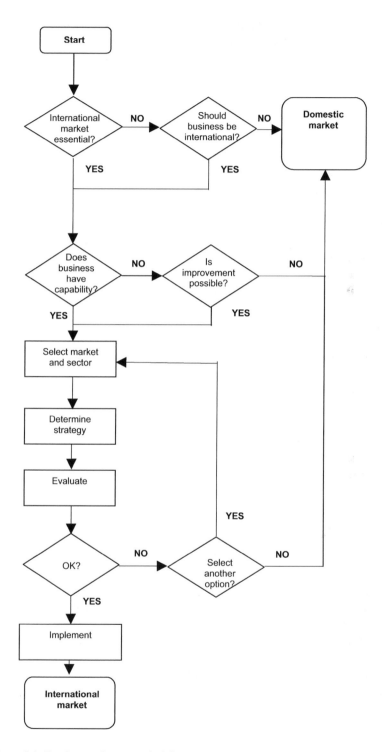

Figure 5.1: Foreign market entry decision process

Where international involvement is relatively small it is likely that the majority of the marketing effort will be conducted from the home company headquarters. Larger scale overseas operations will require the devolution of marketing functions to departments and subsidiaries who will be responsible for their own marketing plans and budgets. The evolution of an organization to a full-scale global player reverses the trend towards devolution by establishing centralized marketing activities geared to gaining competitive advantage through global economies and standardization for the whole group.

Strategies to be adopted will be rooted in the relevant international market-place and the services and products a company is able to offer. The marketing approach will be different for consultants, contractors, manufacturers, materials and equipment suppliers.

The broad definition of marketing describes it as:

'A management function that organizes and directs all activities concerned with converting customer purchasing power into effective demand for a product or service and its delivery to the customer so as to achieve the business objectives set by the company'.

The above statement requires marketing to be divided into six functions, as detailed below.

- **Market assessment** utilizing prior knowledge of the market and market research. This function will identify and scale the size of the potential market in terms of its diversity and depth. Areas of potential growth will be identified alongside areas that are stagnant or in decline. The degree of competition will be evaluated and price trends will be examined relative to the estimated capacity of the industry in each country and across regions or globally, if applicable. International and national trends in the type of construction by clients and the procurement method used will be analysed and then split between the public and private sectors. A profile of competitors will be compiled, together with an analysis of strengths and weaknesses linked to market share. Scope for new products and services will be looked at, given identifiable trends in culture, society, living standards, fashions and traditions.

- **Development of a marketing strategy**, the aims and objectives of which should be firmly rooted in the international market defined by the nations involved. The strategy should be integrated with the capacity of the business in terms of its expertise, productive capacity and ability to finance the scale of operation as envisaged by the strategic objectives. A nation by nation sales forecast will be developed in the long, medium and short terms. The development of corporate and subsidiary marketing plans will be required to control and monitor the overall effect of the marketing effort at corporate and tactical levels.

- **Promotion and advertising** will be conducted nationally and internationally to make potential clients aware of the quality and value of company services and products. This is especially important in new international markets where clients will be unaware of new players and will be distracted by existing suppliers with new promotions and deals who will be aiming to improve their market shares. Accentuating strengths and understanding those requirements most valued by clients will be key factors in attracting attention. Promotion and advertising budgets will be determined in the marketing plan and it is essential that these be used effectively to achieve maximum impact by way of introduction to products and services on offer.

- **Obtaining work and sales** are vitally important aspects of any business and a wide variety of approaches can be taken depending on the nature and type of business. Manufacturers and materials suppliers are more likely to use a traditional approach by engaging a sales force consisting of technical experts and high pressure salesmen whose sole task is to move as much of a product range as possible. Design consultants will be more likely to use personal contacts and networking to hook clients; alternatively, they might work through partnerships and alliances with other consultants who come together to form multidisciplinary teams working on one or more projects. Either way, once clients are on board they are nurtured through personal contact aimed at providing excellent service and value for money. Construction companies offering a design and build or turnkey service will take much the same approach as consultants. However, those contractors offering a straight construction service will be more likely to operate using the traditional tendering process based on approved lists of contractors. Recently, more emphasis has been given to the development of integrated supply chains where long-term partnerships are built up for the benefit of all concerned.

- **Monitoring of turnover** against forecasts and feedback to management on the performance of strategies adopted are key activities necessary to determine business performance. Analysis can be broken down by country, subsidiary, department, project, service and product. This will allow trends to be established and predictions of future performance to be made in the light of perceived prospects, market conditions and the performance of competitors. It will be the responsibility of management to exploit positive trends and to eliminate or mitigate adverse circumstances.

- **Customer service and satisfaction** is an important element in obtaining repeat business that generates long-term client relationships. Clients expect value, quality and excellent in-use performance. Current best practice involves a zero defects policy backed by guarantees. The trend is to eliminate defects, but where they occur an effective means should be in place to rectify them with minimum inconvenience to the client. Where possible, construction companies aim to exceed customer expectations, thereby building up client confidence and trust.

- **Public relations** are a crucial part of the international construction business. Particular attention is now given to issues concerning the sustainability and conservation of resources and the natural environment. Considerable mileage can be gained in the public eye if the company is perceived to be genuinely concerned about the welfare of national inhabitants and their quality of life.

International construction services and products

The potential to grow within the various international construction markets will be influenced by a company's ability to establish competitive advantage by the coordination and integration of marketing strategies between countries, regions and globally. The successful transfer of 'know-how' from one country to another will also be a significant factor. To assist the implementation of the correct strategy construction services, products and materials should be classified according to the extent of their applicability to national, regional and global markets. Figure 5.2 illustrates that where services and products are judged to be country-specific then there will be no scope for expansion into the wider international market. In the event that they can be applied regionally, with or without adaptation, then there will be a much larger potential market. A key factor will be the nature and extent of nationally accepted standards and codes of practice. A system of internationally recognized independent testing and accreditation is important to the acceptance of new products, materials and equipment.

The ultimate case is a global market where services, products, materials and equipment can be produced to accepted international standards that open up a world market for a standard product. Illustrations of successful ventures of this type are provided by the company profiles of Lafarge and the Caterpillar Corporation who have managed to exploit world markets. Although materials and product suppliers are more developed globally there is considerable potential in the globalization of design services and construction expertise. Advances in technology and developments in communication and travel systems have made possible a scenario whereby innovation, research and development can more easily be brought into play. Potential exists for the development of clever designs and processes to achieve higher productivity and economy of scale.

Market research

International business is in a constant state of change and development. What was successful last year may prove to be less so in future unless changes are made to reflect the demands of the market. It is therefore important that companies participating in the international construction market remain aware and vigilant about what is happening around them. Hence the importance of market research and analysis necessary to determine the size and profile of the market and the manner in which it is changing.

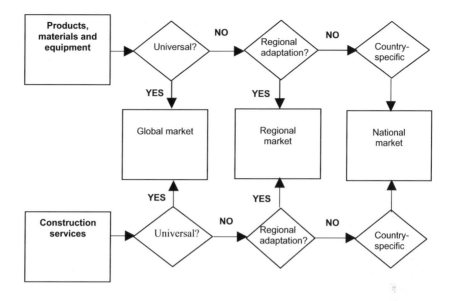

Figure 5.2. Market classification of construction services,
products, materials and equipment

The function of market research is concerned with investigating the needs of the market relative to what the business currently has to offer. Where there are mismatches these should be identified and appraised to establish whether changes are necessary to marketing strategy and plans. Emphasis should be given to collecting information and data about the market to inform the development of corporate strategy aimed at maximizing growth and profit potential.

Market research data can be divided into three principal types, namely:
- primary
- secondary
- published material.

Primary data

Primary material describes data that is generated by research undertaken to find out more about specific clients or markets. In the majority of cases, international companies involved with construction will be more interested in industrially based research rather than consumer research that examines mass buying habits, fashions and trends. Therefore it will be important to gain access to potential major clients to ask them about their spending plans and the type and quality of service or product that they require. It will also be necessary to seek views on the existing products and services to establish what needs to be improved and by when.

Attention should be given to existing clients who must regularly be asked about what they think of services and the product range supplied. This activity is important because consumer reaction reflects changing needs and competition in the market-place, which if detected at an early stage will minimize potential adverse affects.

Investigation should also be conducted into the services and products available from competitors with a view to establishing to what extent competitive advantage has been maintained. Where competitors, especially in technology and performance, have made advances then action must be taken to halt a possible decline in market share. This type of investigation is more difficult since it will not be possible to enquire of competitors directly. Opinions should be sought from clients that establish their relative values for other services and products. It may also be possible to analyse technical performance by purchasing products for evaluation.

Traditionally, survey work required to collect primary data is undertaken by questionnaires, face-to-face interviews or by arranged interviews over the telephone. More recently the trend has been to use the Internet to seek views through structured web pages, which can be designed to be simple and quick to complete.

Data will be analysed according to the size of sample and its ability to indicate what is happening in the market as a whole. Where sample sizes are sufficiently large, appropriate statistical tests should be applied to validate the significance and reliability of the data collected.

Secondary data and published material

Sourcing and reading relevant reports and investigations undertaken by others in the market may obtain secondary data. Data can also be acquired in the form of market surveys and profiles, journal articles, newspaper reports and press releases. This type of investigation requires a broad trawl of media publication, trade magazines and literature, academic publications, technical reports, performance test reports and innovative developments in process and technology.

Data should be filtered and restructured into categories with headings capable of being analysed in a manner that will point to the current state of the market in terms of volume, trend, competitiveness and potential profitability.

Virtually every country throughout the world will have its own statistical office where data is collected year on year about the economy, demography, health, trade and many other areas. This is necessary for governments to establish where they have come from, where they are at present and where they would like to go in future. Data is collected through a periodic census of the population and through both the public and private sectors concerning all aspects of health, education, transport, infrastructure, trade and business. Most countries produce construction and housing statistics that provide annual and, in some cases, quarterly figures about all aspects of production, employment, sectoral spending and trends. These are a very lucrative and useful source of information to scale and judge the extent of the market. Other useful statistics relate to existing and projected public spending on infrastructure, public housing and services.

Adequate and competent market research plays an important part in providing the necessary intelligence and information on which to base sound business judgement. Without this type of information decisions will be more dependent on assumption, which in the majority of cases will increase the amount of risk. The generation and provision of good market information and intelligence is vitally important when entering new and maintaining existing markets.

Innovation, research and new product and process development

The survival and success of a company will be directly related to its ability to continue to meet the needs of the market and to compete effectively with competitors. Arguably the most effective way to do this is by being in possession of essential expertise and products that no other company can provide. Evidence shows that organizations and countries that invest in innovation, research and development are economically stronger and possess competitive advantage over others that are not so forward thinking. This section seeks to outline the nature and importance of new services and products produced with the assistance of innovation and research.

Innovation

Creativity forms the basis from which innovation evolves. According to the Collins English Dictionary creativity can be identified in three ways, namely:
- possession of the ability or power to bring into existence;
- characterization by originality of thought or inventiveness; and
- stimulation of the imagination beyond what already exists.

Creativity in terms of human thinking, either individually or collectively, can be defined as the original, self-disciplined and rational thought of unfettered minds that have the desire to discard the shackles of convention and paradigm. Innovation is therefore the realization of creativity. Creativity that leads to innovation might be influenced by environmental, economic, social and political causal factors that arise as a result of perceived need and or threat.

The stimulation and ignition of a creative idea is unique to a moment in time where an infinitely variable number of factors and circumstances are brought into play from the past and the present to create a vision of something new. From this moment there extends a process of creativity requiring a stream of solutions, ranging widely in complexity and nature that leads to the realization of innovation. The Oxford dictionary defines innovation as 'make changes in something already existing, as by introducing new methods, ideas, or products' It comes from the Latin *in* meaning 'into' together with *novare* 'make new'. The change brought about by innovation can be incremental or 'big bang', or somewhere in between. It may be perceived as revolutionary, implying a change, which at its most extreme can be in completely the opposite direction. Under such circumstances, the innovator is elated by self-belief, but others will be less convinced, and unless they can be persuaded conclusively the situation may be perceived as uncertain and threatening. Hence, the more radical the change the more difficulty the inventor has in persuading others that the proposition is a good thing! There is also the danger that extreme invention leads to fanatical belief on the part of the innovator, which, unless properly founded, leads to bias and illogical judgement.

Research

Research is aimed at making a contribution to knowledge and will take many different forms leading to a conclusion. Traditionally, it is usual to state the aim of the research and the necessary supporting objectives. One or more hypotheses can be stated against which the results of the investigation and analysis can be measured to determine the outcome and conclusion. The research will be conducted according to a stated methodology, which critically appraises existing knowledge and then investigates by means of experimentation, survey and testing to contribute new knowledge that is further analysed and evaluated before conclusions are drawn.

Research is classically defined as 'pure' or 'applied'. The former being concerned with research into theory and principles, which normally have no direct application to everyday life, whereas the latter is directly related to application intended to bring tangible benefit. The term 'blue sky' is used to identify research which delves into the unknown in order to discover something entirely new, which may or may not have any useful direct application. In reality, there are many hybrid forms between pure and applied and it is also possible for one to convert to the other as the investigation progresses.

Research can be defined as:

- a systematic investigation to establish facts or principles or to collect information on a subject;
- carrying out critical investigations into a subject or problem; or
- a careful search or inquiry intended to discover new or old facts by the scientific study of a subject.

The definition of research is therefore broad and hence it can be used to describe the search for information and facts that already exist so that they can be utilized for a particular purpose. This may be as mundane as purchasing a new computer or as vast as discovering new physical properties which control the universe.

Relationship between innovation and research

Given what has been said previously, there may or may not be a relationship between research and innovation. Good research can be considerably assisted in its formative stage by creativity leading to relevant innovation of thought. However, new knowledge attained by research is derived from careful and systematic investigation, analysis and evaluation. Claims made, as the result of research must be backed up by proof and where this is not possible in its entirety then qualification and delimiters must be brought into play. The quality of research is the result of judgement by publication, peer review and citation. Not all research is good and research peers, through refereed publication, usually deal with this robustly. It should also be recognized that research is a continuing process involving the advancement of knowledge and understanding. Hence research held to be highly regarded in the past could be completely discredited by future research that reveals a greater level of understanding. Generally, this process is regarded by academics to be healthy and indicative of the strength of intellectual advance. To the uninitiated this can appear to be contradictory and confusing.

Creativity and innovation need not involve research, although it should be recognized that research could provide the environment and the basis for some forms of innovation. Where an individual or a group creates an idea that directly relates to physical presence or circumstance then research may not be involved. The process of nurturing an idea to innovation reality may require the assistance of research, however this may not be the case were existing components are brought together and utilized in a different way. Such processes may include trial and error through cause and effect, utilizing practical experimentation. At this point it is worth introducing inventiveness and ingenuity, which are human qualities capable of producing innovation reality without the need for research. Successful innovation is required to demonstrate tangible benefit, but it does not necessarily have to be fully understood according to proof and principle. Whereas, valid research must always be subject to proof and qualification.

It can therefore be concluded that innovation does not have the same academic paradigm as research, although one may complement the other depending on nature and circumstance. Therefore innovation is more generically applicable and can be undertaken by those without academic credentials, but who have the ability to create something new through ingenuity, inventiveness and practical application. This assertion is very important for the international construction industry because of its complex and practical nature. In essence there is the need for both innovation and research and it will be of benefit to the industry to clearly understand the difference between the two. Using this differentiation, the whole of the global construction industry should be engaged in innovation and research to promote wealth and well-being through technological, managerial and behavioural advance.

New product and process development

Innovation and research contributes to the development of new products or processes. Moreover, for an international construction company to lead in its field and to maintain advantage over its competitors it is essential that resources be invested in innovation and research. The most important element is the development of a culture that naturally seeks out challenges and problems and then encourages those involved to seek solutions by pushing back the boundaries of existing knowledge. Not every initiative or research project will be a success, therefore there needs to be a critical mass of activities that will deliver a percentage of successful outcomes, thereby making the overall effort worthwhile.

New product development is normally concerned with the design and development of new materials, components or assemblies that have features which competitors do not possess, or who cannot match the level of performance required. Equipment manufacturers will also be striving for improved performance and greater efficiency.

Construction naturally lends itself to innovation in design and will be subjected to value analysis to judge benefits in terms of the aesthetic, function, value and cost. Most construction projects are unique and there is scope for innovation. The growing trend towards increasing efficiency by the use of standardization and prefabrication places greater emphasis on innovation, research and development from the outset.

Innovation, research and development can be applied effectively to the total process of construction. This may be typified by improved design management and innovative procurement systems aimed at reducing risk and speeding up the construction process and working practice.

An area of specific importance is the continuing need to improve safety during the construction process and in the period of post-occupation by clients. Innovation and research has a major role in international construction by improving working conditions and the quality of workmanship.

New product and process development is an important area in the global construction market where sustainability and the conservation of resources are of growing importance. In conjunction with the need to cut pollution and reduce carbon emissions into the atmosphere these demands will encourage companies to invest in innovation and research and seek collaboration with universities and research institutes to find competent and adequate solutions to future problems and needs.

Methods of procurement for construction projects

The method of procurement selected for an international construction project will depend on the type of project and client needs. Geographic location and the proximity and availability of the necessary expertise and resources will also be influencing factors. There may be potential to introduce new practices of procurement, but this normally requires the additional task of selling the advantages of deviating from commonly accepted practice and adequate reassurance that risk will be kept to a minimum.

More recently, the global construction industry has followed a trend towards the use of private funds for large-scale public infrastructure and building projects. The provision of expressways, bridges and railways are good examples alongside the construction of hospitals, university student accommodation and prisons. This approach is changing the traditional business of construction by extending involvement into the operation of buildings in order to generate revenue to recover the initial capital outlay and to make a profit. The advantage to public clients is that projects can be brought forward without all the cash being available from the public purse and the risk is defrayed to private companies.

Some international construction companies have developed by providing a complete range of services from project inception to final handover. There has also been development in practices adopted by designers and constructors who have formed partnerships and joint ventures to undertake just one, or a series of projects. Post-occupation services involving facility management can be provided as part of a private–public partnership (PPP), or as an independent service. This section provides the basis for selecting the most suitable from the most widely used procurement methods applicable to international construction.

Traditional procurement

Traditional procurement normally involves the client initiating the appointment of an engineer or an architect who will oversee and coordinate the specialist design input required. Where specialist design consultants are available locally then they should be considered for selection alongside foreign design consultants. There are many examples of global design consultants who establish local offices staffed by a mixture of home country, third country and local staff. The advantage gained is that they may be viewed as quasi-indigenous consultants and as a consequence they will provide strong competition in acquiring work.

The design process commences with the client brief and progresses to the point where contractors can be invited to tender for the project. Figure 5.3 shows this process in its simplest form. Tenders may be open to bids in response to public advertisements, or they may be closed involving selection from a previously approved list of contractors. It is now common practice to involve contractors at an early stage and in some cases an outline design is asked for as part of a design tender. The latter case is a time-consuming and expensive process and, as a consequence, contractors will only be attracted to tender if the odds of winning are improved. Hence, it is normal to restrict the number of contractors who are invited to bid. However, it may be possible to stage the process, whereby the outline design and estimate is used as the basis for the early award of a contract, after which the scheme design is produced and the final contract sum is negotiated. Alternatively, the scheme design can be produced by a client-appointed principal designer who will engage specialist design consultants as required as part of the design team. In this case the contractors will tender on the basis of the drawings and specifications produced, together with other documentation deemed to be required. Where specialist design and detailed design takes place after the appointment of the contractor, then provisional sums will be allowed in the contract sum to cover the cost.

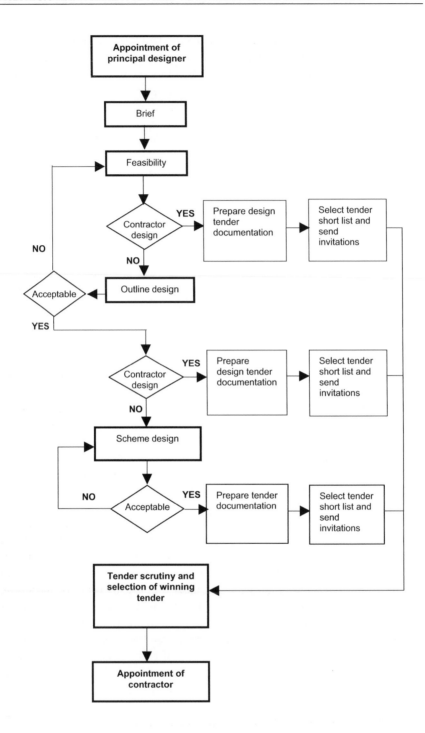

Figure 5.3: Traditional procurement process

It is important to appreciate that the traditional process consists of a variety of approaches that can be adapted to suit the circumstances in hand. There is no single universal solution to suit all cases. The traditional process may therefore be defined as one where a contractor is initially appointed on the basis of a tender which may or may not form the basis for further negotiation in order to reach an agreed contract sum.

Design consultants are typically appointed using a standard contract form, an example being that of the International Federation of Consulting Engineers (FIDIC) in association with the European International Federation of Construction. This contract contains special provisions to accommodate a nation's legal system under which the contract will be executed. The principal design engineer is employed as the client's representative with powers of certification.

Contractors may be appointed under a variety of standard forms of contract that exist throughout the world, which may be suitably adapted to account for local requirements and conditions. The precise form of contract will be subject to agreement between the contractor and the client.

Non-traditional procurement methods

These may be broadly defined as those methods that do not involve tendering in competition according to drawings, specifications and other documentation; instead projects will be awarded according to a range of criteria that concern client satisfaction, quality and value for money. By implication, the client becomes more involved in the delivery of the project. However, this may not be the case where a consultant is appointed to act as the client's representative. The client will also be interested in the degree of risk associated with a particular procurement method and its suitability given the nature and circumstances of the project. It is therefore important that careful consideration be given to the most appropriate choice.

Recently, clients have become more interested in the total life cycle costs of buildings and infrastructure mainly because of research that has shown that the initial capital cost is much smaller than lifetime operational costs. Recognition of the importance of sustainability and the conservation of non-replaceable resources has encouraged clients to look more carefully at energy consumption, atmospheric pollution and the reduction of waste. Another important trend is for governments and their public service departments to bring forward projects by attracting private investment under arrangements known as private–public partnerships (PPP). This is a generic procurement route that has become very popular, albeit controversial, and is now universally adopted in a variety of forms in most countries throughout the world.

Selection of a non-traditional procurement method

It is important that a client either has the prerequisite knowledge to select the most appropriate procurement method for a project, or is provided with impartial advice from a trusted adviser regarding the best option to select. In either case, clients are faced with an array of non-traditional procurement routes and variants thereof from which to select. This section identifies the most common options and then goes on to analyse the advantages and disadvantages that guide the selection process. For this purpose, categories have been developed that broadly categorize the methods as follows:

- design and build
- fee contracting
- private–public partnerships.

Design and build is now established as a major procurement route that suits many international construction clients who want a reliable and moderate risk process resulting in delivery of a project within budget and on time. Other terms used to describe this approach include 'turnkey', 'package deal' and 'one-stop-shop'. Because of public accountability it is more likely to be suited to private commercial clients who have very clear and specific requirements regarding the achievement of their business objectives. This procurement route lends itself to aggressive marketing where competition is not only concerned with price. Therefore, negotiation of the contract sum will take into account quality and a variety of value added factors including phased handovers, optional design features, process requirements, etc. Figure 5.4 illustrates the basic factors, which identify procurement by design and build.

There is a generally held view that design and build best suits fairly straightforward designs, e.g. warehouses, factories, offices, where standard designs are available and the design and construction teams are familiar with the processes and systems adopted. Moreover, there is no reason why sufficient design and construction expertise should not be built up to effectively deliver more complex projects such as hospitals and laboratories.

Fee contracting is an arrangement where the client engages a contractor on a fee basis for the management and delivery of the project. Essentially, the client enters into a contract where it is agreed to reimburse the contractor for the full cost of the project, plus a percentage of the final contract sum to cover the fee for supervising the work. This is a high-risk procurement route where the client carries the full responsibility for cost overruns. This route may be appropriate where a client has a very expert in-house team or where there is a degree of uncertainty that will discourage contractors from submitting competitive tenders for the work. Figure 5.5 illustrates the basic factors that determine the nature of fee management contracting. The more successful variants of fee contracting have been developed around a strong partnership between the fee contractor and the client, founded on understanding and trust generated over a series of projects.

The most common form of fee contracting is the management contracting procurement route where the client appoints a management contractor as a professional consultant at an early stage of the project. The management contractor then becomes part of the professional team and will support the design team with construction expertise aimed at improving efficiency. The provision of this service will be based on the expertise of the management team and their track record, which will be presented to the client prior to appointment. There may be a process of prequalification, prior to a competitive presentation before final appointment.

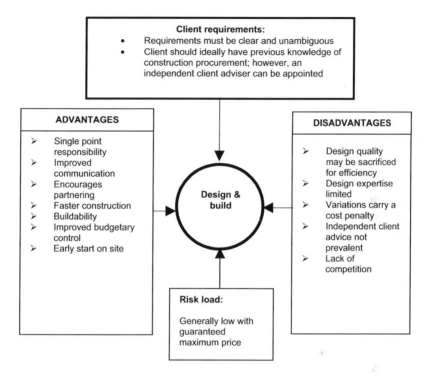

Figure 5.4: Design and build

The management contractor will be expected to appoint works contractors who will undertake discrete packages of work. The contractual arrangement will be between the management contractor and the works contractor. However, it is important to realize that the client is duty bound to reimburse the management contractor for all costs incurred. Therefore, under this arrangement the client mainly carries the risk. This procurement route has largely fallen out of favour with clients in the global construction market, but where conditions are right it may provide an appropriate solution.

A major criticism of management contracting has been risk aversion by some clients who have attempted to unload risk to the management contractor. One way of doing this is by insisting that the reimbursement of package contractors will be subject to a maximum tender figure, hence any cost overrun, other than agreed variations, will be the responsibility of the management contractor. This has led to adversarial relationships, which have impacted on the popularity of this route in recent years.

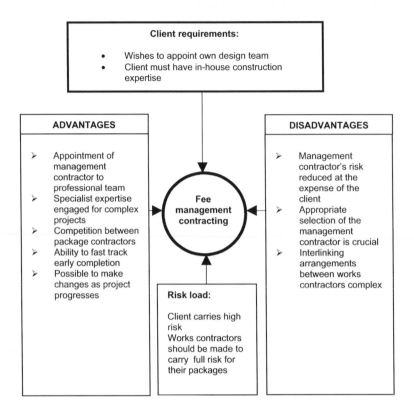

Figure 5.5: Fee management contracting

Construction management overcomes these problems by the client placing direct contracts with each of the specialist suppliers. This implies that the client is familiar with construction and has a close relationship with the professional team. The expert construction manager is therefore appointed as a consultant whose task will be to effectively manage and control the construction process, as well as integrating the design team. This procurement route shares many of the advantages and disadvantages that are claimed for management contracting. Overriding influences in the selection of this route concern the complexity of the project and the strength of the risk involved.

Private–public partnerships (PPP). The term private–public partnership describes a generic project procurement route involving collaboration between public bodies, such as local authorities and central government, and private companies. This concept is predicated on the belief that private companies are often more efficient, better managed and less bureaucratic than their public counterparts. The intention is that by creatively using the management skills and financial acumen of the business community, taxpayers will receive better value for money from public services.

The Private Finance Initiative (PFI) was created in the United Kingdom during the early 1990s and it is applied to construction projects whereby contractors pay for the construction costs and then rent the finished project back to public sector clients. There are different approaches ranging from just building, to build–own (BO), to build–own–operate (BOO), to build–own–operate–transfer (BOOT) and design–build–fund–operate (DBFO). The objectives behind PFI are geared to sharing the potential risks of procuring, operating and maintaining a built facility, linked to economies of scale that can be obtained by operational service providers. This means that the public service can run its core business without having to provide a specialist in-house resource to operate and maintain the constructed facility.

Typically, the PFI contracting organization responds to a client brief and offers a contractual package to operate the constructed facility for a number of years in exchange for rent payable by the client. At the end of the agreed rental period the ownership reverts back to the client. It is normal for the contractor to set up a company comprising the designer, constructor, operator and the provider of funds. In this manner the project becomes a corporate business in its own right. Essentially, PFI has been designed for the public sector based on the established private sector initiative of BOOT.

For PFI to be a viable proposition there must be a high degree of certainty about the demand for the project and the income stream to be generated over the stated period of time. Therefore, the projects ideally suited to this form of procurement are infrastructure facilities such as tunnels, expressways and bridges that impose tolls, or living accommodation where fees are charged, e.g. for students. Projects of this nature would normally be funded through the public sector purse and therefore the introduction of PFI offers considerable economic advantages in reducing public expenditure, at least in the short term, by outsourcing to the private sector in this manner.

Other public facilities such as hospitals, prisons and governments offices can use the same procurement route but in these instances the income stream is less visible and hence there is more risk involved for the PFI contractor. It is therefore essential that the right operating revenues are established in relation to the capital cash injection at the outset.

The advent of PFI has, not surprisingly, been quick to gain in popularity since public clients can bring forward projects for which they do not currently have the necessary cash. On the other hand, contractors relish the thought of a reliable long-term income stream to provide stability to their businesses.

Despite the apparent advantages there are considerable risks where projects brought forward by the public sector are likely to be unsuited to PFI arrangements, especially where the income stream is uncertain and operating costs are hard to predict. Governments must take a responsible attitude towards the projects selected and it is the responsibility of PFI contractors to be wary and to undertake sufficient investigation and analysis to ensure that risk and nasty surprises are kept to a minimum. Figure 5.6 illustrates the basic factors that determine the nature of PFI.

The introduction of PPP as a generic procurement route changes the nature of the construction business. In the event that this form of procurement continues to develop and grow in popularity throughout the world, then the global construction industry will need to adapt further to meet this demand. It would seem at this time that there are considerable benefits to be gained from outsourcing the operation of public sector facilities to the private sector in exchange for private capital investment. Because this form of procurement is relatively new and due to the extended period of typical PPP projects, only time will tell whether this notion is correct.

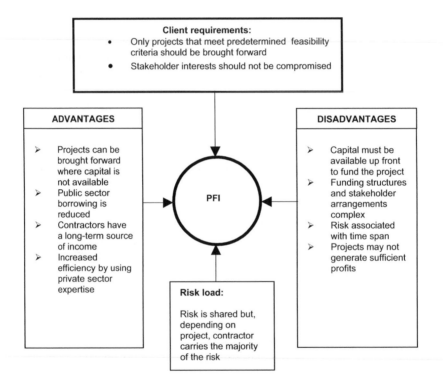

Figure 5.6: PFI

Procurement risk

The prerequisite to selecting a procurement route is the identification of risk in all its contexts. For the evaluation of risk to be useful it is essential that all relevant risks are taken into account and therefore the quality and comprehensiveness of this exercise will be of considerable importance to business judgement. It is also vital that risks are clearly associated with the project(s) under consideration.

The analysis of risk can be categorized as quantitative, qualitative or a combination of both. The extent of the analysis will depend on severity, impact, frequency of occurrence and the complexity of different types of risk. The outcome of this process will be a complete picture of the risk profile, which can then be evaluated prior to decisions about courses of action. Figure 5.7 identifies that if risk is accepted there will be a need to determine whether it should carry a premium or not. In the latter case, a further decision should be taken as to whether the risk should be entirely ignored. If steps are necessary to transfer or avoid risk then it should be established whether a cost penalty is incurred and, if so, this should be built into the price? Alternatively, insurance against risk might be taken out and, again, the cost of the premium should be taken into account.

The objective of risk appraisal is to identify the risks and to make a judgement regarding their acceptability. If it is decided to transfer or avoid risks then this will normally carry an extra cost which will impact on profit margins. There are no set rules other than that of judgement based on the best possible information supported by experience and intuition.

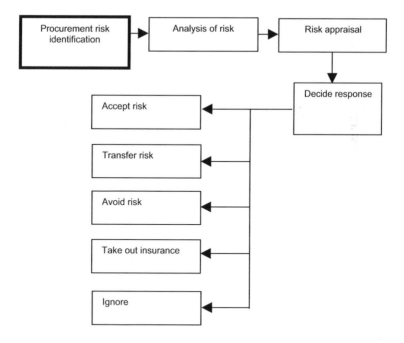

Figure 5.7: The risk appraisal process

Market tactics

The overriding goal must be to seek and establish competitive advantage over rival companies operating in the same area. This can be achieved in a number of different ways using just one or a combination of factors that exploit current demand. Although the long-term strategic direction may remain unchanged, the tactics necessary to achieve targets will be in a constant state of flux. It is therefore important that market intelligence provides a continuous commentary on small shifts in the market that require repositioning to take advantage of change.

Typical perceivable changes in the market might include:

- revisions to government policy relating to trading conditions and taxation
- short-term fluctuations in demand
- shortages in construction resources
- unexpected development in technology
- new entrants to the market
- withdrawals from the market
- shifts in fashion.

It will always be an advantage to anticipate such changes. However, if this is not possible then fast reaction after the event is necessary, therefore an organization should be nimble in its attitude and sufficiently flexible to accommodate change. This requires close liaison between marketing and the business activity. Figure 5.8 provides a framework of the questions that should be asked under such circumstances.

Source/ production	Marketing	Finance
Can it be supplied?	Can it be sold?	Availability?
Capacity	In what quantity?	Cash flow?
Cost	At what price?	Profitability?
Quality	Which clients?	Terms of reimbursement?
Supply chain	How?	Payment terms
Availability	When?	When?

Figure 5.8: Integration of marketing with the business

To achieve effective integration there must be strong communication between corporate management and those responsible for the development of marketing strategy and tactics. In a small organization the functions of corporate management and marketing will very probably be carried out by the same management team, but in a larger company it is usual for marketing to be dealt with by a separate team of experts who will provide information and advice on business decisions.

Case study 5.1: Private Finance Initiative (PFI) — Consort Healthcare

Consort Healthcare was established specifically to bid for PFI contracts under policies implemented by the government in the United Kingdom. The subject of this case study is the Edinburgh Royal Infirmary Project, and it is worth noting that between 1995 and 2000 Consort gained considerable experience in bidding for hospital contracts under PFI.

This case demonstrates that persistence pays off, since PFI is not an easy procurement route and requires considerable expertise in teamwork, planning, financing and project management in general. Consort's battle to win the Edinburgh Infirmary contract began in mid-1995 when it became one of 20 groups in consortium to apply for and submit a prequalification tender. It took one year to reduce the competition to two serious bidders and by this stage Consort had a team of five persons working full-time on the bid, which was submitted in June 1996. Subsequently, Consort and the rival Laing Group were asked to re-bid and, in October 1996, having invested total of £200,000 in the bidding process, Consort was nominated as the preferred bidder.

Between October 1996 and August 1998, a series of complex negotiations, checking and inspections took place. The project agreement between Consort and the National Health Service (NHS) Trust (the Client) had to be finalized. This involved the legality of the contractual arrangements with the University of Edinburgh and issues relating to taking over the old Edinburgh Infirmary site and three other smaller hospitals whose functions will eventual move to the new hospital when it opens. As part of the consortium, Morrison Construction was to develop the old sites and the title of these required careful scrutiny. Edinburgh University's involvement concerned the New Medical School, which would be located in the new hospital. Concurrently, Consort was finalizing a construction contract with ERJV, a joint venture between Balfour Beatty Construction, Haden Young and Morrison Construction and its subcontractors, BICC and Haden Building Management who would eventually manage the Infirmary's estate and facilities.

Among the sensitive issues involved before a loan for the project could be finalized was the transfer of the non-clinical staff from the employ of the NHS Trust to Consort. Further, it was agreed that a contribution from Morrison for the old hospital sites would be included as a credit in the Consort balance sheet. The bulk of the £210 million cost of the new Edinburgh Infirmary would be met by a loan from a group of six blue-chip lenders headed by a Consort member, The Royal Bank of Scotland. The other members of the loan group included the Nationwide Building Society, Halifax PLC, Deutsche Bank, ABN-Amro and Rabobank.

Over the next two years, risk was reduced by the careful consideration of contracts, forecasts and economic models that resulted in the satisfaction of the financiers and the drawing up of a master agreement for the loan.

Although the contractual stage was long and drawn out, it is worth remembering that the private sector bears the risk of cost overrun and delay and therefore it was essential to get everything right. Consort insisted that it did not want work to start before all contracts had been signed. Notwithstanding this, Consort was able to secure a special agreement underwritten by the NHS Trust for ERJV and the architect to continue design work, thus saving in the region of one year and approximately £5m in construction costs.

The advantage in starting a project on a greenfield site where everything was sorted out beforehand was enormous and this provided Consort with the opportunity to achieve substantial cost and operational savings. In the agreement the NHS Trust lays out its requirements for the hospital, but it is the responsibility of Consort to interpret these, hence the design accounted for the concession companies' liability to maintain the hospital for a period of 25 years. Hence, efficient in-use functional performance and life cycle costs formed a key factor in the selection and detail of the design.

Internally, the hospital has been designed to allow patients to flow through the hospital, commencing in a preliminary assessment area before they are directed to discharge or admission to casualty or the wards. All highly serviced areas such as acute care, attendant laboratories and diagnostic facilities are grouped together for operational convenience. Careful design has also made better use of space without impairing care and efficiency.

Edinburgh Infirmary will be Europe's largest teaching hospital and the first phase was completed by October 2001. At its peak there were 2000 construction workers and 100 subcontractors on site. The final phase of the hospital is due for completion in January 2003.

Author's commentary

The lengthy contractual phase of a PFI project would appear to militate against the speed of delivering a project and value for money. It is therefore important to realize that PFI is only suitable for certain types of project.

An important prerequisite of any PFI project is that it must have a sure and substantial income stream over the period of the concession, e.g. 25 years, to enable investment to be recovered and for reasonable profits to be made. Public facilities such as toll roads and bridges, hospitals, student accommodation, etc. are examples where PFI has potential. Given the risk involved and the length of the concession, it is important to spend time in the contractual phase to make sure that problems are identified and dealt with, since unresolved difficulties at the start of construction will have the potential to multiply their impact over the concession period. Those organizations entering PFI for the first time must realize the scale of the commitment required and the need for teamwork with partners and the client. Correctly undertaken, the potential for success is good, but this will not be achieved without considerable effort.

Case study 5.2: Bovis Lend Lease

Lend Lease is a business that spans the capital and creation aspects of most key real estate markets. The corporation has crafted a situation where it can deliver on its vision to provide the best real estate outcomes for clients across the globe. The acquisition of the Bovis Group in 1999 created the Bovis Lend Lease Corporation, which is now one of the world's leading companies in the property management and construction services industry. The corporation employs 7000 persons in 93 offices worldwide and on a regional basis it offers the delivery of a service that guarantees completion on time and to budget and an enhanced commercial result for clients.

Bovis Lend Lease achieves competitive advantage by being able to offer customers a single service through an integrated set of specialisms which include risk management, pre-feasibility studies, master planning, project management, process design, construction delivery, financial structuring and engineering and development management.

The experience and reputation of Bovis for winning repeat business and the implementation of non-adversarial relationships with clients such as Marks and Spencer, the UK-based international retailer, has complemented and supported the Bovis Lend Lease principle of customer service.

Bovis Lend Lease constantly strives to seek new and better ways of working with clients across the full range of the real estate market, which has helped to build important and long lasting relationships with clients across the world. By creating such relationships, Bovis Lend Lease have been able to achieve a broader understanding of client needs which in turn has assisted in adding value to the solutions and service provided.

In order to generate repeat business Bovis Lend Lease needs to go further than satisfying the factors of time, cost and quality: results must exceed the expectations of clients, but not their budgets. The corporation's unique selling point (USP) is its ability to deliver the same high standards across multiple industry sectors in many different countries, balancing capital outlay against technical specification and design criteria against life cycle costs.

In 1997, BP made a corporate decision to partner with an organisation that would undertake the building and maintenance of its retail outlets across Europe. Bovis Lend Lease was able to demonstrate to BP its commitment to cost savings and quality criteria that were vital to BP's capital expenditure programme. The corporation was also able to articulate the advantages gained from adopting a local approach in the countries where it operated. Hence, BP selected Bovis Lend Lease whose first task was to benchmark costs from country to country. By applying procurement leverage through its supply chain and developing improved methods of construction the corporation was able to reduce outrun costs by over in 50% in four years. In addition to improving the quality and speed of construction, the results supplemented a comprehensive set of pan-European standards and procedures. BP has subsequently entered into a global alliance with Bovis Lend Lease to provide outlets in the USA and Japan where it has a vigorous expansion programme. The remit has been expanded to include environmental protection standards and methods of reducing life cycle operating and maintenance costs.

The ability to develop creative solutions by integrating operational, design and delivery requirements with a range of complex and sophisticated projects using its specialist skills and expertise in the interest of client needs is at the core of the Bovis Lend Lease brand.

Author's commentary

The acquisition of Bovis by Lend Lease would appear to have been a good business move. The combination of global real estate expertise and the skill of a construction company with a reputation for client satisfaction and repeat business makes for a powerful global group with the ability to meet the high expectations of clients operating on a global basis.

The case study illustrates that project cost represents only one part of the added value dimension to a client's business. The sophisticated global client is increasingly seeking single-source suppliers who, in addition to providing quality and efficient delivery, also provide added value through life cycle performance and maintenance. The use of benchmarks is a valuable tool for kick-starting the relationship and it reassures the client that a better deal cannot be obtained elsewhere.

Traditional competitive tendering discourages construction companies from taking a full interest in a more sophisticated view of client needs, and involvement finishes with the expiration of the defects liability period.

Summary

Marketing is a multi-faceted and essential part of the strategic corporate management and the production of an international construction organization. It provides the necessary intelligence about the market to inform senior managers about the development, potential, trends and areas of decline within the scope of the corporate business portfolio. The analysis and evaluation of new and existing markets will provide information on which decisions can be based regarding investment and the deployment of resources.

The needs of the market will be constantly changing, with consequent reaction from the competition in the form of new products and services. Successful companies, in addition to reacting to change, will also seek to influence the market in order to create trends brought about by innovation, research and development. New products and services will need to be brought to the attention of clients through direct contact, advertising and by generating a good reputation. The objective will be to gain market share and position by means of competitive advantage achieved through superior products and services that provide added value to the business prospects of clients.

The selection and adoption of the most appropriate procurement route for international projects requires consideration of all the relevant factors. Whatever alternative is selected, the outcome should exceed client expectations and provide the basis for negotiating future projects based on trust and partnership. The examples provided by the case studies demonstrate the importance of building long-term relationships and trust between all parties concerned. This is made more demanding in the international arena where different cultures and ethical values come into play. Therefore, there also needs to be recognition of cultural differences and the means should be set in place to adequately accommodate and mediate between differing views and values.

Marketing is also concerned with the promotion of brand and image that play a vital part in corporate identity and image. It is essential that clients and the public be constantly at the forefront of the marketing effort.

Developments in the use of private investment to fund essential public projects are contributing to a worldwide change in the nature and prospects of the international construction business. Successful PPP projects require considerable teamwork and the need for an integrated, non-adversarial approach to project procurement and supply chain management. The development of new innovative services and products applicable to international construction will be essential to meet future challenges presented by increasingly demanding and complex client needs. Environmental, conservation and sustainability issues will compound this requirement.

Further reading

Babbar S. & Rai A. (1993), 'Competitive intelligence for international business', *Long range planning*, **26**, No. 3, 103–113.

Bogner W. C. *et al* (1999), 'Competence and competitive advantage: towards a dynamic model', *British Journal of Management*, **10**, Issue 4, 275–290.

Balfour Beatty home page (on-line www.balfourbeatty.com).

Bovis Lend Lease home page (on-line www.bovislendlease.com).

Cox A. & Townsend M. (1998), *Strategic procurement in construction*, Thomas Telford, London.

Cox V. L. (1982), *International marketing, planning and execution*, Construction Press.

Harrigan K. R. (1984), 'Joint ventures and global strategies', *Columbia Journal of World Business*, Summer, 7–16.

Harris R. (2001), 'Supply chain management in construction', Civil Engineering Trends Archive (on-line www.emeraldinsight.com).

Horvath L. (2001), 'Collaboration: the key to value creation in supply chain management', *J. Supply Chain Management*, **6**, No. 5, 205–207.

Kapila P. & Henderson C. (2001), 'Exchange rate risk management in international construction joint ventures', *J. Management in Engineering*, **17**, Issue 4, 186–191.

Kotler P. (1997), *Marketing management*, (9th edn), Prentice Hall, New Jersey, USA.

Ogunlana S. O. (1999), *Profitable partnering in construction*, E & F. N. Spon.

Osbaldeston M. & Barham K. (1992), 'Using management development for competitive advantage', *Long range planning*, **25**, No. 6 December, 18–24.

Rowlinson S. & McDermott P. (1999), *Procurement systems – a guide to best practice in construction*, E & F. N. Spon.

Perra-Mora F. & Harpoth N. (2001), *Effective partnering in innovative procured multicultural projects*, **17**, Issue 2, 60–68.

Walker D. H. T., Hampson K. and Peters R. (2002), Project alliancing vs project partnering: a case study of the Australian national museum project, *J. Supply Chain Management*, **7**, No. 2, 83–91.

Warwick Manufacturing Group (1999), *Implementing supply chain management*, Project Progress Report 1, University of Warwick.

Woodward D. & Woodward T. (2001), The efficacy of action at a distance as a control mechanism in the construction industry when a trust relationship breaks down: an illustrative study, *British Journal of Management*, **12**, Issue 4, 355–384.

Zayas T. M. & Chang L. M. (2002), *Prototype model for BOT risk assessment*, **18**, Issue 1, 7–16.

Chapter 6

International construction finance

Introduction

The increasing rate of globalization has brought about major changes to international finance. Improved systems of communication have facilitated the world's financial markets in becoming more interactive and this has encouraged greater integration. The emancipation of financial cash flow, primarily across the borders of advanced industrialized countries (AICs), together with the deregulation of financial institutions and financial innovations have increased the relationships between national money and capital markets. Hence, financial markets have tended towards common approaches due to increased integration brought about by cause and effect. This development is not universal since least industrialized countries (LDCs) with weak economies and a high level of borrowing have found it necessary to impose tighter exchange controls and other measures intended to isolate their domestic markets from the world financial market. The financing of international construction activities, especially in LDCs, is complicated by fluctuations in foreign exchange rates, governmental exchange controls and the risk associated with undertaking work in a foreign country.

It is usually the case that foreign governments will welcome and encourage inward investment, especially where the cash is in a hard currency such as the US dollar and the Euro. This will be particularly so where the local economy is weak and inflation is high. In the event that the local currency is not internationally traded then this will pose a number of difficult problems, which must be overcome to protect investment. In such situations great care is required to ensure the security of the investment and the need to earn an adequate return given the risk involved.

Foreign exchange controls require a thorough investigation and where it is not possible to transfer profits, or the original investment from the country, then serious consideration should be given to the desirability of such a venture. Investment might range from a single project to the acquisition of a major foreign company and appropriate measures will be necessary to anticipate difficulties and to control risks.

This chapter identifies the sources of international finance and then investigates financial strategies to acquire and manage subsidiaries, joint ventures and individual projects. Attention will be given to the peculiarities of international construction and the management of exchange rate risk. The chapter concludes with a brief outline of assistance available to exporters of services and products.

Sources of finance

Most businesses operate with sufficient working capital in the form of cash to support operations on a short-term basis. The remainder of a company's wealth is invested in land, facilities, personnel, equipment, and materials necessary to undertake work; there may also be investments in associated businesses and subsidiaries.

In order to undertake a new venture involving significant investment, cash will need to be raised by using reserves within the firm or by disposing of assets, or by borrowing. Therefore, investment can be classified into short-term to support operations, medium-term to purchase equipment or facilities and long-term associated with expansion of the existing business, or by acquiring new business in order to diversify.

This subject covers a vast range of variations and it is a complex issue in its own right, hence this section gives an outline overview, which can be augmented by the reading references provided.

Short-term finance

Short-term finance will, in the first instance, be serviced from working capital. However, when the limit is reached it will be necessary to seek out and exploit the cheapest forms of short-term borrowing. The most obvious starting point is the use of trade credit where the period of grace before payment is exploited. This is a matter of fine judgement so as not to lose the confidence of reliable suppliers of goods and services. It might also be worth losing discounts for prompt payment where these are cheaper than interest rates charged for bank overdrafts. Given protracted lead times before delivery and the extra risk involved, scope for exploiting trade credit may be more limited when trading internationally rather than in the domestic market.

Where the limits of working capital are exceeded then it will be necessary to borrow cash. The most common form is normally an overdraft from the firm's bank which may or may not be secured against company assets or collateral deposited by a guarantor. A credit limit is usually agreed and interest is calculated on a daily basis. Overdrafts are usually only possible where the credit rating is good and the interest charged would be set according to the prevailing bank rate, nature of the business and the risk involved. A period will be determined for the overdraft facility and the bank will reserve the right to ask for repayment in full at any time. Normally, clearing banks will provide for small overdrafts; however, where larger amounts are involved then it may be best to approach a merchant bank.

It is possible to sell debt for an amount less than the face value. The advantage of adopting this policy is that cash is immediately available, either as working capital, or for investment in assets or other activities that will show a higher return over the debt maturity period. The main means of selling debt is through factoring and bills of exchange or commercial papers. The difference between the initial purchase price and the maturity value is known as the yield and represents the total discount. It is possible for more secure forms of debt to be traded during the maturity period and may therefore be considered as an investment by those purchasing debt for a proportion of this time.

Medium-term finance

Bank loans can be obtained over a fixed period and will be repaid by instalments at an agreed rate of interest, which is usually higher than that for a bank overdraft. Loans can be renegotiated and it may be possible to extend the repayment period. Such loans are normally secured against company assets or a bond put up by a guarantor. It will be necessary to engage the services of a bank that has the facilities and experience to cope with a comprehensive range of financial transactions within and across international borders involving two or more currencies. The introduction of the Euro and the creation of the Euro Zone have made this process considerably simpler, cheaper and less risky for those operating in and between member states.

Finance houses operate hire purchase and leasing arrangements. Under hire purchase schemes the finance house retains the ownership of assets until the completion of the last payment of a nominal sum, which effectively transfers ownership. Such agreements therefore do not need to be secured since default automatically gives the finance house the right to repossess the assets. The cost of borrowing is usually high since the interest is annualized and calculated on the full purchase price. Companies not able to obtain bank overdrafts may have no option but to adopt this method. An alternative might be to lease assets for an agreed monthly payment. After a set period of time the asset will be taken back by the finance house and disposed of at residual value. There are normally conditions attached to the lease about care and usage and provision will be made for the lessee to purchase at the end of the period, renegotiate the terms for an extended period or to lease new replacement assets. There may be tax benefits associated with leasing, however the most significant advantage with both hire purchase and leasing is that costs are known in advance.

Where companies need to raise capital it may be possible to sell assets and then lease them back. In this manner the investor benefits from the rental and the vendor gains valuable liquidity to invest elsewhere or for use in supporting the continuation of the business.

Long-term finance

The capital of a company can be restructured by issuing shares and secured stock to raise finance for major ventures or acquisitions. Shares in a company may be sold to private subscribers where share certificates are issued bearing a nominal capital value, which may or may not be the same as the asking price of the share. A proportion of profits earned will be distributed to shareholders in the form of dividend; the remainder of the profit may be ploughed back into the business, thereby enhancing the chance of earning more profit in future. Shares may or may not carry voting rights regarding the conduct of the business normally discussed at AGMs and extraordinary meetings. Founders and preference shares will carry the right to participate in profits before ordinary shareholders. Preference shares normally carry a fixed rate dividend because there is less risk involved. Normally, the liability associated with the shares is limited to their face value.

Shares can be sold to the general public provided that the company has acquired a stock exchange quotation. Conversion from a private to a public company is an involved and expensive process, since it will be necessary to have the issue price underwritten in the event that all the newly issued shares are not taken up. The share price will be traded by stock exchanges around the world according to the success and business prospects of the company. Usually higher profits and the dividend paid will be measured by the price earnings ratio (PE), which is a major indicator of the value of the investment.

Additional capital may be raised from existing shareholders by using a rights issue, where existing holding shareholders are offered the right to buy a ratio of shares at a discount. Capital can also be returned to shareholders by creating another category of shares, i.e. B shares, or by making cash payments and then reissuing new shares.

Secured stock, normally referred to as debentures, does not participate in the ownership of a company. Debentures are, in effect, loans to the company at a fixed rate of interest which is payable irrespective of profit. Hence, they have prior claim on company assets in the case of liquidation and therefore carry less risk than equity stock. Debentures in publically quoted private companies can be bought or sold in the market and the price will be largely influenced by the fixed rates of interest offered. Some debentures provide for conversion into equity stock.

Sources of finance for individual projects

In order to secure finance for an individual project it will be necessary for the project to be developed to a stage where its potential and viability can be determined with a fair degree of certainty. This should ideally include a scheme design and related project objectives based on a full appraisal of the market demand and potential income generation. The process of realizing the project will need to be shown by a master plan, including the resources required to completion and the budgeted costs. Other relevant factors relating to the environment, including available technologies and skills should also be included.

Sufficient information should be provided to enable potential funders to assess the potential for profit and the risk involved. The sources of finance will include project sponsors and partners, domestic and merchant banks, development banks, and the fixed interest capital market.

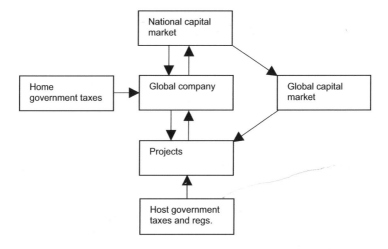

Figure 6.1: Relationships between the factors influencing the cost of capital

Cost of capital

Companies operating in the international construction market that have access to low cost capital will have competitive advantage where they finance profitable long-term speculations. In addition, competitors who believe that a company has the facility to outspend them because of low cost capital will be deterred and hence reputation alone will indirectly contribute to increasing long-term returns. Given the importance of the cost of capital to competitiveness in international markets it is important to understand the influencing factors shown in Figure 6.1.

Capital originates as savings within a nation's capital market from which corporations borrow using intermediaries and by issuing debt and equity directly into the market. Companies then allocate their available capital to projects. Home governments tax and regulate transactions between the corporation and the national capital market. Host governments will tax and regulate and may subsidize flows between the corporation and individual projects.

There will be cost differences between different national capital markets and therefore those that have access to cheaper capital will be at an advantage. Recent integration of world financial markets facilitates global companies to profit from short run disparities in the cost of funds between markets through financial arbitrage.

It is therefore vital that international construction companies seek to establish the cheapest cost of borrowing capital to exploit investment opportunities within the complex series of markets that form the global construction industry. Global companies have the advantage of scanning alternative market opportunities in various countries in order to find the option that is most suitable to fit available resources and expertise.

Companies able to create added value within the global market-place will attract the attention of sophisticated international providers of capital. There is also the opportunity to exploit profit by cross-border arbitrage concerning the differences between the cost of capital. Large-scale activity in this area has the tendency to drive the cost of capital to a common global standard and hence the advantage in this regard tends to decrease under such circumstances.

Corporate linkages, taxation, government incentives and potential conflicts arising from individual projects complicate international investments. Therefore adequate analysis and evaluation must be undertaken for all foreign investment possibilities in order to select those that provide the basis for sustainable competitive advantage.

International and global companies find it necessary to negotiate with national governments to provide financial incentives to make foreign direct investment in a venture or project. This might include tax subsidies, loans and guarantees that will have a significant impact on the economic value of a project and will need to be considered in the evaluation of the investment proposal. Host country financial incentives are likely to be available for technological development and the establishment of new manufacturing facilities that will create jobs. Government subsidies have the potential to reduce net capital contribution and therefore increase the rate of internal return on capital employed.

The international financial system

The main measure of a country's economic output per year is the gross domestic product (GDP). It consists of goods and services produced for home consumption (C), investment (I), government use (G) and exports. The flow of goods is measured as they are purchased, rather than when they are produced. Some purchases will consist of goods imported from abroad and hence imports (M) are deducted from exports (X). Therefore:

$$GDP = C + I + G + (X - M)$$

The nation's balance of payments is a statistical record of all economic transactions between a country's residents and the rest of the world. These are broken down into three accounts:

- current account (CA)
  - trade and merchandise (exports/imports)
  - services (invisibles)

- — investment income (capital working abroad)
- — unilateral transfers (foreign aid, outbound transfers of cash)
- private capital account (KA)
  - — foreign direct investment
  - — long-term portfolio investment (international transactions in financial assets with maturity of greater than one year)
  - — short-term capital flows (assets with a maturity of less than one year, e.g. treasury bills and commercial paper)
- Official Reserve transactions (ORT) — central bank transactions in international reserve assets
  - — gold
  - — IMF credits and special drawing rights
  - — foreign exchange reserves.

Every year a country adds up its credits and its debits. Where the debits exceed credits the balance is in deficit, which will mean a reduction in ORT or short-term capital flows. Provided that a country has sufficient resources then it can, as in the case of the USA, continuously run up a current account deficit. Those countries that are less well off will reach a point were they run out of resources and therefore cannot finance debt any longer; in effect they become bankrupt. This situation is further complicated by policy relating to the supply of money and the amount of inflation generated, which will impact on currency exchange rates and control. The impact of countries that fall into financial difficulty will extend to foreign investors and banks, which could be forced to write off investment capital with consequential knock-on effects in the wider world economy.

The International Monetary Fund (IMF) is a multi-government agency whose role is to promote exchange rate stability and to facilitate the flow of international currency exchange. It also seeks to eliminate exchange restrictions and it makes temporary loans to members with appropriate safeguards in order to rectify problems associated with the balance of payments concerned with national exports and assets compared with imports and liabilities.

Economically strong countries such as the USA, Japan, Germany and the UK have, over the past twenty years, found it unnecessary to use the IMF to borrow money. Instead, where trade deficits have required funding in the short term then borrowing has been from private money. In contrast, LDCs have incurred considerable debt in recent years and the IMF's involvement in resolving such difficulties has been in close association with the World Bank.

The international financial system relies heavily on cooperation between the major economic powers. This is vital to the health of the global economy, and the debt incurred by LDCs, which must be carefully monitored and controlled. The IMF and the World Bank have a major role to play in creating economic stability in the world's less prosperous countries.

Sources of funding in developing countries

In developing countries it is unlikely that large projects will be funded from a single source, since government funds will invariably be inadequate. It is therefore common practice for the governments of developing countries to seek aid from external sources. There are a number of funding agencies that operate on a global or regional scale who provide loans either in part or in full. The largest and best-known organization is the World Bank, which was founded in 1944 as the International Bank for Reconstruction and Development (IBRD). Since then it has set up an institution called the International Development Association (IDA) which acts as the Bank's concessional lending arm for very poor countries who had a per capita income in 2000 below US$ 885. The Bank, based in Washington DC with offices in most major countries throughout the World, provided US$ 17.3 billion in loans to more than 100 developing economies to improve living standards and to reduce poverty. Figure 6.2. shows the leading recipient countries of IDA funding.

The World Bank has now expanded into a group of organizations that complement each other in addressing the need to provide aid to developing countries (Figure 6.3).

More than 180 member countries that are shareholders and who carry ultimate decision-making power in the World Bank are the owners of the Bank.

Top IDA borrowers 2001	Commitments: US$ millions
Ethiopia	667
Vietnam	629
India	520
Pakistan	374
Uganda	358
Kenya	350
Bangladesh	280
Madagascar	268
Senegal	255

Figure 6.2: Top IDA recipient countries
Source: World Bank 2002

The International Development Association (IDA)

The IDA relies on subscriptions and contributions from member countries. As at 30 June 2001 the spread of subscriptions and contributions is shown in Figure 6.4.

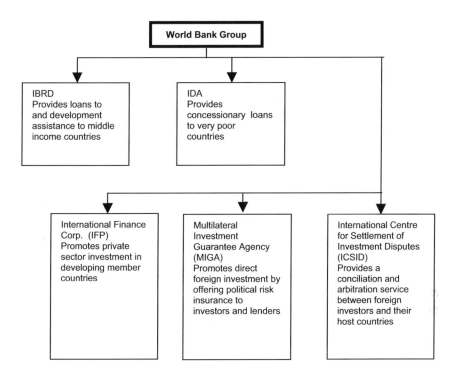

Figure 6.3: World Bank Organization

Member	US$ millions	Percentage
USA	25,841.78	23.77
Japan	24,078.10	22.15
Germany	12,308.06	11.32
UK	8013.06	7.37
France	7468.47	6.87
Canada	4767.53	4.38
Italy	4409.98	4.06
Netherlands	4026.42	3.70

Figure 6.4: IDA subscriptions and contributions
Source: World Bank 2002

To take full advantage of IDA resources it will be necessary for applicants to meet specific criteria:

- *Eligibility*; applicants must be able to demonstrate relative poverty as defined by the GNP per capita being below US$ 885, and a lack of credit worthiness to borrow on market terms and good policy performance;

125

- *Performance ratings:* on an annual basis World Bank staff assess the quality of each borrower's performance. There are 20 performance criteria grouped into four clusters that determine the borrowers' performance rating;
- *Lending and performance:* IDA management monitors lending to each country and actual lending per capita is correlated with performance levels.

There is a strong trend towards lending to countries where policy performance demonstrates effective resource use. Funding can also be obtained from regionally based development banks whose general objective is to speed up development by providing funds for capital investment. In the majority of cases regional governments have set up these banks. Examples include the following:
- Asian Development Bank (AsDB)
- African Development Bank (AfDB)
- Arab Fund for Economic and Social Development (AFESD)
- European Development Fund (EDF)
- Inter-American Development Bank (IADB).

Applications for project loans to be considered by investment banks must progress through a sequence of phases that eventually lead to rejection or acceptance and the implementation of a project. These will vary according to practice and procedure; however, the outline of the World Bank project cycle shown Figure 6.5. is a good example.

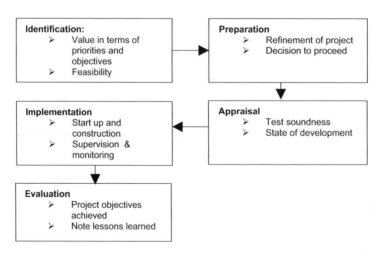

Figure 6.5: Project cycle

Corporate and financial strategy

It is essential that an international construction company develop a strategy to maximize its investment and reduce exposure to risk. This will require careful analysis of the countries and regions in which it will potentially be beneficial to acquire work. It may be advantageous to set up a subsidiary or to acquire a company infrastructure to manage and administer projects and other business interests. This is especially the case where competition is low and there are strong government incentives in the form of free land and tax breaks. Sight should not be lost of the global geographic spread of the company's activities in terms of their complementary and harmonious advantages. There may be virtue in limiting operations on a project-by-project basis controlled from the headquarters of the parent company with adequate support services devolved to the site. This would be particularly applicable where there are uncertainties, which might require a fast withdrawal after the project is complete.

In recent years, a growing number of international construction companies have been forming joint ventures to take on large projects, which require a broad range of expertise and considerable capital investment. By working in partnership the risk is spread and therefore reduced. At the heart of a joint venture is development of trust and continuous improvement brought about by collaboration. Maturing working practices and procedures assist efficiency and can result in advantages for all concerned. Joint ventures can mature into strong alliances where two or more organizations become committed to mutually beneficial goals and business strategies. Such close relationships can eventually lead to merger or acquisition. Entering into a joint venture with a local partner may also be advantageous where the financial risk is shared and advantage is gained from local knowledge and business networks.

Financial evaluation of mergers and acquisitions

A sound strategy for mergers and acquisitions is based on a company's diversification programme and the corporate planning process, since these will be used to justify actions taken. Drucker (1986) laid down five rules based on case studies for successful acquisitions:

1. the acquiring company must contribute to the acquired company;
2. there must be a common core of unity;
3. the acquiring company must have respect for the acquired company;
4. the acquiring company must supply management to the acquired company in the short term; and
5. the management of both companies should receive imminent promotions directly resulting from the merger.

Although the number of case studies involved was limited, Drucker's work has been established as relevant to a large number of mergers and acquisitions that have subsequently taken place.

The rationale behind mergers and acquisitions is that it is usually cheaper to buy a company with the required expertise, assets and products, rather than to build up a new facility up from scratch within the existing organization. This notion must be tested by a valuation of the target company to establish its asset value and potential as a partner organization. Valuation is not a straightforward process and there are many intangible and unproven factors that require estimation. Due diligence has already been described in Chapter 4, and this will provide the necessary information to make a valuation of the company as it exists. The next stage will be to estimate the short, medium and long-term prospects of the acquired organization and an assessment must be made of the value added as a merged or acquired company. The model shown in Figure 6.6 provides a framework for this analysis.

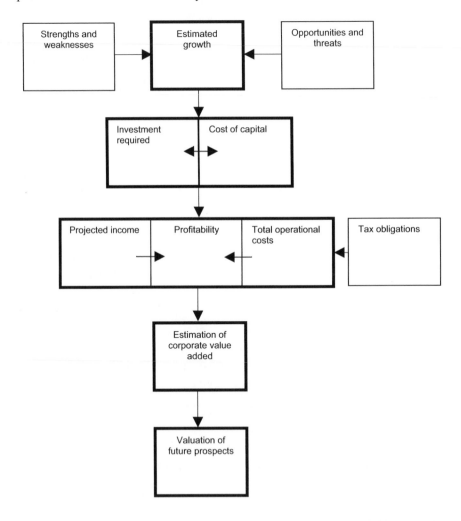

Figure 6.6: Valuation of future prospects for a merger or acquisition

The total valuation that determines the price that should be paid will be based on the company's rate of internal return as a going concern and the valuation of future prospects as a merged or acquired company. Conversely, those selling the company will have conducted a similar exercise to determine the asking price and the difference will be the perceived total value of the merged company, which will then become the subject of negotiation. In the event that a sale must take place it is worth remembering that a company divestiture will ultimately only be worth what somebody is prepared to pay.

Financial management for multinational construction companies

Commensurate with the growing maturity of an international construction company will be the need to exert appropriate financial control by measuring performance against budgets and targets. The degree of financial autonomy given to overseas departments and subsidiaries will depend on previous track record and market stability, together with other factors relating to turnover and profitability. The following sections illustrate some of the financial management strategies that might be adopted.

Financial management strategies

A key factor will be the degree of financial control required and the degree of consistency in the application of system and procedure that will be used. There are three basic approaches, which are described below.

Federal foreign subsidiaries

Under these circumstances the subsidiary companies existing in each country will operate according to general financial and accounting rules and procedures (Figure 6.7). Decisions will be taken locally and performance will be measured against other subsidiary companies. This approach is likely to be taken where businesses are well established and they are operating in a stable, low-risk environment.

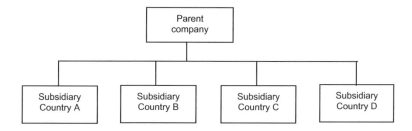

Figure 6.7: Federally related foreign subsidiaries

Functional foreign subsidiaries

This solution integrates foreign subsidiaries into the financial management and control systems of the parent company (Figure 6.8). In this manner more rigorous control can be achieved and it is argued that the system utilizing Internet and Intranet communication is more efficient. Critics of this approach will argue that it can be constraining due to the variety of conditions that exist in different countries.

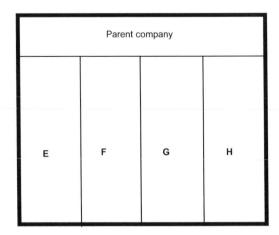

Figure 6.8: Functionally related foreign subsidiaries

Geographic solution

This is a hybrid solution which applies the above strategies according to the maturity of a company and the stability of the national environment within which it exists (Figure 6.9). Loose control can be maintained where there is less risk, thus enabling greater local freedom of decision to cope with specific circumstances.

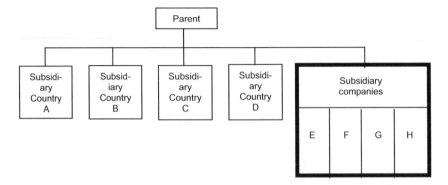

Figure 6.9: Geocentric subsidiaries

Fund positioning

A major concern of a multinational construction company will be the positioning of funds to provide sufficient working capital. Where funds are available from within the organization this may be achieved by the parent company increasing its equity capital in a subsidiary, instead of borrowing from external sources. In return, the subsidiary will pay the parent interest or dividends on this investment. Alternatively, loans can be made between subsidiaries. The chosen course of action will depend on government regulation, taxation and exchange rates.

Transfer pricing is a technique whereby products are valued internally within the organization. This allows prices for goods to be changed according to economies and regulations of the countries involved in the transactions in order to maximize profits, effect cost reduction or simply to facilitate the movement of money.

Where investment is desirable in a country that carries risk associated with instability and the acquisition of assets, it may be a good idea to deposit funds with a bank that has fundamental ties with the country concerned. In this manner a loan can be made by the bank to support the subsidiary's operations. This will effectively block an attempted acquisition since any such action would attract retaliation from the bank.

Foreign exchange risk management

Purchasing power parity theory states that the exchange rate between two currencies will be determined by the relative purchasing power of these countries. Moreover, this may not always be the case when the perceived economic outlook might over- or undervalue the currency. In recent years, the strongest of the world's economies have been skilfully controlled by relating the rate of inflation to interest on borrowing. Major industrialized countries exhibit a high degree of integration within financial markets and, consequently, the factors affecting interest rates are transmitted across national borders. Hence, exchange rates are more stable. This has been achieved by controlling the supply of money in a national economy relative to the demand for money and hence the price level is determined. Changes in price level determine the rate of inflation, which in turn influences the nominal interest rate. The nominal interest rate represents the cost of holding money, which will have an effect on the demand for money (Figure 6.10).

Exchange rates are directly affected by the supply of money, especially where governments elect to use seigniorage (printing money) to finance their spending. The rate of borrowing and inflation will also have an effect on interest rates.

The introduction of the Euro has done much to simplify and stabilize exchange rates. On the other hand, in countries with a lesser degree of integration, in particular LDCs, there is more likely to be a lack of coordination of macroeconomic policies. This contributes to less stable currency exchange rates that result in sharp swings in competitiveness and business prospects.

Countries that apply strict exchange controls to isolate their domestic economies from the international financial market face additional difficulties concerning the ability to attract foreign investment and conduct foreign trade. This should be viewed in the light of difficulties associated with China's phased membership of WTO and the commensurate introduction of Yuan into the international financial system.

When dealing in foreign exchange it is important that steps are taken to minimize exposure to losses resulting in variations in exchange rates caused by inflation and speculation. Accelerating or decelerating payment in local currency depends on whether the change is detrimental or beneficial and the rapid depreciation of equipment and other assets normally deals with inflation risk. Where hyperinflation exists in the host country then the best policy will be to deal only in hard currency such as the US dollar or the Euro.

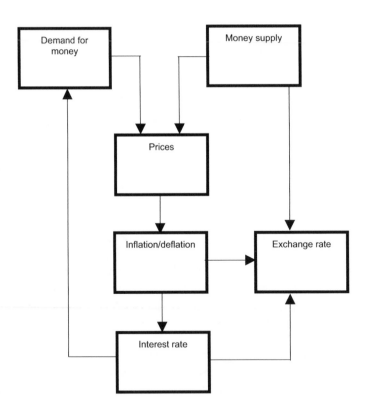

Figure 6.10: Influencing factors on the exchange rate

Hedging strategies can be employed to give protection from adverse trends in exchange rates. Forward exchange contracts can be used where goods or services are to be supplied at a given future date. The exchange is agreed in advance, hence the purchaser gains if the exchange rate rises above that agreed; conversely, the purchaser loses if the rate falls below the agreed rate. The advantage of this arrangement is that it is known in advance how much will be paid, irrespective of the exchange rate. This arrangement is good for preparing estimates for lump sum fixed price contracts. Alternatively, currency options can be taken whereby the purchaser has the right to buy or sell a specified amount of foreign currency at an agreed rate within a predetermined time period. This arrangement tends to be more flexible than a forward exchange contract.

Dealing in foreign exchange is a highly specialized and involved business that requires considerable knowledge, expertise and, above all, acumen. Where an international construction company's involvement is extensive it could well be worth employing a specialist team whose role would be to minimize risk exposure and to take advantage of beneficial trends to advance profits.

Assistance to exporters

Export credits and insurances

Foreign trade is considerably more risky than dealing in the domestic market because of unfamiliar practices, legal requirements, economic and cultural difficulties. Export credits are a form of home government support for foreign trade. All major exporting countries will have some export credit facilities, which normally take the form of either insurance or financing.

Export credit insurance is mainly concerned with the risk of non-payment due to commercial or political reasons. Risk can be comprehensive or for specific purposes. A premium will be payable, which will typically be around 10% of the contract value.

Export credit finance consists of supplier credit that allows the client to defer payment until after the contract is complete. The vehicle for allowing such credit is normally a promissory note that can be purchased by the supplier's bank in a similar manner to a bill of exchange. The risk is normally underwritten by the respective export credit agency. Buyer credit is where the export credit agency underwrites the risk of default between the lender and the buyer.

Export assistance

In order to encourage exports of goods and services, governments will provide assistance in a variety of forms. Most usual will be the provision of soft loans with long-term low interest to cover specific projects. These are normally considered on an individual basis and the grant of the loan will be subject to meeting formalized criteria.

Aid and trade provision may also be available according to previously laid down criteria and rules which normally favour developing and poor countries.

Case study 6.1: Agency funding for developing countries

A selection of case studies is described that are typical of cases worthy of funding to reduce poverty and improve living standards.

World Bank: Gujarat, India – emergency earthquake reconstruction programme

On 2 May 2002, the World Bank Board approved a loan through the IDA of US$ 442.8 million, with a grace period of 10 years and a maturity of 40 years.

The project is intended to assist the second phase of the earthquake relief programme as a follow-up to the US$ 261.6 million already provided immediately after the earthquake. The aim of the loan is to complete ongoing reconstruction and provide for sustainable measures that will restrict damage and reduce loss of life if the region is unfortunate enough to experience a similar event in future. In reality, the loan will finance further assistance to hundreds of thousands of people whose lives were shattered by the 2001 earthquake, through a participatory approach that will require communities and government, both local and national, to play leading roles in planning and implementing reconstruction works, especially for the most vulnerable groups.

The second phase will support the reconstruction and repair of houses in rural and urban areas, repair and strengthening of public buildings, roads, bridges, dams and irrigation infrastructure. Reinforcement will be provided to undamaged government buildings and critically important public buildings such as schools, hospitals and fire stations in earthquake zones. Funding will also support the establishment of an emergency management programme.

Asian Development Bank AsDB: metropolitan waterworks and sewerage system, Manila, The Philippines

The initial listing for this project was 15 October 2001 with approval confirmation in 2002 and a completion date of December 2004. The total cost of the loan amounted to US$ 5.9 million.

In 2001, the Metropolitan Water Sewerage System (MWSS) provided in the region of 4000 million litres per day from the Umiray, Angat and Ipo river basins to concessionaires for distribution to the population and industry. Despite measures to reduce wastage, the supply of water will fall well short of demand by 2003. The intention of the loan is to access new water supplies from the Wawa River, Laguna Lake, Angat Aqueduct improvement and Marikina North-East.

The main objective of the project is to provide the MWSS with a flexible loan facility to engage consultants to prepare public and private sector projects, as above, for new water source development. The loan will also include for capacity building to strengthen the financial management of the MWSS. The intention is to improve the living conditions and health of the population in Metro Manila by means of providing safe water supply and the project will facilitate the expansion of the service area, particularly for the urban poor.

African Development Bank AfDB: the Tema-Aflao Rehabilitation Road Project, Ghana, West Africa

On 17 April 2002, the African Development Bank approved a loan of US$ 18.32 million to finance the Tema-Aflao Rehabilitation Road Project.

The objective is to provide improved road transport and reduced travel times and vehicle operating costs. This will enhance traffic flow and improve trade on this section of road that forms part of the Trans West African Highway providing regional integration between Ghana, Burkina Faso, Togo, Benin, Nigeria and Niger. The project will contribute to poverty reduction and strengthen regional unification by providing integrated and sustainable road transport in the area. The upgrading of the road will assist the local population to increase its agricultural production and provide better access to education and health facilities. Other benefits include easier access for traders and farmers to income generating markets and will encourage tourist traffic to the Volta River estuary.

The project will involve the rehabilitation of 41 km on the Akatsi–Aflao section with a single tarmac concrete surfaced carriageway 7.3m wide with dressed shoulders and edge marking. The road will bypass Akatsi town.

The total cost of the road rehabilitation is expected to be US$ 27.03 million and therefore will be co-financed in association with the Government of Ghana. The AfDB loan will cover part of the foreign exchange cost of the project.

AfDB operations commenced in Ghana in 1973 and during the period to 2001 the Bank had committed US$ 789.77 million net of cancellation on 60 operations. Of this amount, US$ 574.22 million had been dispersed.

Author's commentary

LDCs depend heavily on agency bank loans for justifiable projects that often involve the expenditure of hard currency to engage consultants and import expertise and materials to undertake the projects.

A major problem is that AICs and NICs are continually increasing their productivity resulting in cost reductions in real terms. Without commensurate productivity improvements in LDCs they fall further behind, resulting in lower real term incomes and reductions in national economic strength. It therefore becomes virtually impossible to fund entire projects from internal sources that require the importation of expertise and resources. This situation is made worse by downturns in the world economy resulting in reduced foreign direct investment.

Case study 6.2: Skanska Financing: Stockholm Centre of Physics, Astronomy and Biotechnology

Skanska Financial Services has devised an innovative approach for the financing of the Stockholm Centre of Physics, Astronomy and Biotechnology in association with the Royal Institute of Technology and the University of Stockholm. A bond loan was raised to finance the construction costs and a 25-year lease was signed by the Swedish Government to cover the interest and amortization payments for the loan, which equates to real interest bonds amounting to 1.2 billion Swedish Krona. The outcome means that the tenant will pay a rent that is lower than the level possible with a more traditional leasing agreement.

Ohman Fondkommission arranged finance for the project and, in simple terms, this means that the Swedish Government pays rent corresponding to the interest and amortization payments for the bond loan. The rent is then converted into real interest bonds that are then sold on the stock exchange. The purchasers include a dozen or so investors, including pension funds. The credit rating of the institute, Standard and Poor's, assigned the bond loan its highest triple AAA rating because of the Swedish Government's high credit worthiness and the structure of the agreement.

After 20 years the tenant has the right, but not the obligation, to acquire the property and redeem the bond loan. Alternatively, the lease may be prolonged.

Further, in addition to the leasing agreement signed by the Swedish Government, Fysikhu Stockholm KB (newly formed to own and finance property and to lease it to the Swedish Government), Skanska and the tenant have concluded a separate management agreement for the building.

The result is that students and staff have gained an ultra-modern building to house the Centre for Physics, Astronomy and Biochemistry.

Author's commentary

Securitization is a common method of funding commercial premises in the USA and the UK, however, this was the first occasion that Skanska had used this solution to fund a project with the Swedish Government as the tenant. For this solution to work, the project must be of sufficient magnitude and the credit rating of the client must be high.

There would appear to be further scope to successfully apply this funding approach successfully to other building and infrastructure projects.

Summary

Financing and monetarily controlling international construction ventures and projects is often more complicated and involves more risk than those in a domestic market. Fluctuating currency exchange rates, government exchange controls and the need to acquire resources from international sources creates difficulties and risks that require close monitoring and control.

Where ventures and projects are to be funded by borrowing then it is important that banks and financial lending institutions need to be convinced about an organization's capacity and competence to undertake the commitment with the least possible risk. Interest rates will be charged according to the perceived risk and it is therefore important that applications for funding are prepared in a comprehensive and clear manner to achieve the best possible terms. Similar practice should also be applied to requests for medium and long-term finance.

Where work is to be undertaken in LDCs, it is likely that finance for the project will be derived from government and development agency sources such as the World Bank and regional development banks, e.g. AsDB, AfDB. These agencies lay down precise project cycles and procedures that are put in place to control the quality and progress of the work as well as the payment procedures for completed work. Where an international construction organization is borrowing to finance resources locked up in the project between stage payments, account should be taken of delays caused by the respective agency approval system and procedures.

Financial transactions using hard currencies, e.g. US$, Euro, Yen and Pound Sterling, are less prone to risk and will be preferred to local currencies, especially those that suffer from high inflation and are not internationally traded. Local currency will be required to pay for indigenous resources and services. Therefore it will be necessary to operate at least a dual currency system. Hedging and covering purchases from international sources will need to be implemented to provide protection against adverse trends in exchange rates.

The strategic financial management of international construction companies is an important aspect of corporate control. The amount of financial control devolved to subsidiary companies will depend on the nature of the company and its geographic spread. One approach is to provide autonomy were subsidiaries operate independently according to financial regulations and procedures. The alternative approach is to integrate the financial procedures of the subsidiaries with that of the parent company. Global companies with interests and many subsidiaries may elect to use both approaches in a hybrid solution. In all cases it will be necessary to allocate company funds to support business activity most effectively and at the same time reduce exposure to risk.

Where governments are keen to encourage the generation of foreign income, various forms of support will be made available through consulate assistance, export credits and insurances to cover additional risk.

Further reading

Asian Development Bank home page (on-line www.asdb.org).

African Development Bank home page (on-line www.afdb.org).

Beamish P. W. (1992), *Multinational joint ventures in developing countries*, Routledge, London.

Beidleman C. R. *et al.* (1990), 'On allocating risk: the essence of project finance', *Sloan Management Review*, Spring Issue, 47–55.

Blommeart A. M. M. *et al.* (1991), *Financial decision making*, Prentice Hall, NY.

Brownlie S. & Harris F. C. (1989), 'A review of finance for large-scale construction', *Construction Management and Economics*, **5**, No. 2, 115–121.

Caves R. E., Frankel J. A. & Jones R. W. (1999), *World trade and payments*, 8th edn, Addison Wesley, MA.

Drucker P. (1986), *The frontiers of management,* Heinemann, London

Mankiw N. G. (1997), *Macroeconomics*, 3rd edn, Worth Publishers, Basingstoke UK.

Porter M. E. (1986), *Competition in global industries*, Harvard Business School Press.

Price A. D. F. (1995), *Financing international construction projects*, ILO, Geneva.

Tiong R. L. K. (1990), 'BOT projects: risks and securities', *Construction Management and Economics*, **8**, No. 3, Autumn, 315–328.

World Bank home page (on-line www.worldbank .org).

Chapter 7

International management culture

Introduction

Culture can be defined as acquired knowledge based on assumptions and perceptions used to generate social behaviour. When considered at a national level it provides a broad definition of social culture. In this manner values and attitudes are blended together into a national set of ideals that are passed down from one generation to the next. Experience and advances in knowledge that are gained over time will, under normal circumstances, slowly modify such values. There will, of course, be significant step functions in cultural change that occur from time to time and are usually brought about by such factors as war, scientific breakthroughs and fashion. This process of change is responsible for a widely held view that past values will eventually reach a point in time where they are considered to be outdated and old fashioned. It is also important to appreciate that variations exist within cultures and that individuals vary considerably according to age group and the extent to which they may be atypical of their national culture. It is therefore important not to confuse personality with culture.

The successful management of an international construction company will require understanding of the different aspects of culture as it applies to personnel employed from different countries who are involved in the conduct of projects and other business activities. Barriers between cultures should be recognized and ways must be determined to minimize adverse affects and to accentuate advantages to be derived from the potential to create new cultural approaches to the conduct of business activities.

A major danger is to succumb to ethnocentrism, embracing the fundamental belief that one's own cultural approach is superior to that of others from a different cultural background. Typical examples include the imposition of home country practices that would be considered as alien, filling the top jobs with home nationals, application of differential pay scales for doing the same job and no investment or commitment to local society.

The conduct of business in the international market is made much more difficult than within a purely domestic market by the introduction of different cultures. A key part of coping adequately with this extra challenge concerns an increased awareness of and a sympathetic attitude to different ways of doing things.

The chapter commences with the need to build a cultural map in order to increase understanding of the issues and elements that drive different cultures. Using cultural mapping as a base, a framework is developed to enable the application of appropriate management practice. The prospects for intercultural management are examined in the context of a globalized society where local cultures and values are assuming new importance. The means of profiling and identifying the nature of cultures are explained and some conclusions are drawn from previous research.

Cultural mapping

A prerequisite to building a cultural map is to develop a hierarchy of issues and orientations, starting with those fundamental issues that are common to all cultures. These are the perceptions of what is good and right as opposed to the forces of wrong and evil. From these will descend fairness and justice, pride and guilt and a sense of belonging and loyalty. These are powerful emotions which, when challenged directly, can cause turmoil and, in the worst cases, devastation. Figure 7.1 shows a pyramid of cultural hierarchy with the human race at the apex and the individual at the bottom. In between are the cultural orientations that are brought about by nationalistic attitudes and beliefs, which in turn divide further into various sub-cultures.

The prime characteristics of national culture can be grouped as shown in Figure 7.2 and will be generated directly from the universal issues and resultant forces which form the foundation of all cultures.

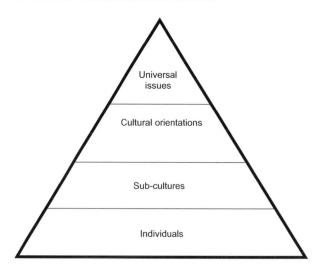

Figure 7.1: Cultural hierachy pyramid

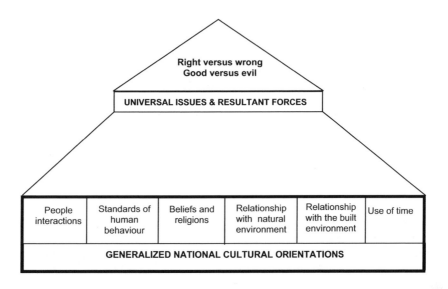

Figure 7.2: Group of generalized national cultural characteristics

At the heart of culture lies the universal issue of 'right or wrong', which provides the foundation for morals and ethics that are interpreted differently by individual cultures. Moral principles are diverse and what in some cases may be considered to be honourable in one culture, might be judged to be completely wrong in another. Moral values are therefore considered to be absolute in nature, but their interpretation is fundamental for each culture. Human rights stem from ethics, which are universal, even when there are no established moral grounds. The Universal Declaration of Human Rights provides the foundation for ethical behaviour irrespective of culture.

People interactions

Each national culture will have its own system of society, which will have been built up over previous generations. As a general rule, the older the society the more structured and rigid it has become. Hierarchies and social classes have a large influence on the standing of groups, families and individuals. Each social layer will have its own sub-culture that will set it apart from other groupings. The aristocracy will have taken steps to maintain its position through the use of wealth and influence to ensure the continuum through future generations. Only revolution or the failure of certain groups or families through human failings have seen parts of the aristocracy lose its status. In many advanced industrialized countries democracy and free trade have ensured a more liberalized approach whereby individuals and families succeed on merit.

In Asian communities, especially Chinese society, ultimate respect is traditionally given to elders, irrespective of their competence and knowledge. Therefore, position and standing within society demands respect and should not

141

be questioned. The Chinese are very aware of the need to maintain honour and dignity in the face of adversity and extreme sensitivities come into play in attempting to avoid loss of face.

African society is dominated by the tribal and family systems, which have evolved because of poverty and the complete absence of a welfare state. Such a system does create strong sub-cultures, which naturally encourage fragmentation and sectarianism and it is therefore necessary that strong leadership be shown from national governments to maintain national unity. In the absence of such leadership real dangers exist of civil conflicts resulting from disagreements and disputes.

The increased availability and affordability of global transportation has encouraged migration of the world's population to other countries for family reasons or to seek increased prosperity in countries that are able to support better living standards. Industrial growth and falling birth rates in AICs have created shortages of skilled and qualified personnel. Shortfalls have been made up by encouraging applications from suitably qualified individuals from overseas. Policies have also been implemented by many countries to provide safe havens for foreign refugees. These actions, especially in the USA and the UK, have resulted in the creation of multicultural societies where families still have roots in their country of origin, but live and interact with the indigenous population and persons from other cultural and ethnic backgrounds. The integration of various cultures in a national society eventually has an impact on cultural change and short-term differences need to be accommodated by a greater level of understanding and awareness, not least in the business environment.

Language is a natural expression of culture through communication. It is vital to know the meaning of idioms, colloquialisms and clichés, as well as nuances and implied meanings. In this manner it is possible to convey subtle meanings that will comply with cultural expectations denoting attitude and behaviour. When translating from one language to another it will be necessary not only to understand the subtleties of both languages, but also to interpret correctly the true meanings between them. Failure to achieve this demanding requirement will lead to misunderstanding and, in some instances, embarrassment. Even the same language will be differently applied from country to country creating different meanings for similar words or phrases.

The three most common languages in the world are Chinese Mandarin, Spanish and English, the latter being the dominant language of business, medicine, engineering and science.

The ability to express oneself precisely and clearly in any language is a prerequisite to good communication. The art of oral and written communication forms the foundation for all human activity, especially in coping with complex and difficult situations. It is said that it is better to be able to express matters clearly in one language than to be only partially competent in two or more languages.

A strong education system will considerably influence culture, since people who are fully literate will be more widely read and will be more aware of historical matters and the current situation nationally and globally. Moreover, education will provide the ability to analyse and evaluate situations, thus enabling informed judgements to be made. In advanced or developing industrialized societies these qualities will be essential in medicine, science, engineering and commerce.

There is evidence that schooling throughout the world is increasing and the level of illiteracy is diminishing, however there is a growing demand for tertiary education, especially at universities, to cope with the increasing requirement for highly skilled graduates in all disciplines.

Standards of human behaviour

Recognition must be given to differences in custom and manners. What might be extremely polite in one culture could be completely the opposite in another. A business operating in foreign countries needs to acquire a rapid understanding of customs and manners to improve the chances of business success. Managers within an international construction company will need to fully understand user lifestyles and requirements to inform the design and construction of commercial buildings, infrastructure and homes in order to facilitate customs associated with cultural practice.

Customs will also dictate the way that companies market themselves and advertise their products and services. The employment of a reliable local marketing and advertising agency alongside a local joint venture partner would be one way of accommodating this requirement. The appointment of a local partner will also help to avoid misunderstanding and potential damage to business relationships.

Beliefs and religions

Beliefs and religions within the host country will differ from those in the home country and it will be necessary to identify and examine the differences with a view to developing a better understanding. This will inform the development of appropriate strategies and courses of action to mitigate potential difficulties and to increase social cohesion.

Values associated with human behaviour will have a history of development brought about by events, religion, conflict, immigration and many other factors. Values will also be attributed to lifestyle and interaction with the physical environment. National social policy and the strength of families will also have an important influence on social values.

Attitudes associated with interpersonal relationships, honesty, fairness and decency will play a significant role in the stability of society. Attitudes towards work and the desire to improve are powerful forces in the development of national business culture.

Artistic taste will influence all aspects of design, especially those representing the long held traditional style. Even new styles will have been influenced to some degree by culture. Therefore, the design of built facilities requires careful consideration concerning harmonization with the local culture and environment. Successful marketing will need to accommodate highly valued traditions and styles alongside what is acceptable to society.

Religions practised in most parts of the world have a considerable influence on the way that people behave towards each other within that culture and towards people from other societies. There will also be an influence on the hours that people work. In Islamic countries, regular daily prayer must be performed which is usually carried out during working hours and it will be necessary to designate areas where prayer can take place. It should also be remembered that during Ramadan workers are not permitted to eat during the day and there are other fundamental restrictions to personal behaviour during this period.

Religious festivals of all creeds are celebrated throughout the year. The most notable festive seasons are Christmas, Easter, Lunar New Year and the end of Ramadan. Where staff employed celebrate all of these festivals then arrangements will be required to cover for absent colleagues. There are also certain work ethics that encourage people to work hard, for example, the work ethics of Confucianism in Asia and Shintoism in Japan. Such ethics require people to live industrious and virtuous lives and not to squander hard earned cash. Religion will also affect what people can eat and how and when they socialize. The perceptive company will need to recognize these necessities and make allowances accordingly.

It is therefore important that a firm operating in a foreign country and with a multicultural workforce should take the trouble to understand the nature and requirements of the various religions. An analysis should then be undertaken to work out how best to adapt company systems and procedures to accommodate fundamental religious requirements. The implementation of such proposals should be subject to negotiation and agreement by all concerned.

Relationship with the natural environment

It is now generally recognized throughout the world that natural resources such as oil, gas, minerals and hardwood are finite. Hence, it is vital to ensure that steps are taken to conserve and recycle resources where possible. A growing concern in advanced and developing industrialized countries is the amount of rubbish that is consigned to landfill and steps are now being put in place to collect sorted rubbish at source to increase the feasibility of recycling. Research is also gathering pace in the field of reprocessing waste materials into useful products such as wallboards and insulation.

Less developed nations will not be in possession of such advanced technologies. Nevertheless, because of the relatively poor state of these economies, products that would normally be trashed in a wealthier economy will be innovatively adapted for different uses. A good example is the second-hand market for corrugated iron sheeting in LDCs.

Awareness of the political and social importance of adopting policies and practices that promote sustainability in all countries is a vital attribute. This will directly impact on the materialistic culture, which is geared to technology and the economic infrastructure that determines living standards. Where countries are technologically advanced, people tend to be far more materialistic and more demanding than those of poorer nations who will be more concerned with fundamentals. Therefore, different approaches are required, but the principle of sustainability remains the same in both cases.

Attitude towards conservation will depend on the economic and technological standing of a nation, together with the value attached to maintaining the natural beauty of the environment. Invariably, there are conflicts between economic gain and environmental conservation and there are many instances where environmental conservation has been sacrificed. There is usually a middle way, which will conform to cultural demands and will maintain a heritage for future generations.

Conservation can be considered in terms of resources, climate, geography and heritage. Concern has been expressed about climate change and disruption brought about by the emission of greenhouse gasses. Global warming and the rise in sea levels due to melting of the polar ice caps are matters of considerable concern, especially for low-lying countries, for example Bangladesh which has a long history of natural disasters caused by flooding.

On an international level there is still considerable disagreement concerning the approach to limiting the amount of carbon and sulphur that is pumped into the atmosphere. Europeans are calling for more regulation and carbon taxes, whereas the USA prefers a less regulated approach. The outcome of earth summits on the environment have proposed the introduction of a carbon credits system, whereby countries that have used up their carbon allocation can purchase credits from other countries who have under utilized their quota. Such an arrangement would potentially be to the benefit of LDCs. Meanwhile, fast developing nations such as China, Taiwan and Brazil are burning more fuel and, in the latter case, large areas of rainforest are being cut down to make way for agricultural and urban development.

The conservation of energy and the adoption of clean power generation sources such as hydroelectricity, wind farms and, possibly, hydrogen are of considerable importance. International policy generally supports a reduction in the use of non-replaceable energy sources by more efficient transport systems, better-insulated buildings and more efficient power generation.

It is becoming increasingly important that construction companies operating in the international market are aware of the issues concerning conservation, both globally and for individual countries where business is conducted. By producing designs for buildings and infrastructure that promote conservation and efficiency it will be possible to gain competitive advantage in areas other than straight cost, especially when whole life cycle performance is taken into account.

Relationship with the built environment

The built environment is often taken for granted in the sense that it is slow to change and, consequently, people adapt their attitudes to the extent that they do not see what really exists. It is not until groups or individuals experience a superior environment that these deficiencies become apparent. However, the built environment has an enormous impact on culture and the way society works. The design layout and quality of living and recreation space will have a major impact on social behaviour and the way in which property is looked after and maintained.

Acceptable standards relating to living and working space will have evolved over many years and will be an inbuilt part of the culture. A good example is provided by people in Asia who are used to living in much smaller areas than people in North America. Also, Asians relate far more closely to the community and are happy to be in close proximity to others. The culture in Western countries is quite different, where personal space is valued as a place to retreat from the hustle and bustle of working and social life.

The built environment is in a constant state of development and it is therefore important that such development is properly planned and is in harmony with what already exists. Hence, the heritage of ancient or notable buildings and structures needs to be considered sympathetically. Cultural attitudes to the protection and conservation of old buildings are of considerable importance when proposing schemes for redevelopment. Therefore knowledge of cultural attitudes can be taken into account in scheme design, which will add another unique factor to how the scheme is viewed other than its cost.

Use of time

Culture will determine how long people work and how they use their available leisure time. The work ethic in Hong Kong is a good example of how hard work can be effectively combined with quality time for relaxation. The driving force in Hong Kong is to make money and people are prepared to put effort into achieving this objective. It is not unusual for employees to work in excess of sixty hours over a six-day week. However, as a rule Sundays are culturally orientated to family and leisure activities. In addition, Hong Kong enjoys an exceptional number of annual bank holidays because they still celebrate both Chinese and British holidays such as the Queen's birthday and Christmas.

In West Africa, working hours tend not to be so long and a more casual approach is taken to the time employees arrive and depart from work. In African countries where there is a substantial Muslim population, Friday afternoon will be given over to prayer and most of the population takes Saturday and Sunday as rest days.

Foreign staff working in remote areas where there are few distractions will usually adopt long working hours simply for something to do. Under such conditions it is important that employers recognize the need to provide for periodic time off, either to return home or to visit a major nearby city to let off steam. Oil companies are familiar with such practices and adopt a three weeks on two weeks off working pattern for offshore oilrig workers.

Companies operating overseas will need to conform to local working hours and practice, but allowance will still need to be made for the cultural differences of staff and the special needs of personnel who are working away from home for long periods.

Cross-cultural management

The prime role of cross-cultural management is to facilitate synergy between actors from different cultures who are brought together to perform specific tasks. This involves the transfer of knowledge, values and learning into the multicultural domain. The main difficulty with cross-cultural management in a successful international or global construction company is the domination of its corporate culture over attempts to localize the organization where responsibility and control is ceded to local managers rather than to expatriate staff. In the drive for corporate global dominance it has been argued by Ghoshal and Bartlett (1998) that global organizations concentrate on the deployment and the use of resources in pursuit of business aims and objectives.

Globalization encourages companies to become knowledge-based learning organizations with customer orientation, stakeholder commitment and the achievement of competitive advantage as guiding principles. The growing role of the Internet demands that management copes with complexity and change at a speed determined by the capacity to transmit electronic information. Associated with this is the need to be responsive to the requirements of local markets. It is therefore important that the company adopts a universal language and system to facilitate easier business communication.

Localization may be defined as an attempt by a global company to become part of the country, region or city where its operations are based, and to become part of the lives of the local people that it employs. The roles adopted by the local office and its managers must share the same strategic directives and goals as the company. This raises the issue of corporate citizenship since a balance must be achieved between being an international presence and gaining the right to become a full member of the local business community. Therefore there is likely to be conflict between business economics and moral obligation. It has been argued by Barham and Heiner (1999) that localization is about adding value to the local community by becoming a domestic player, thus being able to gain advantage by access to local skills and know-how.

Corporate citizenship extends to the whole organization and it is concerned with the relationship between companies and society, both globally and locally. Managers operating at the highest levels will be responsible for making decisions that span national boundaries. They must therefore be aware of international socio, economic and political factors that are likely to intervene and affect business strategies. Approaches should be adopted that avoid sensitive areas that would be likely to cause conflict and resentment. Therefore it may be stated that the prime factors to be considered involve:

- the maintenance of a steady state between business and society;
- creation of regional alliances;

- adoption of a robust and consistent system of management and control;
- mitigation of risk; and
- planning for the future.

The latest thinking concerning cross-cultural management draws attention to the imposition of western and Japanese cultures on local nations by the process of business globalization. It points to companies, notably from the USA and Japan, which have assumed that corporate cultures developed within their own societies are best and therefore fall into the trap of ethnocentrism by overriding local cultures. Such assumptions are often made with insufficient knowledge of the benefits to be gained by retaining cultural practices that have been developed over generations to cope with local conditions. There is a strong body of opinion in academic and business domains that globilization, instead of creating uniformity and standardization, is in fact having the reverse affect. Greater awareness created by improved communication and the Internet is accentuating the importance of local culture and the need to develop enriched solutions that are appropriate and effective. It is therefore suggested that the corporate aims and objectives of global companies must be rethought and should be more sympathetic to local conditions and needs.

Cultural dimensions

Cultural research conducted by Hofstede (1980, 1991, 1993, 2001) in the Netherlands was based on a study of IBM's employees in 40 countries and regions. The outcome established four dimensions to culture, and it is worth exploring these in terms that reflect similarities and differences, which have the potential to categorize and cluster nations with like cultures. Although the research was limited to one global company it has proved to be highly relevant and robust and has been validated by other research. This ground-breaking research is now recognized as a classical study of its kind. The four cultural dimensions and the data from the research were used to produce an index of scores for each dimension calculated from the average answers to questions presented to a range of IBM employees.

- **Dimension 1 — Power distance** -high power distance is associated with an acceptance by lower grade staff of an unequal distribution of power in an organization where members of staff in authority are to be obeyed without question. Subordinates accept that managers make the decisions and they do not expect to be required to take responsibility. In a low power distance culture, inequalities and status symbols are minimized and subordinates expect to share in decision making.
- **Dimension 2 — Individualism versus collectivism** -individualistic cultures reflect personal aspirations as an employee and as a private person. There is a desire for challenging work and freedom to undertake the necessary tasks. Collective cultures emphasize being a respected team member and a strong feeling for the common good.

- **Dimension 3 — Masculinity versus femininity** -a highly masculine culture is defined by individual recognition, promotion and high rewards, whereas highly feminine cultures are characterized by good cooperative relationships with colleagues and managers. Job security and living standards are also held to be important within masculine or feminine cultures.
- **Dimension 4 — Uncertainty avoidance** -involves preoccupation with uncertainty where frameworks, system and rules are introduced to cut down risk and introduce stability into the working environment. This could be attributed to a lack of confidence compared with those societies where personnel are not overly concerned with uncertainty and adopt less well-defined and more flexible working practices.

The analysis illustrated by Figure 7.3 shows that the AICs selected tend to be culturally individualistic compared with the selection of NICs and LDCs which tend towards a more collective culture, and there is a strong correlation across all cultural dimensions. AICs showed a wide disparity in dimensions 3 and 4, but power distance is more closely related in the middle of the index.

The USA, UK and Australia have similar cultural profiles, which helps to explain the close relationships between the three nations. Japanese culture distinguishes itself as highly masculine and displays high uncertainty avoidance while tending towards a collectivist culture. The cultural profile of Japan is very different and this helps to explain the more aggressive style in which Japanese global companies are managed. Swedish culture tends to be the complete opposite to that of Japan. There is no virtue in trying to judge which approach is right or wrong; however, the comparison of cultural profiles according to the cultural dimensions does help to build a picture of the general manner in which a company conducts its business and finds solutions to problems. Care should be taken not to confuse these generalizations with specific cases that may be atypical.

This research has encouraged other researchers to investigate further similarities that are useful to identifying the nature of a country's culture. Hofstede (2001) advocates the introduction of a fifth dimension of long versus short-term orientation because of its association with economic growth. He also expresses the need to extend his research to new countries not covered by the previous study.

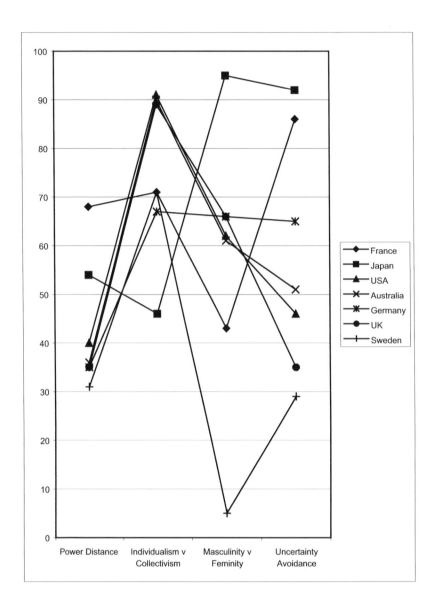

Figure 7.3: Plot of the cultural dimensions of 15 nations contained in Hofstede's study
Adapted from Geort Hofstede, 1991 & 2001
(*a*) Selection of AICs

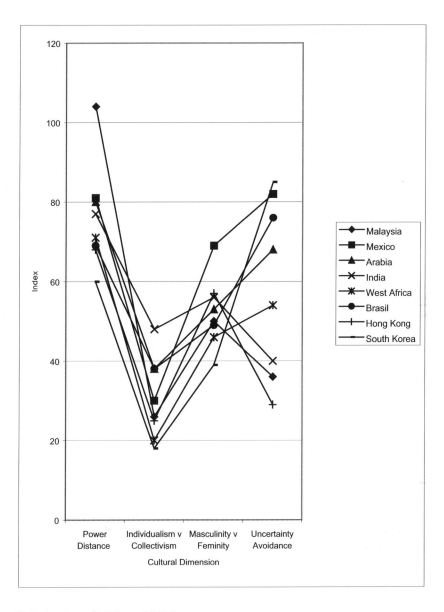

(*b*) Selection of NICs and LDCs

Collectively, this work provides useful knowledge about cultural attributes that will help an international construction enterprise to evaluate its intention to invest in a foreign country. Once a decision has been made to proceed, then this knowledge will be critical to the adoption of management strategies and decisions.

Individualism and collectivism

A study made by Triandis (1995) sought to provide a better understanding of individualistic and collectivist cultures. He suggested that collectivist cultures encapsulate individuals within 'ingroups', hence attitudes, beliefs, dimensions, definitions and values are shared by group members. Further, it was recognized that there are different collectivist groups that can be classified as friendly or alien, i.e. 'outer-groups'

Individualist cultures are centred on 'self' and the relationships with other individuals are treated as friends, acquaintances or enemies. A distinction was then made between vertical cultures that emphasize hierarchy and horizontal cultures that stress equality. These can then be further developed to include collectivism and individualism (Figure 7.4).

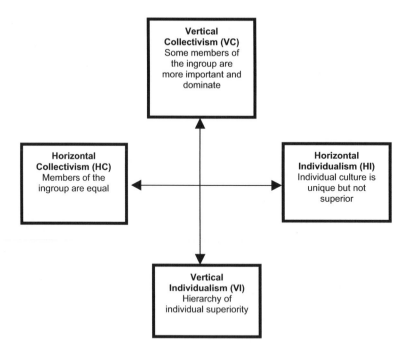

Figure 7.4: Vertical and horizontal individualism and collectivism

It is argued that cultures are not collectively or individually monolithic and variation can be determined by the frequency of occurrence, while recognizing that higher social classes within a culture are more likely to be individualistic whereas lower classes are more collectivist. By means of example, South Asian cultures tend to be collectivist, while USA and Sweden tend to be individualist cultures. Triandis *et al.* (2001) extended this work to examine the relationship between culture and deception using a multilevel analysis of eight cultures. Four were perceived to be collectivist (Hong Kong, Japan, Korea and Greece) and four judged to be individualist (USA, Australia, Germany and the Netherlands). The results of the analysis showed that cultures with high VC are most likely to deceive, whereas cultures with HC and VI have a tendency to moderate deception, while HI has the least tendency to deception. A further generalization is that individuals will lie when an important aspect of their self-concept is threatened and that some individuals in collectivist cultures were more likely to lie in a situation where their independent self could be threatened.

This work provides a different approach to that of Hofstede and it is supported by Trilling (1972) who argued that authenticity is higher in cultures where people in the main decide for themselves about identities and roles.

Working cultures

Where an international construction company has had no previous experience of working in a particular country then it will be important to research and establish which work ethics are in place and the impact that these will have on the operation of the business. Some work ethics are extremely rigid and are dominated by procedure and time, whereas others may be more objective-driven where working hours and practices are more flexible. As a general rule, more rigid work ethics are found in Asian countries whereas Westernized countries need, on average, to be much freer in their attitudes. Clearly, systems and working practices will need to be adapted so as not to clash directly with established culture. It may be possible to provide training to establish new working practices that will be of benefit to all concerned.

Culture will, to a large extent, determine what motivates people to work effectively and productively. It will therefore be important to establish the prevalent motivational factors, which should then be ranked in order of priority. In one country pay may be a high motivator, whereas in another it may be the quality and condition of the working environment. A good indicator of a positive work ethic is the degree to which the workforce displays a dynamic approach and attitude to work. Countries with such positive attitudes to work will be high on the list of preferred investment locations for those companies operating on a multinational basis.

Phases of cultural development of an international construction company

At the commencement of international business activity there is a tendency for a company to conduct its foreign business for the benefit of the home country and to impose home country ways of working. This approach is known as ethnocentrism and it is a tendency present in companies whose home countries display cultural dimensions of high masculinity and high uncertainty avoidance, e.g. Japan.

Normally, as a company expands its international business to more and more countries, by mergers, acquisitions, joint ventures, etc., then the tendency is for less account to be taken of the home country's interests. Subsidiaries become more autonomous and more local managers are employed who, while absorbing the company's corporate culture, will still react to host country factors. This development is known as polycentrism.

The continuation of this trend leads to geocentrism where all considerations relate to the well-being and survival of the company itself. National pressures are regarded as impediments and constraints and they are dealt with on their merits. At this stage of development the nationality of employees and managers is of no significance and people are regarded and appointed according to merit. Moreover, the company can be regarded as truly global in its culture and operation.

Towards convergence

While national identities and cultures are important, progressive development towards globalization lends some support to the convergence argument. The most obvious support comes from developments in technology, especially the rapid development and expansion of information technology that is helping to create a global culture in consumerism, fashion, sport and life style. The second level of support comes from the integration of the financial markets and the convergence of nations into federations and trading blocks. The growing influence of international bodies such as WTO and GATT is also a factor. Finally, convergence is supported by the universal adoption of successful management strategies, organizations and systems, techniques and styles. These cross-cutting developments provide the vehicles to increase the pace of globalization and the benefits that derive from standardization and economies of scale.

This approach enhances the human desire to be different and therefore local needs and cultures will continue to play an important role in global markets. It can therefore be argued that convergence increases the need for localization while at the same time deriving benefits from globalization.

Case study 7.1: Skanska management development and training

Since 1995, the Skanska Management Institute has been training its managers at all levels. The company has recognized that employees with international experience are increasingly important as key people for projects in various countries. International mobility of key personnel is an essential aspect of a global company like Skanska. Moreover, the company needs internationally experienced employees who can join projects quickly and managers who can apply an international perspective. This is achieved by adequately training existing employees and recruiting new staff by means of Skanska's European Job Centre that started operations in 2000. To encourage external job seekers they are able to enter their applications in a database via the Internet.

The Skanska Development Institute, located just outside Stockholm, conducts a one-year leadership programme that adopts a methodical approach to training its managers based on twelve critical managerial dimensions derived from interviews conducted within the company. As part of a summer school, professional actors are used to facilitate realistic role-playing exercises designed to provide appropriate insight into reactions to various situations associated with leadership. Managers attending the programme are selected from different countries and will come face to face with their strengths and weaknesses as leaders.

Although the programme majors on leadership, the role-play exercises and subsequent discussion among attendees soon reveals cultural differences that are exposed and discussed. The intention is that the participants are made aware of the need to appreciate and recognize cultural differences and then to adapt their own management and leadership style to cope with the situation.

There are no absolute solutions to these situations; rather, the dialogue between observers and participants in the role-play process is intended to create a higher level of awareness. Participants are also subjected to an exercise that showcases personal interaction styles in the group dynamic process. Self-confrontation, where weaknesses as well as strengths are exposed, can be difficult, but those who have experienced the course have attested through their feedback that it has been helpful and stimulating.

Author's commentary

Where managers have no experience of working in a particular country or culture then an important prerequisite is that they are properly briefed before they are assigned and afterwards when they arrive to take up their new roles. There should also be a period where the manager seeks to learn more at first hand about the various aspects of cultural behaviour as set out in this chapter. This may be achieved in a variety of ways, the most usual being to develop good relationships with close subordinates from whom assistance can be sought. Above all, a manager operating in a new culture should err on the side of caution until an adequate grasp is gained of the differences and how they affect the management and leadership style.

The importance of the Skanska development programme is that it raises the level of awareness of cultural differences and it emphasizes the important bearing that this has on the leadership style to be adopted in the management process.

Case study 7.2: Working on community projects in Bangladesh

The Housing and Hazards Group (H&H) is a group of Bangladeshi and British engineers and architects who are committed to bringing new choices to the people of Bangladesh regarding the way they build their homes. Traditionally, houses — which comprise 90% of dwellings — are constructed using natural building materials such as mud, bamboo and straw. The increasing population and additional demands from urban dwellers has applied pressure on resources and the traditional housebuilding materials that were once free now have to be paid for. Consequently, new houses are using fewer materials and existing houses are falling into disrepair. The outcome is that houses are increasingly prone to the natural disasters that regularly visit the region, such as the floods of 1998, which destroyed 900,000 homes.

H&H have recognized that the housing projects implemented in Bangladesh over the past three decades have usually been in response to a natural disaster, rather than planned projects to encourage and initiate sustainable change. Low-cost prototypes using primarily western technology have proved to be much more expensive than rationalized housing and they do not meet the cultural needs and aspirations of individual families.

Through experience, H&H have established that by making small improvements to the critical parts of the traditional house a significant difference in its integrity and performance can be achieved. It has been established that by adding a few percent to the cost of the traditional house the householder can be provided with a kit of parts designed to make improvements that can reduce lifetime cost by increasing longevity and reducing vulnerability to natural disasters.

In order to meet the challenge of bringing this knowledge to the grass roots and to offer choices to real people, young British engineers have been encouraged to live in the village communities and carry out participatory action learning.

The case cited is of a young Arup and Partners engineer who, in 1996, lived and integrated with the people in a remote village in the Dinajpur district of northern Bangladesh. By embracing the culture and working with local builders the engineer was able obtain funding from the British Council for a course of participatory workshops. The aim was to develop a critical view by discussing current building practice with local people and then to encourage them with advice and suggestions to develop their own improvements to increase the effectiveness and quality of their housing, thereby reducing vulnerability to natural disasters. In this case, the builders put the ideas into immediate action by creating a sewing skills centre using the innovations judged to be the most appropriate by the workshop participants. The participants were then able to critically evaluate the as-built performance and the cost of the innovations. Because most of the community was illiterate, the results of the ongoing workshops were communicated to the wider local population through songs performed in public meeting places.

Author's commentary

Local culture does not happen by accident, rather it is built up over a long period of time to assist people to live their lives in what may be very hostile environments. To impose rapid wholesale solutions has not generally been successful and this is typified by infrastructure and health facilities that have been provided in developing countries with little thought to cultural reactions and how such facilities can be maintained to provide optimal performance.

By embracing the local culture, as in this case, sympathetic advances can be made by applying appropriate know-how in a way that the locals can appreciate and take advantage of, leading to a stage-by-stage process of continuing harmonious development.

Summary

Social culture is an important issue that needs to be thoroughly considered and addressed by multinational construction companies. Normally, a company will be very familiar with its own home culture, but it is important to realize that this may not translate very easily or appropriately into other countries where the company has work and business interests. Moreover, there will be differences in translation from one country of operation to another. Hence it is likely that a company that operates on a multinational basis will also need to adopt and accommodate a multicultural approach. Part of the answer is to find a common set of values that represent the company culture to which all employees can subscribe. In effect this provides the common denominator for all aspects of human communication and interaction, while recognizing that cultural requirements exist that need to be satisfied.

A prerequisite to the successful management of cultural differences is an awareness that these exist in the first place and the realization that if senior management does not effectively deal with them then it is highly likely that difficulties will be experienced. The factors affecting cross-cultural management have been described and research has been cited that throws some light on how cultures can be classified and evaluated to inform corporate decision-making.

Because of the sensitive nature of the cultural differences referred to in this chapter they will only be apparent in extreme cases. More likely will be the development of tensions and behavioural undercurrents that will have a detrimental effect on teamwork and trust. The Skanska case study illustrates an example where a global construction company has recognized the need for managers to adapt effectively to different cultures and has implemented a programme of training to address these issues by role play and analysis of individual performance.

In the next chapter emphasis will be given to international human resource management and the policies and procedures designed to encourage best practice in the management of people, their self-development, conditions of employment, safety and general welfare.

Further reading

Arup home page (on-line www.arup.com).

Barham K. & Heiner C. (1999), 'Identifying and developing international market competence', (ed.), *Financial Times Handbook of Management*, London, Financial Times/ Pitman Publishing.

Deresky H. (1994), *International management: managing across borders and cultures*, Harper Collins, New York.

Ferraro G. P. (1990), *The cultural dimensions of international business*, Prentice Hall, Englewood Cliffs, NJ.

Ghoshal S. & Bartlett C. A. (1998), *Managing across borders: a transitional solution*, Random House, London.

Hickson D. J. & Pugh D. S. (2001), *Management worldwide — distinctive styles amid globalisation*, 2nd edn, Penguin Books.

Hofstede G. (1980), *Culture's consequences: international differences and related values*, Sage Publications, Beverley Hills, CA.

Hofstede G. (1991), *Cultures and organization: software of the mind*, McGraw Hill, Maidenhead, UK.

Hofstede G. (1993), *Cultural constraints on management theories*, Academy of Management Executive, Vol. 7, No. 1, 81–93.

Hofstede G. (2001), Culture's consequences: international differences and related values, 2nd edn, Sage Publications, Beverley Hills, CA.

Holden N. (2001), 'Why globalizing with a conservative corporate culture inhibits localization of management', *Int. J. of Cross-cultural Management*, Vol. 1(1), 53–72.

Matteau M. (1993), *Towards meaningful and effective intercultural encounter*, Hull, Canada: Intercultural Training and Briefing Centre, Canadian International Development Agency.

Skanska home page (on-line www.skanska.com).

Triandis H. C. (1995), *Individualism and collectivism*, West View Press, Boulder, CO.

Triandis H. C. *et al.* (2001), 'Culture and deception in business negotiations: a multi-level analysis', *Int. J. of Cross-cultural Management*, Vol. 1(1), 73–90.

Trilling L. (1972), *Sincerity and authenticity,* Oxford University Press

Chapter 8

International human resource management

Introduction

The human resource is arguably the most valuable asset possessed by any business and its management requires special skills that must cope with all types of human behaviour. The management of people requires the ability to lead, motivate and command respect from employees who require a sense of purpose and appreciation of their efforts. The maintenance of a productive working environment involving good relationships between management and fellow employees plays an important part in developing the commitment that is vital to maintaining competitive advantage.

During the past century there have been considerable changes in management style, leadership, group dynamics and social behaviour. The paradigm of scientific management as proposed by Frank Taylor, based on authoritarian principles, was paramount early in the twentieth century. The needs of individuals were suppressed by the requirement for advances in efficiency brought about by the application of scientific techniques such as time and motion study. Progressively over the past 75 years there has been an increasing recognition of the advantages to be gained by adopting more behavioural management styles as proposed by, amongst others, Maslow, Hertzberg and Child that adopt a more democratic approach to management and decision making. These changes have had a key impact on the tasks performed in the management of human resources.

Human resource management (HRM) is a key function that specializes in the management of people who are employed by an organization to achieve strategic business objectives. HRM practice requires integration with corporate strategy and it recognizes that employees are critical to achieving corporate business objectives and sustainable competitive advantage. HRM also specializes in assisting managers to achieve efficiency and equity in objectives.

This chapter extends HRM into the international context and seeks to establish the importance of interaction with corporate strategies and management. The functions of international human resource management (IHRM) are outlined and related to cultural issues.

Influences on IHRM

Human resource management policies operated by the home company may need to be modified according to the culture of the nation in which business is being conducted. Local employment legislation will also have a profound influence on practice and procedure, especially where the intention is to employ a large number of expatriate employees imported specifically for the purpose of conducting business.

Figure 8.1. indicates the prime influences of national and legal requirements, which together with the combination of scientific and behavioural management approaches will influence the manner in which management is executed. This in turn will have a direct impact on the manner in which IHRM is conducted. Hence it may be assumed that each country, and sometimes each province, will need to be treated differently.

Employment laws and legislation will change from country to country and it will be essential for these to be fully appreciated regarding employees' rights and the constraints that will be imposed on business practice. There should also be a consistent policy of non-discrimination where all employees are treated equally without regard to gender, age, ethnic background, religion or disability.

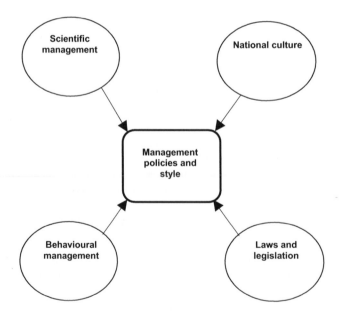

Figure 8.1: National influences on management policies and style

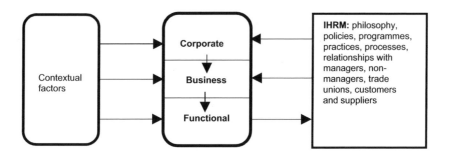

Figure 8.2: Hierarchy of strategic decision-making and its relationship
with IHRM

The relationship between IHRM and management decision-making

The hierarchy of decision-making within a global construction organization commences at corporate level where the fundamental direction of the organization is determined. It then progresses down to the national business level where strategic policies are determined and localized factors are taken into consideration in the establishment of business aims and objectives. In order to realize stated business aims, functional decisions will be necessary which will involve the prime operating components of the organization. Human resource management policies will be implemented to enable processes and practice in accordance with corporate policy. This will require the development of close working relationships with managers and non-managers on the ground, trade unions, customers and suppliers (see Figure 8.2).

IHRM plays a crucial role in the delivery of the mission and strategy associated with a venture into foreign business. Figure 8.3 shows the importance of linking the mission and strategy to be adopted to the systems, organization and human resource management processes. This will need to be addressed under the influence of economic, political and cultural forces emanating from the contextual environment.

IHRM is required to fit with modern management concepts and it is therefore important to create a means whereby HRM policies can be linked to management systems, processes and techniques. Figure 8.4 illustrates a communication stem linking management ideologies, supply chain policies and techniques such as Just in Time (JIT) and Total Quality Control (TQC). The intention is that the overall outcome will provide flexibility, high efficiency and quality, while at the same time reducing waste. This approach equates with the Japanese model of production management.

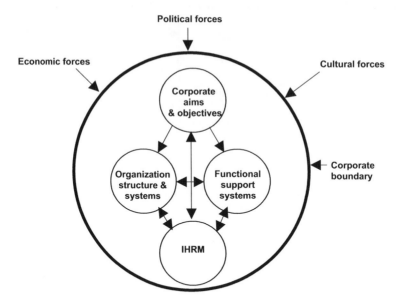

Figure 8.3: Integration of HRM

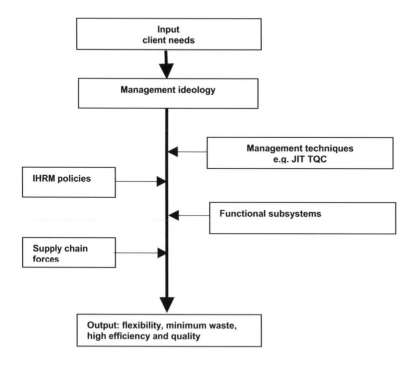

Figure 8.4: IHRM management outcome stem

Sources of personnel for international construction companies

There are three basic options for employing personnel, namely:
- home country nationals (expatriates)
  individuals residing abroad who are citizens of the parent country of the organization
- host country nationals
  local individuals who are employed by the organization to fulfill specific roles
- third country nationals
  this category of employee comprises citizens of countries other than the parent country or host country. Normally these individuals will have relevant specialist skills and experience.

The proportion of each of these staff categories will depend on many factors, however it is more common for companies in their initial stage of internationalization to depend on home country staff, especially managers. This pattern tends to change with time as more host country nationals are employed.

Models of human resource management applied to international construction

In order to achieve corporate business aims and objectives it will be necessary to adopt a suitable approach to IHRM befitting the nature and scale of the organization, together with the operational environment and the profile of the staff employed. The application of policy will require judgement concerning whether emphasis should be placed on situation factors that impact on IHRM or alternatively on staff performance through development and appraisal. Another approach is to recognize the influence and impact of the socio-technical context of the business and relate it to the cultural business outputs.

The situational HRM model

The situational model shown in Figure 8.5 takes a strategic view of human resource management in meeting long-term objectives stated by the organization as well as the stakeholders' interests. The situational factors will depend on the international context and the particular circumstances pertaining in the country in question. Hence, the feedback loop between policy, long-term consequences and situational factors is a dynamic process of continuous interaction that requires constant observation and consequent actions.

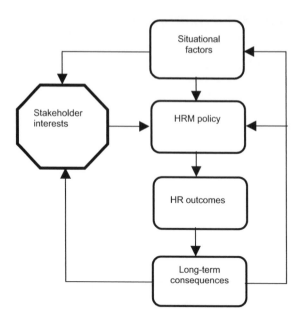

Figure 8.5: The situational model of HRM
Adapted from the Harvard Model of HRM

The staff performance model of HRM

This model concentrates on the selection and appraisal of employees in relation to performance, staff development and rewards. It also highlights the importance of motivating and assisting staff in achieving the performance expected by the organization through properly focused staff development to strengthen the capability of individuals. The development and training of host country employees features strongly in this model (see Figure 8.6).

The socio-technical model of HRM

The socio-technical model, Figure 8.7, is used to establish cultural business outputs that are then related to business strategy and organizational roles facilitated by HRM systems. Because of its emphasis on the socio-technical context related to business culture, this model is particularly relevant to international business. The originators of the model (Hendry and Pettigrew) claim that it provides a sound description of the strategy and decision making required in more complex organizations and then links this to HRM and the environment of the business.

The situational model takes a long-term view of HRM policy in relation to stakeholder interests and situational factors. It is strategic in concept and hence concentrates on policy development and implementation. The outcomes of the HRM policy are judged against stakeholder interests and relevance to situational factors. The staff performance model concentrates on staff selection, staff appraisal and development as a basis for the determination of rewards. It is therefore more functional than strategic. The socio-technical model is strategic and takes into account external contextual issues and their relationship with the business culture. This model is also functional in that organizational roles are fully integrated with HR systems. Whichever model or combination of models is selected it must have the capacity to support the functional systems of IHRM in a balanced manner to meet the needs of the business and its operational environment.

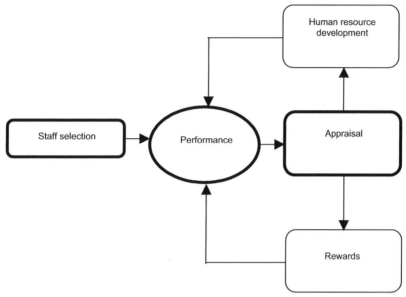

Figure 8.6: Staff performance model of HRM
Adapted from the Fombrum Model

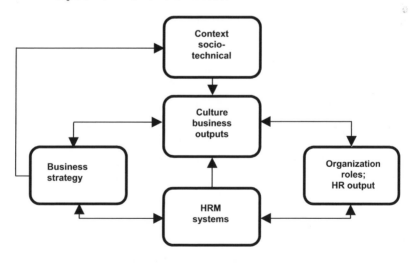

Figure 8.7: The socio-technical model of HRM
Adapted from the Warwick Model of HRM

Functions of international human resource management

International human resource management is characterized by being broken down into a number of interrelated functions associated with all aspects concerning the employment of people within an organization. Typically, the breakdown will be as follows.

- *Human resource planning*

  The acquisition of sufficient appropriately skilled and qualified employees will be essential to the implementation of an international business strategy. The supply of labour must be geared to demand and it is therefore important to forecast future workloads accurately, together with the quantity and type of skills required. The demand for personnel must be based on business plans, future projects and projected sales.

  The number of existing employees and their skill mix will need to be evaluated alongside an assessment of the availability of skills in the market-place. A comparison of supply and demand will highlight shortfalls or surpluses that will require management to make decisions about staffing levels.

  Where projected turnover indicates a steady long-term rise and where demand for certain knowledge and skills exceeds supply then management will be required to look more closely at the possibility of directly employing more staff on a permanent basis. In the event that the situation is less certain and there are relatively short periods where demand exceeds supply then the possibility of engaging employees on short-term contracts or by outsourcing should be considered. Where surpluses are apparent then steps should be taken to reduce the level of employees by retraining, redeployment or redundancy (Figure 8.8).

- *Recruitment and selection*

  Recruitment will either be from within the existing employee base, or through advertising for new employees from the home, host or third countries. Preference will normally be given to selection taking place from adequately qualified persons from within the organization. The first step will be to identify screening factors that will highlight those persons who will be suited to undertake overseas assignments and then to draw up a shortlist of those adequately equipped to carry out the role. Clearly, age, experience and education are important factors, but there are other vital requirements such as adaptability, self-reliance, motivation and leadership that must be present. Health and family status also need to be taken into consideration. The outcome of this process is to appoint a person who will be suited and dedicated to the task in hand.

  Where people are to be recruited from outside the company, then the normal process of advertising, interviewing, tests and selection will be put in place. Importance will be placed on previous track record and experience in the role. Note will need to be taken of any employment requirements and restrictions imposed by the host country.

- *Redundancy and dismissal*
  When it becomes necessary to reduce the number of employees, where possible, this should be achieved by natural wastage or by retraining, assuming that there is sufficient time available. Where a more rapid solution is necessary then redeployment and early retirement should be investigated before resorting to redundancy, which will either be voluntary or compulsory. The latter options will normally involve the payment of compensation and statutory regulations will usually ensure that employees are fairly treated.

  Dismissal of an employee is normally associated with poor performance, malpractice or gross misconduct. Procedures and practice associated with dismissal are covered by employment legislation and employees will normally have the right to be represented by a trade union where they are in membership.

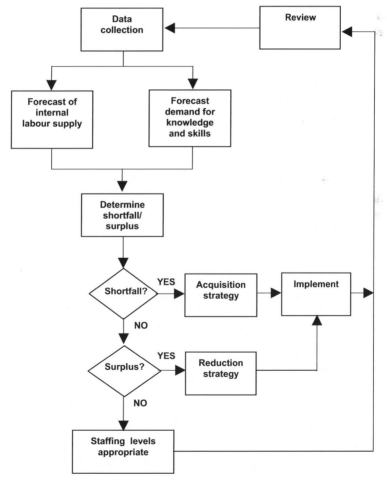

Figure 8.8: Human resource manpower planning process

Where employees feel they have been unfairly treated they can normally appeal to a tribunal and if successful this can result in a company being required to pay substantial damages.

- *Repatriation*

Repatriation is the process of inducting persons back into the home country organization structure after a period of foreign service. The life style and conditions of service overseas are likely be very different to those at home. Generous allowances and a cheaper cost of living might mean that expatriate employees enjoy considerable benefits over and above those employees based at home. There may also be families involved and therefore the education of children and social factors become important issues that must be dealt with in a proper and effective manner.

Some expatriates will find it difficult to readjust to formal company processes and systems and they may have difficulty in coping with the loss of autonomy and freedom. These matters require careful handling and adequate counselling will be necessary by mentors, supported by good human resource management.

- *Staff appraisal*

A properly constructed and applied appraisal system is a key element in enabling staff to attain their full potential. It is also an important aspect of maintaining morale and providing the necessary motivation and commitment to achieve job performance targets.

Staff appraisal is normally carried out on an annual basis where appraisees and their appraisers are brought together to discuss, in a fair and objective fashion, the job performance. The process should be fully documented and transparent and it should be designed to expose difficulties as well as to give praise for achievement. The appraiser should be capable of facilitating actions and staff development intended to correct identified difficulties and able to provide other support if necessary. The outcome of the process should be an agreed set of job performance targets to be achieved by the appraisee in the coming year. These should be capable of being measured either qualitatively or quantitatively.

Staff appraisal for overseas staff must be applied with extra care to account for specific working conditions and cultures. The home country staff appraisal system should be reviewed and adapted as necessary for use in the country in question. Because of the temporary nature of project assignments, it may not be possible to conduct appraisals on a strict annual basis and therefore it will be necessary to fit these in according to the start and completion of projects. In any case, the maximum period between appraisals should normally not exceed twelve months.

- *Staff development*

Staff development represents an investment in employees to upgrade their knowledge and skills in order to make them more effective in performing their job roles. This must be closely linked to the staff appraisal process, which should be geared to identifying training needs.

Training for staff operating in foreign countries can be categorized into standard and tailored training programmes. The former will consist of generic programmes that provide knowledge which can be applied anywhere in the world, whereas the latter are designed to meet the specific needs of individuals assigned to particular regions or countries. The most common types of programme will include the following:

- environmental briefing
- language training
- cultural orientation and assimilation
- self-reliance
- attitudinal flexibility
- prior field experience.

The continual introduction of new technologies will require that staff knowledge is updated and training takes place to build competence in the workplace. This aspect of human resource management needs to be closely tied to the development of new operating systems and processes intended to achieve business aims and objectives.

- *Job evaluation*

Prior to setting remuneration and rewards, jobs need to be assessed to determine their correct value. The process should be mainly related to factual judgements and the degree of subjectivity should be reduced to a minimum to ensure internal equity in pay and rewards.

The usual methods of job evaluation include ranking, job grading, factor comparison and point method.

- *Ranking:* a panel of evaluators will assess the relative importance of jobs by ranking them in order of their perceived importance. The advantage with this method is its simplicity and speed. However, much depends on the knowledge and skill of the evaluators, together with the integrity of their judgement.
- *Job grading:* jobs are graded into a hierarchy, which is then related to a set of pay grades. Compensatable factors will be established such as knowledge, skill, responsibility, working conditions, etc. and these will carry a score according to a scale (e.g. 1 = low, 4 = high). The scores are then accumulated to give an overall rank score that determines the value of the job. Each pay grade will be attributed an overall score range and it is therefore possible to associate job scores with respective grades of pay.

— *Factor comparison:* this is more sophisticated than job grading in that each job factor is allocated a benchmark monetary value, which is then numerically compared across a range of jobs to determine individual monetary allocations. The accumulation of monetary allocations against each job factor will determine the rate of remuneration for the job.

— *Point method*: this method is similar to the factor comparison method except that points are accumulated instead of monetary values with each job accumulating a points total. This method tends to be very popular and is used extensively in practice.

- *Reward system and management including allowances*

  Compensation for undertaking assignments in foreign countries will need to take into account a number of elements, which when accumulated tend to be expensive. It is therefore essential that sufficient consideration be given to achieving the best value to support the need to control costs and improve profits. The basic elements are given below.

  — *Basic salary:* there is a tendency for basic salaries and bonuses to be established on the same basis as the home country. Normally, these will have been subjected to job evaluation and related to established company pay scales.

  — *Benefits:* benefits make up a significant proportion of the remuneration package and will include medical insurance, social security payments and pension contributions. There may be the need to provide dual coverage in the home and host countries; however, international agreements have largely eliminated this requirement.

  — *Allowances:* the most prevalent is a cost of living allowance that compensates for differences in expenditure between the home and host countries. Normally this allowance covers relocation, housing and education for members of the family. Where individuals are posted to countries with undesirable or hard living conditions then a further allowance may be made.

  — *Taxation:* it is possible under some circumstances that individuals will be liable to pay tax in both the home and host countries and it is usual that companies will employ a tax protection system which ensures that only the equivalent of tax payable in the host country will be levied against an employee.

- *Industrial relations* HM

  Industrial relations may be defined as the control processes associated with employment of people, the organization and management of work and the relations between employer and employee. These relationships are heavily influenced by socio-political factors, which have a bearing on the stance taken by employers and the representative of the employees. It may therefore be stated that the core of industrial relations concerns work and interactions between trade unions and the management. Traditionally, trade unions are concerned with remuneration, working conditions, including safety and welfare, together with human resource development. Trade unions act collectively for all employees, irrespective of individual performance. This automatically means that appraisal is a difficult area since it is geared to evaluating the performance of individuals. There are three basic strategies that employers can take towards trade unions, namely recognition, exclusion or opposition. Recognition implies legitimacy and the acceptance of collective bargaining, whereas exclusion means that management have decided to conduct business by curtailing the role of trade unions. Union opposition is a strategy aimed at maintaining the status of a non-union company by introducing alternative measures such as employee participation and human resource policies designed to look after the interests of employees generally.

When operating internationally there is no common formula since labour relations practice varies widely from country to country. It is this variation that represents one of the most important challenges to international construction companies. Therefore labour relations policy needs to take into account national differences in labour relations systems and other factors such as the culture, economy, political and legal systems. Figure 8.9 shows the extent of trade union membership for all industries in a selection of countries worldwide. In general, it may be stated that construction is far less unionized than manufacturing.

Another factor to be taken into account is the extent to which industrial democracy is practiced. This tends to be more prevalent in AICs such as Germany, Denmark and Japan. Industrial democracy is typified by the existence of co-determination, which is a legal system requiring that employees are involved in strategic decision making by having seats on the board of directors. This practice is popular in Germany, Holland, Sweden, Austria and Denmark. Co-determination may or may not be supported by various forms of works councils and shop floor participation.

The degree of employee participation and involvement needs to be given careful consideration. Where employees are likely to be sophisticated and mature then it may advantageous to adopt policies involving greater employee participation. In the case of a less sophisticated and less educated workforce then it is possible that little will be gained from such an approach, other than to create harmony and contentment by virtue of individuals feeling valued. Figure 8.10 illustrates the range of options available.

High (<60%)	Medium (30–60%)	Low (>30%)
Canada	Argentina	France
Cuba	Australia	Germany
Denmark	Austria	Greece
Finland	Brazil	Indonesia
Hungary	Egypt	Israel
Iceland	Italy	Japan
Malta	Mexico	Korea
Sweden	Philippines	Malaysia
	Poland	Netherlands
	South Africa	New Zealand
	United Kingdom	Portugal
		Spain
		Switzerland
		Thailand
		United States
		Venezuela

Figure 8.9: Membership of trade unions
Source: ILO

Increasingly it has become recognized that IHRM systems must be tailored according to the country and the circumstances under which construction work takes place. The driving factors influencing such customized policies include:

- empowerment of employees
- accelerated resource development
- employee welfare
- performance appraisal
- encouragement of innovative and creative thinking.

According to Sparrow and Budhuar, a scenario that might work well in one country could be disastrous in another. It is therefore necessary for employees to be amenable to continual and periodic adjustment to satisfy demands emerging from the nature of construction work, as it moves from one country to another.

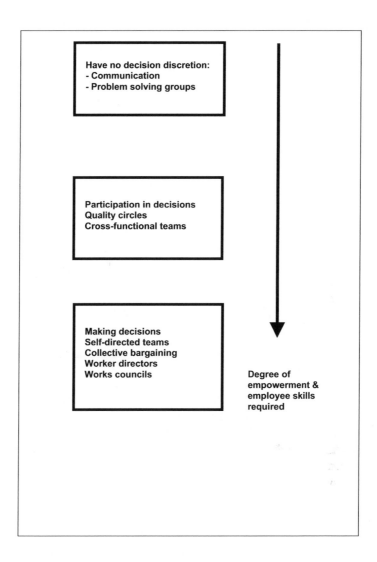

Figure 8.10: Degree of employee involvement

Health, safety and welfare at work

An employer has a duty to ensure the safety of all employees, whether they are directly employed or not. The management of safety is influenced by government legislation, trade unions, economic cost and public opinion. It is therefore reasonable to assume that safety standards will vary from country to country and a company may need to make up its own mind concerning the minimum safety standards that will be applied. There will be benefits accruing from low accident rates and good occupational health, in that employees will be less likely to require time off work and while at work their productivity should be better. Insurance premiums are likely to be less for companies with good health and safety records.

Health and safety policy

Companies originating from AICs are likely to have well-established safety policies, procedures and monitoring systems, which are necessary to meet strict safety legislation and enforcement systems in the home country. These will need to be reviewed when working in other AICs to ensure that differences in legislation, emphasis and practice are taken in consideration.

When AIC companies take on work in NICs or LDCs then it is highly probable that standards will be lower and less well enforced. This raises the issue of whether company home practice will be applied, or whether the minimum standards required in the country will take precedence. As a matter of corporate policy, most responsible AIC companies try to apply their home practice and this raises the need for significant safety training and ongoing enforcement of safe practice in the workplace. The advantage of this approach is that procedures will be consistent regardless of the country in which the work takes place and the relationship and procedures between management will be sound and will benefit from previous experience.

Provision of welfare facilities

The maintenance of proper welfare facilities in the workplace is another important factor that contributes to good morale and a sense of well-being arising from working for a good company. As well as providing the basics such as clean and hygienic toilets and wash facilities, rest rooms and canteen facilities, first aid should be provided by a properly equipped ambulance station with the necessary staff to cope with initial post-accident treatment.

Local employees may also benefit from regular health checks arranged through company medical staff, or they might be provided with private healthcare as a condition of employment.

Mergers, acquisitions and divestments

The restructuring of organizations brought about by the merger, acquisition or sale of a company must take into account the impact that this will have on existing employees. Where the merger is voluntary, then steps can be taken early to prepare the ground, but in the case of a hostile takeover then this may not be possible. In any case, it will be necessary to apply HRM skilfully to achieve the smoothest possible transition to new ownership. The extent of the restructuring will vary from insignificant to complete reorganization. In the latter case, all the previously described HRM functions will be brought into play.

Who is affected will to some extent be influenced by who the acquiring organization is and the extent to which the merger is an equal partnership. The most likely persons to be affected will be board members and senior managers, some of whom may be seeking to leave, while others will be jockeying for position to take advantage of new opportunities.

The smooth transition to the full operation of a merged organization to meet the motivation for the action will be the major consideration for the new management. Therefore the cooperation of employees, stakeholders and other interested parties is of vital importance. HRM should be involved in ensuring that employees are kept fully informed of developments and the positive aspects should be accentuated while the need for less comfortable actions should be fully explained.

Steps should be taken to address differences in corporate culture and work should commence on harmonizing culture and practice within the newly merged organization. It is unlikely that this will happen quickly and therefore longer-term plans should be prepared to encourage cultural convergence and the adoption of new practices.

Case study 8.1: Human resource management strategy, Group Dragados, Spain

Group Dragados is a Spanish company that was founded in 1941. It is strongly orientated to international construction and the services market and has four divisions: construction, services, industrial and concessions. The group also has real estate interests as an industrial shareholder in Inmoboliaria Urbis.

Part of the corporate identity and culture of Dragados is to encourage initiative amongst its employees and to create motivation to achieve company objectives with the assistance of constant professional development. The human resources within the organization and the diversification of the business represent the most important aspects that differentiate the company from its competitors.

Human resources management policy adopted by the Group is strongly orientated to recruiting the right personnel and then managing their contribution and development in accordance with the Group's corporate objectives. Individual development is carried out mainly through a vital training and learning process in which work safety and accident prevention is given special significance. The Group's remuneration objective is to compensate personnel according to their contribution to business objectives.

Dragados has a unique Tutor Plan, which guarantees that new employees easily understand their responsibilities and integrate quickly with the organization. It also ensures a constant flow of knowledge and information from more experienced members of staff. The Group has also implemented a training programme called 'Master Dragados' in which management staff members within the group disseminate their knowledge and experience to high potential professionals. The programme concentrates on how best to undertake the different areas of business management within the Group.

Dragados has a Prevention Department as required by the Law on Work Risk Prevention 1995. This statute was later developed by Royal Decree 39/1997 and contains the 'Regulation and Prevention Services'. The Group has developed risk prevention systems and general procedures that are documented in a manual. The policy is to provide constant, informative training and planning activities aimed to integrate techniques, working conditions, social relations and environmental factors.

The Group has developed an International Human Resources Management information system, the basic function of which is to identify and locate the most suitable personnel to take on jobs and challenges that arise anywhere in the world where Dragados is working. To achieve this the system is able to determine the experience and abilities of individuals and then match them to the specific requirements of individual projects.

Author's commentary

A large global construction company, typified by the case of Group Dragados, must manage and invest in its 'people' who represent the most important resource. Staff development and training provide the foundation for promoting knowledge and expertise that can be brought to bear on the achievement of the company objectives.

Case study 8.2: Balfour Beatty Group safety policy

Balfour Beatty serves the international construction market through four main business divisions: building, building management and services; civil and specialist engineering services; rail and engineering services; and investments and developments.

Safety is a major aspect of Balfour Beatty's human resource management policy. Each business in 2000 was subjected to external independent audit of its organization, management control systems and workplace implementation. Those items identified as requiring attention have had action plans drawn up to rectify shortcomings and strengthen safety prevention. One or more of the following carried out independent external audit:

- The Royal Society for the Prevention of Accidents (ROSPA - UK) Quality Audit System;
- The British Safety Council's 5 Star Audit System; and
- The Railway Infrastructure Contractors Safety Rating System.

Balfour Beatty's safety performance has increased progressively since 1990 when the Group's accident frequency rate was 1.57 per 100,000 manhours. In 2000, this figure had been reduced to 0.51. Isolated problems that have occurred with safety have been fully investigated to identify causes in order that relevant and effective solutions can be developed and implemented. The relevant lessons learned have been incorporated into safety policies and procedures. In 2000, Balfour Beatty increased its commitment to health and safety training with the introduction of over 26,000 training days, compared with 20,700 in 1999. The Group has also introduced a number of initiatives to promote NVQ training to expand the range and depth of safety management competence across the board, with particular attention being given to key supervisors.

Significant parts of the organization remained accident-free in 2000, including two of the company's largest UK projects representing 1.25 million accident-free hours. This performance was equalled by two of the Group's largest projects in the USA. The result of this performance has been a 20% reduction in insurance premiums and a number of prestigious safety awards and honours.

Balfour Beatty is now widely recognized and acclaimed for its pioneering work in providing health-screening services for its employees, including those based on sites that are provided with a mobile service. The Group is also piloting a scheme in support of a Government initiative to combat the impact of drugs and alcohol abuse on workplace safety.

Author's commentary

By its nature construction is potentially dangerous, especially if inadequate attention and effort is given to developing policies, systems, procedures and working practices to prevent the occurrence of accidents.

The outcome of prosecutions and the potentially disastrous effects that accidents have on individuals and their families are well publicized and are a significant deterrent to attracting good personnel into the industry. Furthermore, an employer has a duty of care to employees and evidence of this manifests itself in low accident rates, which in turn contribute to good morale and a sense of well-being emanating from being employed by the company. Clients also wish to be associated with construction companies that can deliver projects without the human misery caused by accidents and injury or death to personnel working on their projects. Balfour Beatty has recognized this responsibility and has taken positive and effective steps to improve its safety performance.

Summary

International human resource management plays a key pivotal role in the successful management of an international construction organization. It relies on adequately defined principles and paradigms related to all aspects of employing and managing people. These will need to be applied and suitably adapted on a country-by-country basis. However, there should be key policies that are able to implement prime human values adopted by the organization.

When operating internationally the extra tasks presented by differences in culture, employment law and management practice in different foreign countries must be fully taken into account. The objective should be to strive for a corporate company system that has sufficient flexibility to account for these differences. This chapter outlines optional functional systems relating to human resource planning, recruitment and selection, job evaluation, staff appraisal and development, industrial relations and health, safety and welfare.

The problems and difficulties associated with posting home employees to international positions must be fully appreciated and steps should be taken to ensure good performance while on assignment and adequate repatriation measures on return to home duties.

IHRM plays a key role in the promotion of good morale and motivation typified by pride in the job and in being an employee of the organization. The importance of meeting the dual needs of the company and the individual by proper staff development and training have been demonstrated by the Dragados case study and the evidence gathered in other organizations demonstrates that this practice is universally applied by all successful global construction organizations.

The safety and health of employees is a key global issue for all construction companies. Construction, by its nature, is a dangerous business and its poor safety record proves this to be the case. The Balfour Beatty safety policy and systems emphasize the need for adequate attention and investment in the implementation of safety policies and practices, alongside adequate training and updating to meet continually changing and demanding working conditions. IHRM policy should therefore reflect key company safety practices to be consistently applied in all foreign locations, irrespective of local legal requirements and legislation that may require less stringent practices.

Finally, it should be stressed that IHRM is an integral part of the total corporate management system and, as such, should be fully integrated and harmoniously developed with all other company sub-systems and functions. This is especially the case in the event of company mergers and acquisitions.

Further reading

Balfour Beatty home page (on-line www.balfourbeatty.com).

Black J. S., Gregersen H. B. & Stroh L. (1998), *Globalising people through international assignments*, Addison-Wesley, Reading, Massachusetts.

Black J. S. & Gregersen H. B. (1998), *So you're going overseas: a handbook for personnel and professional success*, Global Business Publishers, San Diego, California.

Daniel S. J. & Reitsperger W. D. (1991), 'Management control systems for JIT: an empirical comparison of Japan and the US', *J. Int. Business Studies*, **22**, No. 4, 603–618.

Genus A. & Kaplani M. (2002), 'Managing operations with people and technology', *Int. J. of Technology Management*, **23**, No. 11.

Grupo Dragados SA home page (on-line www.dragados.com).

Ibbs W. *et al.* (2001), 'Project change management system', *J. Management in Engineering*, **18**, Issue 3, 159–165.

Klein G. (2001), 'Sources of power: how people make decisions', *Int. J. of Manpower*, **22**, No. 7, 664–674.

Michie J. & Sheehan-Quin M. (2001), 'Labour market flexibility, human resource management and corporate performance', *British J. of Management*, **12**, Issue 4, December.

Richards T. & Mogar S. (2000), 'Creative leadership process in project team development: an alternative to Tackman's stage model', *British J. of Management*, **11**, Issue 4, 273–283.

Shenkar, O. & Zeira Y. (1987), 'Human resource management in international joint ventures: directions and research', *Academy of Management Review*, **12**, No. 3, 546–557.

Schuler S., Dowling P. J. & De Cieri H. (1993), 'An integrative framework of strategic international human resource management', *J.of Management*, **19**, No. 2, 419–459.

Stanton M. (1996), *Organisation and human resource management: the European perspective, Strategies for Human Resource Management* (ed M. Armstrong), Kogan Page, London.

Chapter 9

Organization structure and management systems

Introduction

A construction business entering the international market will be required to assess the changes that will be necessary to the organization structure to accommodate additional demands. Much will depend on the policy adopted concerning the scale of the involvement and the degree to which the organization will be directly involved as opposed to employing agents and third parties. At the outset, the venture into the foreign market might only involve a small group of people who can be easily accommodated within existing organizational arrangements. Over time this situation might change, especially if the venture is successful, and in the event that a decision is taken to expand, the organization strategy will need to be reviewed.

Construction enterprises operating internationally will need to adopt an effective and appropriate organization structure to implement business strategy. An organization structure represents the business infrastructure necessary to conduct and control the various corporate activities and functions of the company and will be influenced by a range of dynamic factors. As a consequence, organization structures must also be flexible in that they must be readily adaptable in order to meet new situations and requirements.

This chapter explains the principles and influencing factors that determine the selection and evolution of organization structures. There is no universal solution to provide the ideal organization structure, instead companies must tailor their structure to meet their corporate aims and objectives. Project organization structures are analysed and the advantages of matrix project management structures are explained.

The relationship between organization structures and systems is discussed and the principles of the systems approach are described. A methodology is proposed for the conduct of systems analysis that can be applied to an existing business to improve efficiency and productivity. Systems theory is then extended to soft systems methodology (SSM) and its application is described. Systems theory is then further developed to include an explanation of critical systems thinking that provides a universal approach to the consideration and integration of all relevant factors that influence the determination of corporate solutions.

Expansion of international involvement

It is common practice for companies entering the international market simply to expand domestic arrangements to accommodate the extra work. The focus of the business will be on the domestic market and international operations will be dealt with on a project-by-project basis. As the international business grows it will be necessary to set up a head office department to coordinate and control projects and their associated procurement, supply chain and financial requirements. If the volume of business continues to expand in a particular country, then it may be necessary to set up a local office to handle functions devolved from head office. Further growth in the business may require the establishment of an independent subsidiary, which has the advantage of giving a local identity to the business and provides the opportunity to engage indigenous partners in a joint ownership arrangement (Figure 9.1).

Development towards a global organization structure

The expansion of an organization to operate on a global scale requires the development of a suitable organizational framework that enables the responsibilities of management to be fulfilled and facilitates contributions to be made by its members in support of the attainment of the corporate mission and objectives. The organization structure should be designed to promote effective working at all levels and should be geared to encourage motivation. Responsibilities need to be clearly defined and there should be lines of responsibility linking the points of decision. There should be adequate decentralization and proper integration of functional roles. Recent trends have been towards flatter organization structures, therefore adequate attention must be given to the degree of autonomy related to the span of control. The essential features of a competent organization structure are:

- proper definition of roles and responsibilities, involving parity associated with authority, responsibility and accountability;
- appropriate decentralization of decision and control;
- ability to adapt to change;
- provision of individual self-development and advancement;
- avoidance of gaps in management coverage by the selection of appropriate spans of control and reporting time-scales;
- avoidance of potential overlaps and conflicts; and
- lines of authority and information should not be confused.

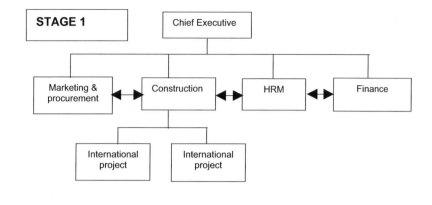

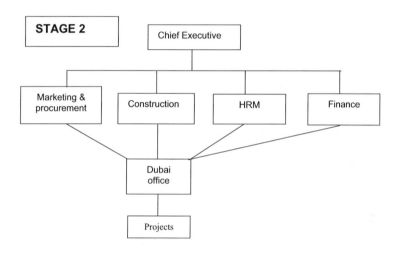

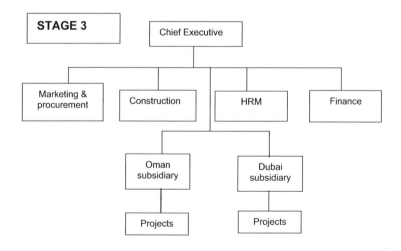

Figure 9.1: Initial stages of international expansion

As the number of domestic and international subsidiaries increases, either by internal expansion or acquisition or a combination of both, it will be necessary to consider the possibility of an international divisional structure which centralizes all international operations (Figure 9.2). The most important advantage is that the load will be taken off the chief executive and it raises the importance and status of international activities by appointing a senior executive with single point responsibility for the international business.

To operate globally, a multinational construction company needs to further develop its corporate organization structure from that of the international divisional structure described above. There are numerous ways in which this can be done, the more usual modes being by product, region, function, mixed, matrix or transnational.

In the global product structure, domestic divisions are given global responsibility for selling a company's products throughout the world. The global area structure introduces another level in the organization structure and the manager at this level will be responsible for all company service or product divisions.

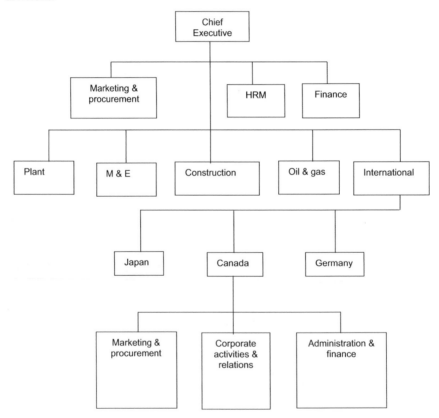

Figure 9.2: International divisional structure

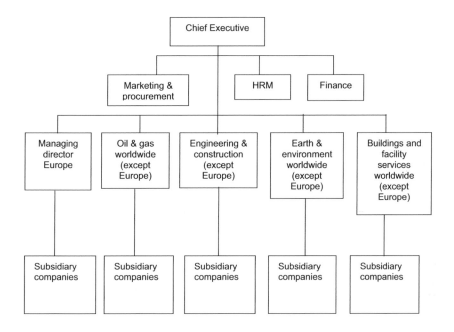

Figure 9.3: Mixed hybrid global organization structure

Each area service/product division will be responsible for all the company functions within its area.

The global functional structure takes the basic tasks performed by the organization which are then subdivided into domestic and foreign production.

The mixed structure, as the name implies, is a hybrid designed to best suit the needs of the organization. Figure 9.3 illustrates a mixed structure that is designed to operate corporately across the board in Europe and is managed separately from the other sectors of the organization that are controlled independently from elsewhere in the world.

A matrix structure initially operates in two dimensions where tasks (functions) and products/services are brought together into one integrated structure. Matrix structures have their emphasis on a systems approach whereby inputs are transformed into outputs.

The two-dimensional matrix can be expanded to three dimensions to give an additional dimension of control by introducing, for example, functional cost centres (Figure 9.4).

Transnational organization structures are those which have been developed to link worldwide business using a network consisting of dispersed subsidiaries, specialized operations and interdependent relationships that use the same information and resources. There is no standard convention for drawing these networks and they can often be complicated. The main criteria for their success relates to clarity of presentation, true representation of the organization and the ability to cope with continuous dynamic change.

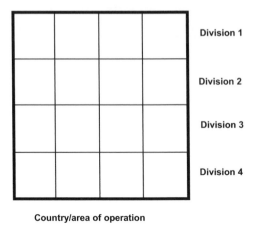

Country/area of operation

Two-dimensional matrix

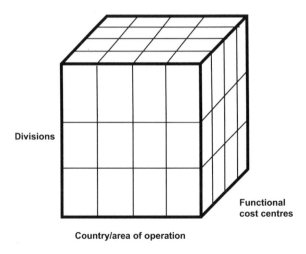

Country/area of operation

Three-dimensional matrix

Figure 9.4: Matrix organization structures

Selection of an organization structure

There is no simple correct solution to selecting an organization structure. The fundamental principles identified previously should be used as a guide and will be influenced by the following factors:

- the medium/long-term corporate strategy and the degree of change in the organization structure required to achieve the growth envisaged, both domestically and internationally;

- the amount of previous experience of working in foreign countries. The greater this experience, the more likely it will be that the corporate organization structure adopted will be more developed and sophisticated;
- the organization structure selected should accommodate local variations caused by tradition, culture or taste which translate into variation in products and services;
- the degree of centralization of decision and close control required by the home organization. Usually, where faster growth is required then there should be more decentralization and autonomy in decision-making given to subsidiaries. This will potentially have greater risk, but will also have the prospect of greater profits; and
- the potential to accommodate changes to the business, without a complete restructure.

Culture plays an important part in the way companies are organized and operated. In countries that have a strong culture of respect for authority it is more likely that chain of command structures will be adopted. These, in modern management terms, tend to be inflexible and bureaucratic and are quick to break down and become inefficient under dynamic pressure. Countries with a strong social class system tend to have strong horizontal communication across social groups, i.e. senior management, middle managers and operatives, however vertical communication between the groups is limited. In parts of the world where strong social democratic values exist it is usual for the chief executive to communicate top down and, at the same time, with those at the bottom of the structure. This may be through a selected person who then conveys the message to the rest of the workforce. Countries which do not have a class structure or strong social hierarchy will often be comfortable with structures that accommodate the notion that workers can communicate freely with top management. There are other important differences in managerial and organizational culture such as:

- recognition of the performance of the individual rather than the group;
- explicit rather than implicit control;
- greater reliance on reports for control purposes;
- adoption of performance benchmarks; and
- expatriate personnel policy versus localization.

It can therefore be deduced that the determination of international organization structures and their control is a vital and often difficult undertaking that must take into account a host of factors, some of which may be in conflict and will require mitigation to optimize the best solution. The corporate international business will be in a continuous state of development and change, hence the performance of the selected structure should be subjected to periodic reappraisal and adjustment to ensure that it maintains the level of performance expected.

Project organization structures

A project may be defined as a combination of human and non-human resources that are brought together within a temporary organization structure to achieve specified project objectives. The project manager will be a key appointment and the degree of autonomy associated with the management of the project will be determined by company policy in accordance with the size, complexity and location of the project.

The context of a construction project is characterized by the following factors:

- normally the project manager will be executively responsible with the necessary delegated degree of autonomy;
- the organizational life of the project is temporary, governed by the dates of its commencement and completion;
- the construction project normally resides within a corporate organization, the majority of whose business is made up of a series of projects;
- functional support services are usually provided from a central source; and
- the various disciplines concerned with the project require the leadership of a project manager.

The application of a traditional chain of command management structure to a construction project does present a project manager with the difficulty of integrating a wide range of independent professional and supply chain inputs, alongside functional corporate services and the need to control directly employed site staff, where applicable.

With the increasing use of procurement routes involving partnering, outsourcing and supply chain management, the use of project matrix structures has gained in popularity. The easiest way to create a matrix structure is to identify an activity work breakdown structure (WBS) for the project and then to allocate personnel to these activities in order to undertake associated tasks to achieve completion. Where the project is broken down into packages, then the structure will simply comprise the allocation of package contractors (Figure 9.5).

The emphasis is on coordination and control, since inputs may be from more than one source and are translated to outputs to activities within the WBS.

However, where the WBS involves many activities then the allocation becomes more complicated and it may be an advantage to use a more complex matrix technique to gain closer control.

Work breakdown structure	Arch.	Eng.	1	2	3	4	5	6
Substructure	●	●	●					
Frame	●	●		●				
Cladding	Input				●		Input	
Services		●				●		
Finishings◄— Output	●						●	
External works	●							●

● = translation function

Figure 9.5: Matrix project structure

Linear responsibility analysis (LRA)

LRA identifies individual roles and then relates them to each other and to the operational system of the project. It also provides a clear managerial view of the project and exposes the points of decision. The translation functions can be broken down into verb descriptions, which define the relationship between the job role and the relevant activity. Typically, the diagram shown in Figure 9.5 can be enhanced by the introduction of translation functions shown in Figure 9.6. There can be more than one translation function allocated to each job input.

The matrix can be further developed into a schematic diagram that represents the operational and systems relationships between the various project activities identified by the selected WBS. The diagram can be enhanced to show and classify the job inputs related to each project activity and it can be further developed to show:

- interdependency between activities;
- differentiation between activities in terms of technology, territory and time;

Symbol	Translation function
✛	Design
●	Undertakes the work
○	Direct supervision
▲	Management control & monitoring
◇	Approval
◆	Advice

Figure 9.6: Typical range of job input translation functions

- sentience relating to professional allegiance and allegiance to the firm; and
- primary, key and operational decision points.

Corporate and project management systems

The organization structure provides the framework for the conduct and control of the business, whereas the efficiency of the operational processes and procedures will be subject to detailed analysis relating to the appropriateness of the systems adopted and their continuing relevance. Systems analysis and organization structures are intrinsically tied together; therefore the process of corporate development will involve a considerable amount of reciprocation, involving the appraisal of cause and effect. This should be carried out with due consideration of the wider environment in which the business is taking place.

Expansion into the field of international construction will require an analysis and re-evaluation of the existing systems and organization structure to establish what should be done to safeguard operational standards, efficiency and quality.

It is essential that those undertaking a systems analysis of an international construction business appreciate fully the relationship between corporate and project systems. Basic systems theory classifies systems as open or closed. Virtually all systems applicable to construction are, to a varying degree, open in that they are directly influenced by the environment within which they exist (Figure 9.7).

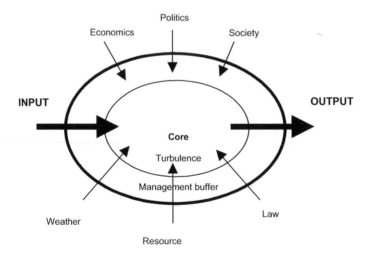

Figure 9.7: Open system theory applicable to construction
businesses and projects

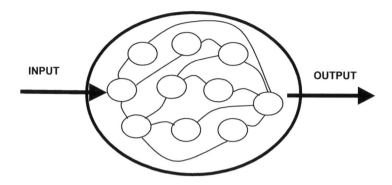

Figure 9.8: Reductionist logic applied to break down the system into
subsystems, to identify and understand their relationships

It is normal to apply reductionist logic by breaking business down into identifiable and interrelated subsystems. Each system is analysed in turn and then explained in terms of subsystem relationships (Figure 9.8).

From this basic theory the embryonic corporate system can be developed within the context of the market and influences from the general environment. Key to the development of the system will be the corporate mission and strategy of the organization (Figure 9.9).

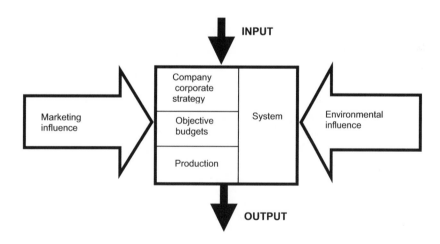

Figure 9.9: Development of the corporate system

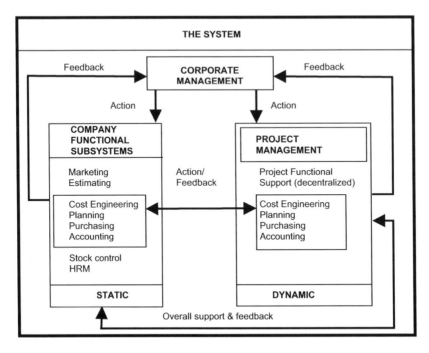

Figure 9.10: The development of the corporate system to interrelate with
dynamic project subsystems

Because construction companies are project based it is necessary to distinguish between 'static' functional subsystems that are concerned with the company business infrastructure and the temporary dynamic subsystems that are required for the management and control of individual projects. It is also important to identify and understand the interaction within and between these two groups of subsystems (Figure 9.10).

The further development of this model to suit a construction organization operating internationally will depend on corporate policy and strategy, together with the extent of involvement. Where a business decides to set up an overseas office then it will be necessary to determine which subsystems will be devolved locally to support ongoing projects. Where a divisional organization structure is adopted, then the above model will need to be developed to accommodate an international arm of the company and an additional set of static subsystems may need to be introduced. Further development of the company on a global basis will require additional levels and subsidiaries of the business to be introduced on a nested basis where the interrelationship of all functions is identified as part of the overall corporate system.

For those organizations already operating on an international scale, it will be necessary to periodically evaluate the performance of the system existing in the light of change and expansion or contraction. There may be other reasons for undertaking a system analysis, for example:

- the introduction of new technologies and processes;
- developments in information technology;
- inefficiency and poor communication;
- inadequate control and monitoring; and
- poor profits or losses.

Normally, systems analysis covers an examination of the relationships between the business and its environment and a critical comparison between the business and its competitors. The outcome might lead to the identification and, if necessary, the restatement of the goals of the business.

The objectives of new systems proposals must be clearly articulated to ensure full understanding and acceptance for implementation by senior management. To achieve this, the systems analysis and the development of new proposals should be undertaken in a thorough and logical manner.

Figure 9.11 provides an overview of the process of systems analysis and development, which leads to the approval and implementation of new systems proposals. Because application is specific to each case, no attempt has been made to provide detailed actions. Instead, a logical step-by-step process is provided for the reader to interpret. The major steps in the basic systems analysis and design methodology are described in the form of a generic framework that is set out as follows.

Definition of new system aspirations and performance

The system objectives will be reviewed and prioritized, after which they will be broken down into quantifiable sub-objectives as necessary. The methods of measurement will be determined and performance benchmarks will be established to form the basis for each objective.

Identification of organizational requirements and constraints according to:

- divisional or departmental breakdown of the business that forms the organizational infrastructure within which the business system model may be developed;
- roles and responsibilities of individuals and groups within the framework of the organisation structure;
- work and information flows that are essential;
- processes and procedures that must take place for various reasons, e.g. quality, sustainability, safety; and
- geographic location and physical dispersion of business activities.

Cross-checks should be made concerning change and casual effects from the general business environment.

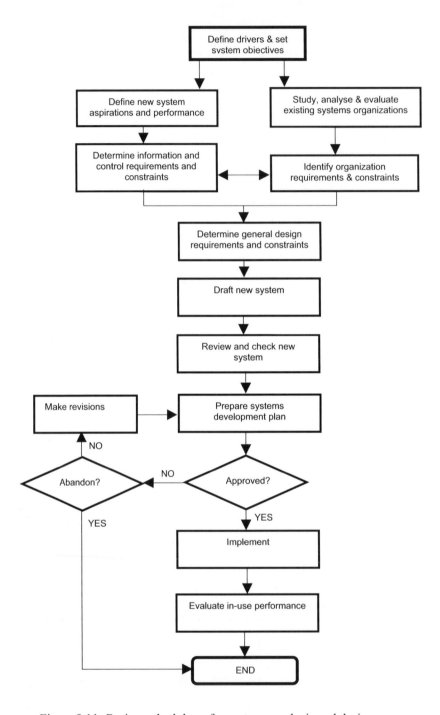

Figure 9.11: Basic methodology for systems analysis and design

Determine information and control requirements and constraints
The following should be identified and fully evaluated:

- requirements and constraints imposed by the existing system (aspects to be retained);
- recommendations by management;
- legal and corporate policy requirements and constraints; and
- internal control measures required.

Determination of general design requirements and constraints
These will set the limitations and rules for the new system proposals and will be evaluated according to maintainability, flexibility, compatibility, expandability and information management. The general design of the system must take into account all factors that are necessary to determine the initial design and subsequent upgrades envisaged over the system life cycle necessary to comply with the business plan. Testing should be according to predetermined benchmarks. Alternatives should be considered and compared to finally establish the optimal solution.

Draft system design
The scope and parameters of the new system will be defined taking into account the previous steps outlined above. The business will then be broken down into appropriate subsystems and the role and function of each will be specified. The interrelationships between the subsystems will be defined and processes and procedures will be determined. Information flows will be developed with suitable data carriers.

The proposed system will be specified and the likely benefits will be evaluated. Finally, recommendations will be made for implementation and evaluation of system performance.

The completed draft will be checked and reviewed prior to submission to management for approval. Management will approve, abandon or require further revisions. If approved, the plan will be further developed for implementation. Once implemented, a process of performance evaluation against benchmarks will begin and a system of continual improvement and development will be implemented.

Developments in systems thinking

Previously, systems theory has been considered as a 'hard' theory concerned primarily with logic and scientific thinking. However, the systems movement in more recent years has come to accept that 'soft' issues concerning human attitude, relationships and motivation, including teamwork and a sense of belonging play a vital role in the development and performance of business systems and organization structures. In particular, project-based activities involved with construction tend to be complex and considerably influenced by a host of physical and environmental factors which are further complicated by the temporary nature of projects. It is therefore unrealistic to take a purely scientific approach to such theories, for example applying reductionist logic. Instead, a view may be taken that development should take place and be implemented to achieve improvement on an incremental basis. In other words, the solution will not be perfect, but by learning from experience further improvements can be developed over time. Thinking of this nature has led to the introduction of soft systems methodology.

Soft systems methodology (SMM)

The process commences with an investigation to gather information by observation, interviews, sampling and the acquisition of secondary data from documents and records. This information is summarized by the use of 'rich pictures' (Figure 9.12) which can be diagrammatic or sketch presentations that accentuate prime features of the business system under investigation. The 'rich picture' should identify problems, conflicts, owners and systems.

The total SMM process shown in Figure 9.13 commences with an investigative stage, which is within the real world. The next step is to create a model of the real world in order to simulate improvement. This is achieved by creating root definitions, which represent an idealized view of subsystems. The aim is to draw out what is to be done, why, and by whom? The beneficiaries and

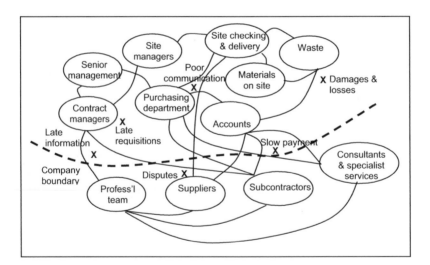

X = problems

Figure 9.12: Rich picture diagram of the interrelationships between the purchasing department of a construction company and its internal and external interactions

losers are determined and the environmental constraints are established. This is achieved by formulating a statement around six elements termed the CATWOE Mnemonic, i.e.

- **C**lients — beneficiaries/victims
- **A**ctors — those who carry out the activities
- **T**ransformation process — input leading to transformation resulting in output
- **W**orld view — constitutive meaning
- **O**wners — who is in control
- **E**nvironmental constraints.

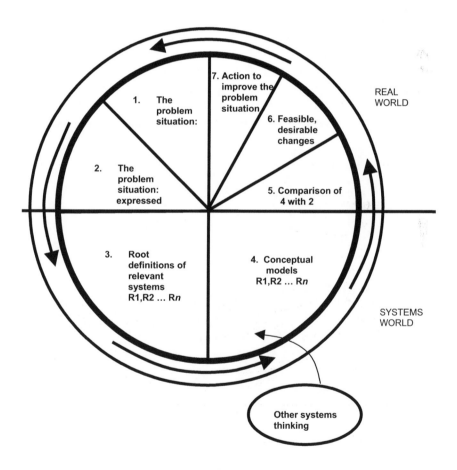

Figure 9.13: The cyclical process of soft systems methodology
Adapted from Checkland, 1991

197

From the root definitions, conceptual models are developed of subsystems that provide a systematic idealized account of human activity, usually in the form of a constructed set of verbs in the imperative mood. Such models contain the minimum number of necessary activities for each subsystem to satisfy the requirement of the root definitions. Only activities to be directly carried out should be included and these should be subjected to ongoing monitoring and control (Figure 9.14).

Each conceptual model represents one element of the total system. It is now necessary to develop the interactions and casual connections between the elements in order to construct a holistic conceptual model for the whole system similar to that shown in Figure 8.8. Once this is achieved then a comparison can be made between the idealized model and the reality of the existing system. In this manner differences can be established which will then be analysed to provide benefits and costs. By understanding the future behaviour of the system captured in the conceptual model it will be possible to select and prioritize the changes worthy of serious consideration.

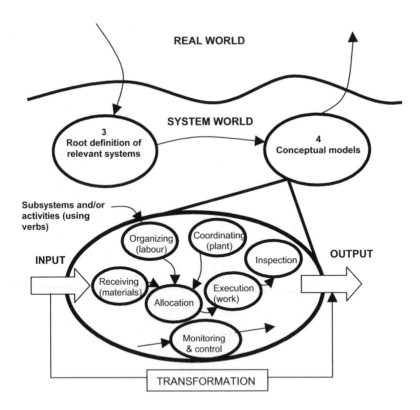

Figure 9.14: Conceptual model representation
Adapted from Checkland, 1991

Before action is taken to implement potential improvements it will be necessary to classify the changes as structural, procedural and attitudinal. The means necessary to make the changes will need to be established and a plan should be prepared for management approval and implementation.

Critical systems thinking

It may be necessary to bring to bear other techniques to enhance systems thinking and the quality of the proposed outcome. Systems analysts, especially in construction, are often presented with complex 'messes' caused by a variety of technical, social, economic, political and environmental factors and it is often the case that the adoption of one systems approach will prove to be inadequate in realizing the best solution. What is required is a combination of systems approaches, both hard (scientific) and soft (behavioural) to be brought to bear in a given combination to solve a particular problem. This implies that the problem can be identified and understood before the means to find a solution can be established. It is not within the scope of this book to describe all the individual system analysis approaches, however reference can be made to Checkland & Carson (1993) and Flood and Jackson (1991) for a more detailed exposition. Figure 9.15 illustrates the process of selecting individual systems methodologies to create a system of systems known as an epistemology to generate creative solutions to complex systems problems.

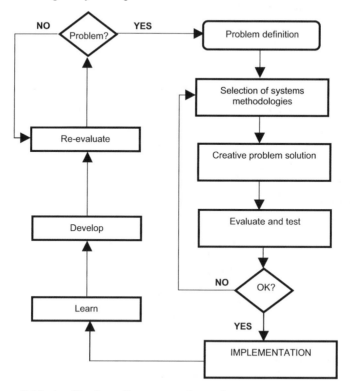

Figure 9.15: Application of systems epistemology

According to Howes (1996) a critical systems approach could be taken by moving from theoretical to 'real world' issues that can be identified and applied within three distinct groups:

- systems
- organizations
- people.

The basis of this approach relies on the linkage between all three groups, in that systems operate within a determined organization structure and people in teams/groups or individuals form part of the organization. Under each group head the following system methodologies can be allocated as shown below:

Systems	Organizations	People
Operational research	Organizational analysis	Critical systems hueristics
Systems analysis	Linear responsibility analysis	Strategic and surface assumption testing
Systems engineering	Viable systems dynamics	Social systems design
Systems dynamics	Interactive planning	

Identification of methodologies by group
Systems
This group is primarily concerned with processes, procedures and techniques aimed at facilitating a set of logically derived methodologies geared to providing order and reason according to need. Each methodology has its own attributes which will, in the majority of cases, contribute to the project process and will augment other systems for the same purpose.

Operational research (OR): consists of a range of mathematically based techniques aimed at resolving specific problems. Examples include, network analysis, linear programming, dynamic programming, queuing theory, probability theory, risk analysis, sensitivity analysis, Markov chains and time/cost optimization.

Systems analysis (SA): represents a logical and detailed approach to examining existing systems in terms of organisation, production flow processes, information flow including documentation. The context is also evaluated in business, economic, technological and social terms.

Systems engineering (SE): can be described as the development of new systems solutions from the specialized primary and secondary aims and objectives. Account is taken of constraints and requirements, including any existing procedures which must stay in place. Cost benefit analysis is carried out at all stages of development.

Systems dynamics (SD): emphasizes a model structure, which supports an interest in prediction and control. There are four principle characteristics namely, order, direction of feedback, non-linearity and loop multiplicity. The primary aim of system dynamics is to stimulate possible scenarios.

The above approaches are primarily equated with the hard scientific approach; however, VSD can incorporate sociological factors, thus providing a soft systems dimension.

Organizations

The prime concern of this group is the evolution of an appropriate framework of roles and responsibilities that will enable the tasks (activities) comprising the project to be achieved effectively.

Organization analysis represents a general approach involving hierarchies, span of control, decentralization, line management and service functions. Linear responsibility analysis takes a matrix approach identification of tasks and roles that are linked by transformation functions. A map of function categories and control loops can be transferred into a sequence network and barriers to communication can be identified by sentience and technology (Walker, 1996).

Viable systems dynamics (VSD): based on a viable systems model intended to deal with complexities through the science of cybernetics. The ordering of organizations and the development of viable control systems are central features. The idea of 'recursion' is fundamental; in that both vertically and horizontally interdependent subsystems are integrated by higher management levels. VSD methodology deals with the ordering of organizations and provides a link to systems through cybernetics. Interactive planning involves all those in the organization concerned with the planning process, thereby achieving a greater understanding and appreciation of the way the organization works in practice. It can therefore be described as participation, thus developing a sense of ownership.

People

The social context, involving people within and without the organization or the project, is a critical area that can easily be overlooked in the quest for efficiency through technology, logic and procedure. Participation, consultation, commitment and ownership are words that form the bedrock of successful team building and group performance. Morale is also a key factor in an age where work in many Western societies is now a social necessity beyond the need to earn money. The methodology of critical systems heuristics falls into two parts. The first identifies twelve critically heuristic categories that are used to interrogate systems decisions and the second part provides a tool for the participation of individuals. The intention is to encourage self-reflection among systems planners. Strategic Assumption and Surfacing and Testing (SAST) is a methodology involving group formation, assumption surfacing, dialectical debate and synthesis. The idea is that through adversarial debate differences can be highlighted which then provide a basis for consensus.

Social systems design has become an increasingly important factor in the application of management science, hence the introduction of a contingency approach and the development of soft systems thinking.

Spanning over all three categories are the concepts of soft systems methodology and contingency theory.

Distinction should also be made between 'hard' and 'soft' systems approaches and their relationship with conventional systems theory. Taking a reductionist approach, a problem is solved by breaking it down into small parts that can then be solved individually (Bertalanffy, 1971). This does not work well in construction due to the interaction between corporate and project activities, which explains the limited success that operational research techniques have achieved in construction. Reductionist logic is normally equated with hard scientific systems based on mathematical analysis that in many cases provide only one optimal solution. In reality there may be many optimal solutions that are created by the dynamics of the environment as they change with time.

The general systems approach recognizes the complexity of business organizations and their related projects, which makes it potentially more adaptable to construction. The recognition of dynamics caused by change is also another important factor. However, problems are generally not wholly 'hard' or 'soft' and hence a combination of the two, to a varying degree, is more applicable. This is known as the contingency approach. The strength of the contingency approach is that this requirement is accommodated by the recognition of the need to adopt both scientific and social science based methodologies.

Soft systems recognize that the initial solution to dynamic complex situations will not be perfect. The advantage of soft systems methodology is its acceptance that improvement is a continuing process by taking advantage of experience gained in the operation of the proposed system in the real world (Flood and Jackson, 1991).

By adopting a critical systems approach to the management of construction projects the following advantages should be realized:
1. critical awareness of the project and its process;
2. social awareness of the groups, teams and individuals involved;
3. freedom to contribute in the most appropriate manner to the development of ownership;
4. encouragement of integration and the development of a fast track approach to achieve team spirit;
5. complementary and informed utilization of systems methodologies linked to organization structures which facilitate the efficient achievement of project objectives and ultimately the efficient delivery of the project.

The achievement of the above will facilitate greater teamwork and better communication, together with a sense of participation and ownership in the realization of the project aims and objectives. Total quality management (TQM) will be founded on systems and procedures, which assist the achievement of customer satisfaction through conformity to performance standards and quality targets.

Case study 9.1: AMEC plc, operational structure

The name AMEC was introduced in 1982 as a result of the merger between Fairclough Construction UK and William Press UK. AMEC plc has its headquarters in the UK and, in 2001, it acquired 46% ownership of SPIE S.A., the international electrical and engineering services company based in France, with an option to purchase the whole company in 2002. In combination, AMEC and SPIE in 2000 had an annual turnover of US$ 8 billion and employed 50,000 people in almost 50 countries.

AMEC is a leading international supplier of specialist services and engineering services for clients in manufacturing, commercial, infrastructure and process industries. Emphasis is given to the application of knowledge, innovation and technology to generate value for clients over the life of their capital assets. The company's key markets are:

- consumer and industrial products
- energy, oil and gas
- forestry
- transportation infrastructure
- pharmachem
- public works and infrastructure
- utilities and telecoms; and
- niche sectors including astronomical telescopes, scientific instruments and exhibition facilities.

In 2000, 47% of AMEC revenue came from the UK, 30% from the Americas, 17% from the rest of Europe and 6% from the rest of the world. As at September 2001, the market capitalization of the company on the London Stock Exchange was £1.07 billion and its profits in 2000 were £98.9 million.

AMEC's ambition is to develop a leading international construction business engaged in the provision of engineering solutions to the infrastructure, commercial, manufacturing and process industries. To achieve this ideal, vital importance is attached to meeting the needs of clients and developing long-term relationships with them. The company will also strive for continuous improvement and excellence in all its activities, and aims to achieve this by encouraging its employees to develop and contribute to their full potential. AMEC is committed to pursuing its ambitions in a responsible manner by contributing to sustainable development of the national economies, societies and environments in which it operates.

The organization structure of the company has been geared to meet the corporate business requirements and ambitions utilizing a hybrid regional, global and divisional structure. Each region has its own divisions that are supported by worldwide business streams. The investment arm of the business is structured as a separate entity that has global responsibility and SPIE is incorporated as a separate autonomous entity.

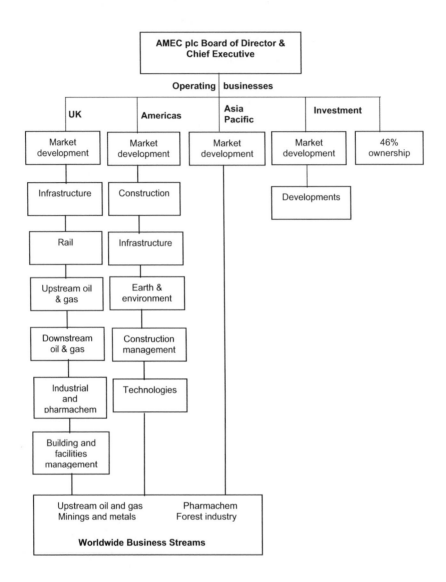

Author's commentary

AMEC has a broadly diversified business with the largest proportion of its turnover residing in the UK. The worldwide business streams operate divisionally within the UK markets, but are extended to provide specialisms in the Americas and Asia Pacific. According to the organization structure, European work is either operated through partial ownership of SPIE or through the UK office.

The structure adopted has the potential to provide an entrepreneurial approach through decentralization of decision-making and provides local managers and their teams with the opportunity to establish how best to achieve business targets set by corporate strategy laid down by the company.

The structure appears to have good flexibility to promote expansion in the Asia Pacific region and in the event of the full acquisition of SPIE it will be interesting to observe developments in operational policy and consequential restructuring of the organization.

Case study 9.2: Skanska organization and management structure

Skanska was founded in 1887 and specializes in construction-related services and project development. The company's turnover in 2001 amounted to approximately 165 billion Swedish Krona and in 2002 the number of employees stood at about 79,000. Skanska has 23 permanent markets, the key markets being Sweden, United States, United Kingdom, Denmark, Finland, Norway, Poland, Czech Republic, Argentina and Hong Kong.

The company aims to be a world leader, being the client's first choice in construction-related services and project development. Its objective is to develop, build and maintain the physical environment for living, working and travelling.

Skanka's key responsibility is to develop and maintain an economically prosperous and sound business, while recognizing responsibilities towards countries, communities and environments, as well as those to employees and business partners and towards society in general.

To achieve the above, the company operates to a Code of Conduct that is implemented through its organization structure and systems.

The Senior Executive Team is supported by corporate staff and two specialist divisions, namely Skanska Teknic and Skanska Financial Services. The organization is divided into two major operational areas: Services & Project Development and Construction Services. The organization chart as at 2002 is shown below.

Skanska retains a strong corporate structure that oversees and supports the function divisions of the company, namely Services & Project Development and Construction Services. Both divisions are comprised of autonomous companies that operate regionally or nationally, or offer a specialist service on a global, regional or national basis.

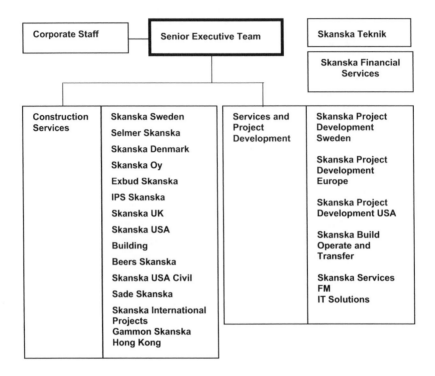

Author's commentary

Skanska has a widely diversified business structure, which has evolved according to market need and opportunities presented for expansion through acquisitions or entry into new international areas of operation. The result is a hybrid global functional divisional structure that is further divided into autonomous business units that operate either geographically or as business subdivisions specializing in particular countries. The fulfilment of corporate aims and objectives of the business are the responsibility of the Senior Executive Team whose prime role is the corporate coherence and identity of the group, to support the achievement of performance targets and benchmarks.

Technical and financial competence are key factors in Skanska's competitive advantage and the contributions made by Skanska Teknik and Skanska Financial Services directly support the Senior Executive Team and all business units within the Skanska organization.

Summary

The organization structure of an international construction company provides the framework for undertaking and discharging management responsibilities. The framework is dynamic and will be in a constant state of change and development, which requires monitoring and control. Systems provide the rationale and plan for processes and procedures required to manage human and non-human resources and information. It therefore follows that organization structure and systems are intrinsically related in providing an integrated business infrastructure.

Emphasis has been given to the need to examine the theory of organization and its application to the development of an international construction business from the outset to a full-scale global enterprise. A range of organization structures have been described that are intended to provide alternative solutions according to business, geographical and environmental factors. Matrix organization structures have been described and developed utilizing linear responsibility analysis.

Attention has been drawn to difficulties that arise through the inherent complexity of construction and related processes that are further complicated by the diversity of projects and geographic location. Reference has been made to the 'mess' that can only be dealt with by an all-embracing approach to identifying problems and then finding robust solutions. A systems approach has been described that logically breaks down the operation of an organization into subsystems performing specific functions that are causally related. The systems involved represent the processes that will be fulfilled by roles performed by persons and automated processes contained within the organization structure. The corporate output of the organization will be the amalgam of the outputs of the subsystems that transform the inputs.

It is proposed that a logical approach should be taken to systems analysis, geared to improving the business performance of an organization and that where appropriate this should be enhanced by the introduction of a critical systems approach where a variety of systems and organization methods are brought together in a unique manner to resolve difficult problems comprehensively.

Further reading

Alder N. (1997), *International dimensions to organisational behaviour*, 3rd edn, Cincinnati South Western.

AMEC plc home page (on-line www.amec.com).

Bertalanffy L. Von (1971), *General systems theory: foundations development applications*, Allen Lane

Checkland & Scholes (1991), *Soft systems methodology in action*, Wiley, Chichester.

Flood R.L. (1993), *Beyond TQM*, Wiley Chichester.

Flood R. L. & Carson E. R. (1993), Dealing with complexity, NY, Plenum

Flood R. L. & Jackson M. C. (1991), *Creative problem solving: total systems intervention*, Wiley, Chichester.

Gelbard R., Pliskin N. & Spiegler I. (2002), 'Integrating systems analysis and projects', *Int. J. Project Management*, **20**, Issue 6, 461–468.

Hofstede G. (1980), 'Motivation, leadership, and organization: do American theories apply abroad?', *Organisational Dynamics*, **8**, No. 2, 50.

Howes R. (1996), *A critical systems approach to construction project management,* CIB International Conference Construction Modernisation and Education, Beijing

Katzenbach J. R. & Smith D. K. (1993), *The wisdom of teams: creating the high performance organisation*, Harvard Business School Press, Boston MA.

Love P. E. D. *et al.* (2002), 'Using systems dynamics to better understand change and rework in construction project management systems', *Int. J. Project Management*, **20**, Issue 6, 425–436.

Skanska home page (on-line www.skanska.com).

Chapter 10

Communications

Introduction

The nature of large-scale international construction projects, using resources from different countries and continents, necessitates a high degree of coordination and communication. Communication can be defined as the process by which information is exchanged and understood by two or more people, usually with the intent to motivate or influence behaviour. This typically involves an exchange of facts, ideas, opinions or emotions. The importance of effective communication in organizations cannot be overemphasised because it is the ultimate means by which behaviour is modified, change is effected, knowledge is acquired and shared, and goals are achieved. Individual motivation and effectiveness depends on communication, so that people understand what they have to do and why. Communication in the organization may involve giving instructions, sending or receiving information, exchanging ideas, announcing plans or strategies, comparing actual results against plans, using rules or procedures, and communication about the organization structure and job descriptions. Information is required for effective management decision-making. Successful communication of information and coordination of interdepartmental as wells as international activities depends on effective information flows and communication between individuals whether co-located or geographically distributed.

The basic components of the communication process, the verbal and non-verbal forms of communication, the formal and informal channels through which communications take place within organizations are presented in this chapter. The implications for organizations that operate globally are discussed with respect to the influences of different languages and culture on communications. The variety of electronic media, in particular the Internet, and their growing potential for communications on international projects is discussed. A case study illustrating the successful use of a web-based project collaborative system to manage a major project with four major partners from two different countries with different languages, is presented.

The communication process

The challenge of effective communication in organizations may be appreciated by looking at the key elements of the communication process indicated in the model in Figure 10.1. Simply stated, the communication process involves the sender, the transmission of a message through a selected channel, and the receiver. The receiver may respond or provide feedback to the sender. The message may be distorted and affected by noise in the communication process. Companies operating globally need to devise mechanisms for minimizing such effects when communicating over long distances, usually in a multilingual environment with the added need to be culturally sensitive.

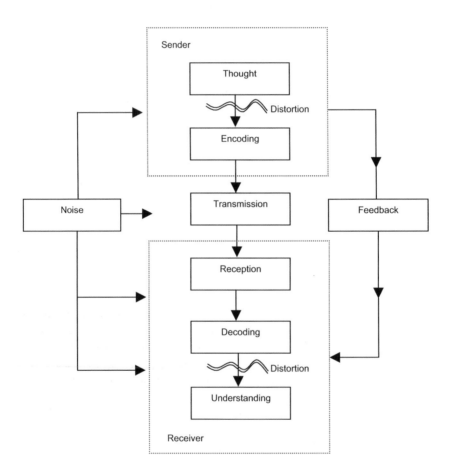

Figure 10.1: The communication process

The sender of the message

Communication begins with the sender or an individual who wishes to convey an idea or a concept to others, to seek information, or express a thought or emotion. The sender encodes the idea in a way that can be understood by both the sender and the receiver, by selecting symbols with which to compose a message. The message is the tangible formulation of the idea that is sent to the receiver. The sender must organize the material of the message into the most coherent form and appropriate device. Consideration should be given to such matters as: should it be written or oral, does it need illustrations or just text, should it be translated into a foreign language?

The channel to transmit the message

The message is sent through a channel, which is the communication carrier linking the sender to the receiver. The message may be oral or written, and the channel through which it may be transmitted can be a memorandum, a formal report, a face-to-face meeting, a telephone call, a computer, or television. Two or more channels may be used, each with advantages and disadvantages. Thus, the proper selection of the channel is vital to effective communication.

The receiver of the message

The receiver is the person to whom the message is sent. The receiver decodes the symbols to interpret the meaning of the message. Accurate communication can occur only when both the sender and the receiver attach the same meaning, or at least similar meanings, to the symbols that compose the message. Thus, it is obvious that a message that is encoded into Chinese requires a receiver who understands Chinese. Encoding and decoding are potential sources for communication errors, because knowledge, attitudes, background and culture act as filters and create 'noise' when translating from symbols to meaning.

Distortion

The meaning of a message can be lost at the encoding and decoding stages. The problem typically arises from the language and the medium used. An example for such a situation is a brief email message requiring further discussion and not action, which can easily give the wrong impression. The translation of a message from one language to another has considerable potential for distortion and care needs to be exercised to avoid this.

Noise

Noise is any factor in the communication process that interferes with exchanging messages and achieving common meaning. Noise includes, for example, interruptions while the sender is encoding, the use of ambiguous symbols in encoding, static on telephone lines as a message is being transmitted, and fatigue on the part of the receiver while he or she is decoding. In the international context, language is an especially important factor in cross-cultural communication; not only verbal expression but also gestures and posture can result in noise, hindering communications.

Feedback

Finally, feedback occurs when the receiver responds to the sender's communication with a return message. This response involves a reversal of the communication process so that the receiver becomes the sender and the sender becomes the receiver. The communication is one-way without feedback and with feedback it is two-way. Feedback is a powerful aid to communication because it enables the sender to determine whether the receiver has correctly interpreted the message.

Forms of communication

The main forms of communications used by individuals within organizations can be categorized as verbal and non-verbal. Verbal communication refers to the oral and written use of words to communicate; the most commonly used forms of communication in organizations. Non-verbal communication refers to the use of elements and behaviours that are not coded into words. Verbal and non-verbal types of communication each play an important part in the effective transmission of messages within organizations.

Verbal communication

Oral communication can range from speech without visual contact by means of a radio, personal pager or telephone to speech with visual contact through television presentation, television link and face-to-face conversation. In the main, it takes place largely through face-to-face conversation with another individual, meetings with several individuals and telephone conversations. It has the advantages of being fast, cheap, the meaning of messages can be underlined by using stress, timing, and pitch, it is more personal than written communication with potential for informality, it is easy to use in that repetition and duplication are acceptable, and it provides immediate feedback from others involved in the conversations. The disadvantages are that it can be time-consuming, difficult to terminate, judgements may be made about the person rather than their message, the audience may ask awkward questions, and additional effort is needed to document what is said if a record is necessary. When using a foreign language, it is necessary to appreciate the potential differences between correct speech and the language as it is used in current practice. This necessitates great caution in the choice of translators and interpreters.

Written communication occurs through a variety of means such as office memorandums, business letters, reports, newsletters, policy manuals, written information on television screens and electronic billboards. The advantages are that they have the potential for formality, provide a record of the message, avoid personal contact, can be disseminated widely with a minimum of effort, and allow the sender to think through the intended message carefully. The disadvantages are that they demand considerable linguistic skills, are time-consuming to produce, can be expensive, are of a relatively impersonal nature, present the possibility for misunderstanding by the receiver, are slower to transmit and mean a delay in feedback regarding the effectiveness of the message.

Non-verbal communication

This is more commonly referred to as body language. It comprises body movements such as facial expressions, eye movements, gestures and postures. In assessing an individual's response to an issue, conclusions can be drawn from observing such body movements. Non-verbal communications can be used advantageously or can give serious offence. The same symbolic gesture can have different meanings in different countries. The vertical movement of the head (nod) means yes to the rest of the world except in Greece and Turkey where it means no (Stallworthy and Kharbanda, 1985). The 'thumbs up' gesture means alright (OK) in the US and Western Europe but is an insult in Sardinia and Northern Greece. Body language can be used effectively to give emphasis to a speech or a delicate negotiation when controlled. It can prove counterproductive or even harmful when used unconsciously or at the wrong moment.

Communication channels

In assessing organizational communication an important consideration is the flow of information throughout the various parts of the organization. Serious effectiveness and efficiency problems can arise from information failing to reach the individuals and groups that need it for their work. Patterns of organizational communication flow are sometimes referred to as communication channels because they represent conduits through which managers and other people within the organization can send and receive information. Communications typically flow in three directions linking different parts of an organization: vertical, horizontal, and diagonal communication. Managers are responsible for establishing and maintaining formal channels of communications in these three directions. Managers also use informal channels of communications by getting out of their offices and mingling with employees.

Formal communication channels

Vertical communication involves the exchange of a message between two or more levels of the organization hierarchy, the formal channel of which is typically represented in a firm's organization chart as shown in Figure 10.2. It can involve a manager and a subordinate or several layers of the hierarchy. It can flow in a downward or upward direction.

Downward communication flows from people at the higher levels to those at the lower levels in an organization. This kind of communication can take many forms, such as meetings, company policy statements, company newsletters, informational memos, and face-to-face contact. It typically involves information from any of the following categories: implementation of goals and strategies; job instructions relating to specific tasks; job rationales explaining the relationship between two or more tasks; procedures and practices of the organization; feedback on individual performance; and efforts to encourage a sense of mission and dedication to the organizational goals. Unfortunately, downward communication across several levels, national boundaries, and multiple cultures is prone to distortion and information may be lost as it comes down the chain of command. The effectiveness of downward communications can be improved through the use of multiple channels, repetition and the encouragement of feedback in the form of upward communication.

Upward communication is the flow of messages from a lower level to one or more higher levels in the organization. This may take several forms such as one-to-one meetings with an individual's immediate superior, meetings with superiors, memos and reports, suggestion systems, grievance procedures, and employee attitude surveys. The information typically pertains to progress of current work, serious unsolved problems and situations in which subordinates need help from superiors, new developments arising within or affecting the work unit or organization, suggestions for improvement and innovation, and employee attitudes, morale and efficiency. The distortion that characterizes downward communication also plagues upward communication. Managers responsible for the international operations of their organizations must expend sufficient efforts in motivating and encouraging upward communication to ensure that subordinates do not filter or block information that is unfavourable to them but important to the organization.

Horizontal communication is the exchange of messages between people of the same or similar organizational level or rank, also known as peers or co-workers. It may be intradepartmental, occurring within the same department or section. It may be interdepartmental, occurring across different departments or

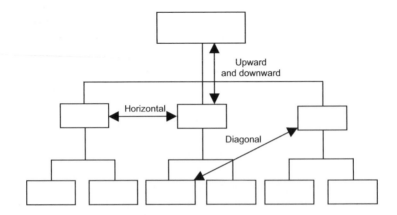

Figure 10. 2: Information flow across the organizational structure

sections. The purpose is not only to inform but also to request support and coordinate efforts for the achievement of organizational objectives. It may be part of a formal work relationship, to coordinate the work of several people, and perhaps departments, who have to cooperate to carry out a certain operation.

Horizontal communication is particularly important in learning organizations, where teams of workers are continuously solving problems and searching for new ways of doing things. However, proper safeguards may need to be taken in order to prevent potential problems because information may not follow the chain of command. Specifically, horizontal communication should rest on the understanding that horizontal relationships will be encouraged wherever they are possible, subordinates will refrain from making commitments beyond their authority and subordinates will keep superiors informed of important interdepartmental activities. Although horizontal communication may create difficulties, it is necessary in many enterprises in order to respond to the needs of the complex and dynamic project environment, particularly when operating globally.

Diagonal communication flows between people at different levels who have no direct reporting relationships with one another. Simply put, it is interdepartmental communication between people of different ranks. Diagonal communication has the potential to speed up information flow, to improve understanding, and to coordinate efforts to achieve organizational goals.

Informal communication channels

These exist outside the formally authorized channels and do not adhere to the organization's hierarchy of authority or related task requirements. Informal communications coexist with formal communications but may skip hierarchical levels, cutting across vertical chains of command to connect virtually anyone in the organization. Two types of informal channel used in many organizations are 'management by wandering around' and the 'grapevine'.

Management by wandering around (MBWA) was popularized by Peters and Waterman (1982) and Peters and Austin (1985). MBWA applies to managers at all levels, who mingle and develop positive relationships with employees and learn directly from them about their department, division or organization. In any organization both upward and downward communications are enhanced with MBWA. Managers have the chance to describe key ideas and values to employees and in turn learn about problems and issues confronting employees.

The grapevine is an informal person-to-person communication network of employees that is not officially sanctioned by organizations. It can be thought of as relating to personal rather than positional issues (Pace, 1983). It links employees in all directions ranging from top management, through middle management, to operational level employees. Employees use grapevine rumours to fill in information gaps and clarify management decisions. They may sometimes create difficulties when they carry gossip and false rumours. The grapevine tends to be more active during periods of change, excitement, anxiety and poor economic conditions.

Cross-cultural communications

Communication in the international environment is complicated by the existence of different languages, cultures and etiquette as indicated in Chapter 7. Culture influences the context within which communication takes place. Context includes situational factors such as the roles of the participants, the nature of the existing relationships, and the non-verbal forms of communication. Kennedy and Everest (1991) place countries on a continuum ranging from low to high context cultures. In high context cultures, the emphasis in the communication process is on establishing and strengthening relationships in the exchange of messages. Countries with high context cultures are to be found in Latin America, Arabia, Africa and Asia, including Japan. The context as well as the non-verbal communications is likely to be as important as the spoken word with individuals from these countries. In low context cultures, the emphasis in the communication process is on exchanging information through the spoken word with less emphasis on the surrounding circumstances or non-verbal communication. Low context cultures are to be found in North America and Europe. For example, in many African cultures, individuals show respect to those high in the social structure by not looking at them in the eye but an individual from a low context culture may ignore or misinterpret such subtleties. Thus, individuals from low and high context countries may experience difficulties in communication if such differences are not taken into consideration.

There are many other ways in which culture influences communications. Colours have different meanings in various cultures. Black is often associated with death in many North American and European countries, while in the Far East white is the colour of mourning. In business dealings it is quite common in most North American and European countries to communicate on a first-name basis, yet in most other cultures, especially those with a highly hierarchical structure, persons generally address one another by their last names (Kirpalani, 1985). In North America and Europe one expects that people mean what they say. The need for precision is illustrated in the popularity of management by objectives, where goals are stated precisely in quantitative, measurable terms whenever possible. In contrast, Japanese communication is implicit, as the meaning has to be inferred. For example, Japanese dislike saying 'no' in communication. Instead, they couch a negative answer in ambivalent terms. In the Chinese culture, words may not convey what people really mean because they may want to appear humble (Chu, 1987). For example, when a promotion is offered the person may say he or she is not qualified enough to assume greater responsibility. But the expectation is that the superior will urge the subordinate to accept the promotion and mention all the virtues and strengths of the candidate, as well as his or her suitability for the new position.

It is necessary for individuals who have management responsibility for the international operations of organizations that operate globally to be fully cognizant of these dangers so that they can help to prevent their colleagues from giving unnecessary offence. Organizations that operate globally apply a variety of measures to overcome communication barriers in the international environment which include providing extensive language training, and the use of translators. Frequently, local nationals who know the host country's language and culture are hired for top positions.

Electronic communication

While developments in transport have played a major role in internationalizing industries and markets by making it possible to transfer resources and goods between countries and continents, it is widely acknowledged that the development of information and communication technology (ICT) is one of the most important driving forces behind globalization. The integration of computers and telecommunications into a unified system for the processing and interchange of business information has opened new opportunities to global business, including those in construction, for the acquisition of global competitive advantage. Contributing to this has been the continuous exponential increase in affordable computing power augmented by developments in connectivity. Local Area Networks and Wide Area Networks are the basis of this connectivity. These, when combined with developments in telecommunications, like satellite and cable links, have significantly improved inter- and intra-organizational communications. These advances have made possible the development of the Internet, which is making a significant impact on business activity through improved linkages in the value chain between businesses, their clients and suppliers.

The Internet

The Internet has revolutionized the computer and communications world and has become the most popular channel for communication. The Internet is a world-wide broadcasting capability, a mechanism for information dissemination, and a medium for collaboration and interaction between individuals and their computers without regard for geographic location. Thus, it is a good way for anyone with global interests to communicate. Its main uses include remote log-in from one computer to another, remote access to files and software on other computers, file transfer, electronic mail, newsgroup formation and access, news distribution, electronic conferencing and the world wide web (www).

Remote access

A facility known as Telnet enables one computer to log into another and use it as if it were a terminal attached to the remote computer. Telnet is a terminal emulation protocol commonly used on the Internet and TCP/IP-based networks (Buchanan, 1997). It is an inherent part of the TCP/IP communications protocol. This implies that a PC can be part of a much larger and more powerful computer system to which it is remotely connected, with access to its data files and the operation of its software. Thus, site personnel working at a remote construction site could use their firm's computer system much as if they were working at the office.

File transfer

A facility known as FTP (File Transfer Protocol) enables the transfer of files from one computer to another across the Internet and TCP/IP-based networks. FTP includes functions to log onto the network, list directories and copy files. It allows the transfer of a whole file from one computer to another without altering the file format. Unlike email programs in which graphics and program files have to be 'attached', FTP is designed to handle binary files directly and does not add the overhead of encoding and decoding the data. FTP is suitable for the transfer of large electronic documents, particularly engineering drawings of various file formats, between remote sites within the same organization or between partners.

Electronic mail

Electronic mail (email) facilitates the transmission of messages over a network. It enables one-to-one and one-to-many communication across the Internet. Thus, users can send mail to a single recipient or broadcast it to multiple users. Mail is sent to a simulated mailbox in the network mail server or host computer from which it is interrogated. An email system requires a messaging system, which provides the store and forward capability, and a mail program that provides the user interface with send and receive functions. The web browser can also substitute for the mail program. The mail program may be set up to query the mail server every few minutes and alert the user if new mail has arrived. Besides simple written messages, email enables users to attach files and other forms of information to their communications. Thus, construction documents and other related electronic media can be exchanged between geographically distributed project partners.

Voice mail

Voice mail is a recording system that enables senders to leave messages for receivers by telephone in its early days and, more recently, via the Internet. Voice mail allows non-verbal cues such as voice quality and tone of voice to be conveyed. It is particularly useful in imparting short messages that do not require further discussions with the intended receiver.

Newsgroup formation and access

Newsgroup (also known as Internet discussion group) facilities act like a public notice board on the Internet to which subscribers can attach either original messages or replies to others. It starts by someone posting an initial query or comment, and other members reply. Others reply to the replies, and so the 'discussion' forms a chain of related postings called a 'message thread'.

Electronic conferencing

There three types of electronic conferencing, namely teleconferencing, data conferencing and video conferencing. Teleconferencing is the simultaneous communication among a group of individuals, in its early days by telephone and recently via computers and the Internet, from different locations. It enables the holding of meetings among group members who are not in the same physical location. Data conferences allow a group of individuals simultaneous interaction to confer over text and graphics documents. This allows designers located in different geographical locations to work on the same drawing simultaneously. Video conferencing enables the holding of meetings with individuals in two or more locations by means of live video. The individuals may use a combination of video, audio and data for the purpose of communication. It allows non-verbal cues such as body language, essential for effective communication, to be conveyed. Video conferencing software, such as Microsoft's NetMeeting and Netscape's Collabra, are now readily available as they are bundled with standard software packages. These tools enable project teams to collaborate, redline drawings and solve problems without having to be co-located, helping to reduce travel costs and improve project communications.

The world wide web (www)

The most famous feature of the Internet is the world wide web. The first important feature of the web is the continuous connection of computer systems called hosts or 'web servers' to the Internet so that information held on them can be accessed at any time and from anywhere. The second important feature is that information is stored using a concept known as hypertext that enables links to be made between one information component and another. Documents are kept in 'web servers' that store and disseminate 'web pages'. The web pages are accessed by users with software called a 'web browser', the two most popular being Internet Explorer and Netscape Navigator. The web page, or web document, may contain text, graphics, animations and videos as well as hypertext links. The links in the page let users jump from page to page or from document to document whether they are stored on the same server or on servers around the world. The web itself becomes a huge hypertext document acting as the largest collection of on-line information in the world.

The web has also turned into an on-line shopping facility by allowing organizations to add electronic commerce (e-commerce) capabilities. In addition, the web has become a multimedia delivery system as new browser features and plug-in extensions allow for audio, video, telephony, 3-D animations and videoconferencing. Most browsers also support computer-programming languages, which allow applications to be downloaded from the web and run locally.

The Intranet

The web spawned the Intranet, an in-house, private web site for internal users in an organization. It is protected from the Internet via a firewall that lets authorized internal users out to the Internet, but prevents unauthorized external Internet users from coming in. Intranets use the same communications protocols and hypertext links as the web and thus provide a standard way of disseminating information internally and extending applications worldwide simultaneously. This has made it possible to create collaborative project environments that allow full integration and linking among many of the tools used in managing construction. An intranet infrastructure, with distributed applications and data, allows authors to publish their own project data, at the appropriate time and to the appropriate location, and provides access to authorized users. Centralized control of project data publishing is no longer required. As a virtual program office, intranets make needed information available to project stakeholders in a timely manner. Project members collaborate in virtual meetings, discussion threads and in action databases. The collaborative information is captured and stored for all authorized users to see and for historical logging. For example, all information about meetings (such as attendees, items reviewed, action items generated) is all automatically tracked in a web-based project management environment.

Extranets

This is a web site dedicated to an organization and its extended supply chain partners and customers rather than the general public. It can provide access to virtually any information that is private and not published for everyone. An extranet uses the public Internet as its transmission system, but requires passwords to gain entrance. Access to the site may be free or require payment for some or all of the services offered.

Project collaboration systems

Extranets are enabling project managers to deploy completely integrated, collaborative project management frameworks that facilitate communication, coordination, and collaboration. Traditional project management environments lack the ability to allow project teams to communicate effectively, whether they are geographically dispersed or co-located. Web-based technologies combined with email and other techniques are rapidly eliminating this problem. Renewed focus is being put on ways to help project teams communicate more effectively across virtual, geographical, functional or technological barriers to improve the productivity with which project issues are identified, discussed, actioned, assigned and resolved. This includes the ability for teams to host and participate in on-line meetings, present and review information electronically, and deliver information in a more efficient and timely manner. Communication is also improved among project participants by providing a means of archiving electronic discussion threads and documents related to project plans over the web. Using web links, direct access can be established between project plans and any related documents, specifications, engineering drawings, etc. These avoid duplication of information and provide a clear audit trail of documents, drawings issue and revisions. They allow users to view most formats of CAD drawing, and other more complex computer files, without the need or the licence to run the particular software application which generated the file. Moreover, users are able to mark up ('redline', 'blueline', 'comment' etc.) revisions, which effectively become an integral part of the original document. This is done in a closed network, where no-one is allowed in without permission, and everyone is identified (through an individual user ID and password) making it possible automatically to track who has seen what, and any comments or changes they make. And, of course, because of the system of individual user IDs, it is possible to introduce an organization hierarchy into the system, which allows documents or areas of the project to be restricted only to people at certain levels of the organizational hierarchy. This not only provides project participants with an intuitive framework for accessing project-related documents, but it helps document project processes and best practices for repeatability.

One of the main advantages of using a project extranet is that it ensures that all members of the project team have access to the most up-to-date versions of the various project documents. This means that traditional mistakes generated from someone working from an old document or drawing are, in theory, removed or at the very least reduced. Moreover, the expensive task of sending or more likely couriering documents from, say, the project architect to all the members of the project team, can be done away with, and the job of printing the relevant material assigned to the person or company actually wanting to use it. Project collaboration extranets have the opportunity to significantly improve the way in which the construction industry works globally, without needing to make real changes in the structure or practice of the industry. More crucially, project collaboration extranets reduce the opportunity for mistakes and disputes, the biggest causes of waste and inefficiency in construction.

There are a large number of different project collaboration products on the world market, and choosing the right one can be a daunting and time-consuming process. Each product will have its advantages and disadvantages. Different organizations will have a desire for different features, and different projects will require different attributes. Criteria for selecting a suitable product may include sustainability of solution provider, customer service, desired functionality and pricing. They typically range from 0.1% to 0.5% of project costs and vendors claim these should be more than offset by savings in the running of a project. A good example of the use of such a facility on an international construction project is presented in the case study at the end of this chapter. Traditional approaches to project management are inefficient in handling the dynamic and fluid nature of today's design and construction processes and their associated extended supply network environments. By using the latest Internet-based technologies, companies can create an advanced, fully integrated, collaborative project management framework that provides a long-term solution for future success on a global scale.

Information exchange standards

The construction industry is composed of many disparate disciplines. Each of these has evolved independently, with its own unique terminology, computer applications, and ways of expressing and communicating information. This often leads to problems in sharing, coordination and communication of information

221

between disciplines. It has long been recognized that what is needed is a common language or an information standard (or protocol) for representing and sharing or exchanging information between the proliferation of computing systems that serve the construction industry. There have been major international efforts to develop information standards for the construction industry worldwide. Some standards are already in use and others are still undergoing intensive research and development work internationally. These standards fall under the following categories:

- electronic data interchange (EDI)
- de-facto CAD
- STEP and the industry foundation classes (IFCs)
- extensible mark-up language (XML) and web standards.

Electronic data interchange (EDI)

EDI is the exchange of structured business data such as enquires, quotations, orders, despatch advice, invoices, goods receipts, bills of quantities/materials, reinforcement bar schedules, etc. between firms by electronic means according to agreed message standards. To make it possible for an application such as a sales order processing system to read a data file and select the pieces of data required, the relevant parts need to be structured. The data detailing 'delivery address', must be allocated a given number of characters known as a fixed length data record. This can comprise, for example, 5 lines of address (each line having 35 characters — address field), a postcode of 9 characters and a country code of 4 characters. The total length of the address record is 188. Thus, if the application wanted to select only the country code, it would jump to character number 185, the first character of the country code field, and read 4 characters, i.e. from 185 to 188. EDI has been very successful in a number of industries that have very high transaction volumes (e.g. banking, retail and manufacturing industries). The impact of EDI on constriction has been limited, with wider use among builder's merchants, material suppliers and manufacturers.

De-facto CAD standards

These are the traditional file formats that are supported by the most popular CAD packages such as AutoCAD and MicroStation. The early and wider adoption of AutoCAD for computer-aided design in the construction industry has led to its file formats, DWG and DXF, to be adopted as the de-facto standards for exchanging drawings and it is supported by almost all CAD packages. However, these standards largely support the exchange of drawings and do not support the exchange of related information such as cost estimates, project plans, etc. This problem necessitated the development of international product model-based information standards.

Standard for Exchange of Product Model Data (STEP) and Industry Foundation Classes (IFC)

STEP, the international STandard for Exchange of Product model data (ISO, 1992) is an International Standards Organisation (ISO) standard. The purpose of STEP is to 'specify a format for the unambiguous definition and exchange of computer-interpretable product information throughout the life of a product'. STEP standardizes conceptual models with different scopes using the language EXPRESS (ISO, 1997) as parts of Integrated Generic Resources (e.g. Part 41: Fundamentals of Product Description and Support and Part 42: Geometrical and Topological Representation), Integrated Application Resources (IARs) (e.g. Part 101: Draughting) and Application Protocols (APs) (e.g. AP 225: Structural Building Elements using Explicit Shape Representation). While the ISO-STEP initiative has made significant progress in the aerospace and process industries, it has yet to make similar progress in the construction industry.

The STEP initiative has influenced the establishment of the International Alliance for Interoperability (IAI) (IAI, 2002). The IAI has over 600 members around the world. It claims to be the vehicle for the construction industry worldwide, including its customers and suppliers, to collaborate in the development of a common language for sharing project and product data. The IAI specifies how physical objects such as doors, windows, walls, beams, columns, etc. and abstract concepts such as space, organization, projects, tasks, resources, etc. in a constructed facility should be represented electronically through the development of Industry Foundation Classes (IFCs) (IAI, 2002). An IFC represents a data structure, with facilitates sharing data across multiple applications. There are three possible ways of sharing data using IFCs: the exchange of files by email or physical medium (files attached to emails or in diskettes), through shared databases and software interface development for information sharing and exchange.

Extensible Mark-up Language (XML) and web standards

XML has been developed by the World Wide Web Consortium (W3C) to enable open exchange of information, including structured data elements over the Internet. It provides a structured data format that can be interpreted and displayed using a web browser, as well as enabling direct application-to-application interfaces. XML is self-describing as it provides a standardized way to 'tag' information according to its meaning (e.g. item, description, price, etc.). However, XML only describes the syntax and structure not the actual tag names. Several national and international organizations have set themselves up to define data tag definitions for specific industry sectors. Some of the more prominent initiatives are presented below.

ebXML

The Electronic Business XML (ebXML, 2002) was a joint initiative between UN/CEFACT (The United Nations body for Trade Facilitation and Electronic Business) and OASIS (Organisation for Advancement of Structured Information

Standard) to initiate a worldwide project to standardize XML business specifications. It was established to develop a technical framework that will enable XML to be utilized in a consistent manner for the exchange of all electronic business data, in order to create a single global electronic market. A primary objective is to lower the barriers of entry to electronic business in order to facilitate trade, particularly with respect to small and medium-sized enterprises and developing nations.

bcXML

The Building Construction XML (bcXML) is being developed under a European Community funded project called 'eConstruction' (eConstruct, 2002). An XML schema, taxonomy and dictionary are being developed focusing on construction products, resources, work methods and regulations. It aims to provide the industry with a powerful but low-cost communication infrastructure that supports e-business between clients, architects, engineers, suppliers (components, systems and services), contractors and subcontractors. It will integrate with e-commerce and design/engineering applications and support virtual construction enterprises over the borders of individual European states.

aecXML

The Architecture, Engineering and Construction (AEC) industry XML (aecXML) initiative was launched in 1999 by Bentley Systems Inc. and subsequently handed over to the North American chapter of the IAI (IAI-NA, 2002). It is developing an XML-based language used to represent information in the AEC industry that will facilitate the exchange of AEC data over the Internet. The information may be on resources (such as projects, documents, materials, parts), organizations, professional services (such as proposals, design, estimating, scheduling) and construction. The extent to which progress is being made on the development of aecXML is not currently clear; however, the IAI has made considerable progress in mapping its IFCs into XML.

There is clearly a proliferation of information standards initiatives and an absence of a coherent vision in the global construction industry leading to overlapping standards with broad scopes and lack of clarity in their specifications and status. This situation needs to be resolved if the simple open exchange of structured data between different applications is to be achieved globally. The developments of structured information standards such as IFCs and XML are works in progress and have yet to make an impact in the global construction industry. However, construction firms are aware of the potential benefits of structured information standards and are monitoring developments with the intention of adopting them once they become available.

Case study 10.1: The use of a web-based project collaboration system by Construtora Odebrecht, Rio de Janeiro, Brazil

Odebrecht's engineering and construction services include heavy construction and specialized technology projects, electromechanical structures and offshore drilling services. Odebrecht, known internationally for over 50 years, has nearly 200 subsidiaries and affiliates working in 14 countries. Odebrecht's infrastructure and public services division engages in toll road and bridge operations, energy transmission, and sanitation projects.

Odebrecht was contracted by Tractebel, one of the world's largest independent power producers, to build a new 450 MW, R$640 million hydroelectric power station in the Tocantins Basin. To handle the project, a consortium of four companies was created: two Brazilian construction companies — Odebrecht and Andrade Gutierrez, and two German companies — Voith and Siemens. Odebrecht was the lead builder on the project, while Voith and Siemens provided the equipment and its assembly. The three-year project required the coordination of over 200 project-related people from various organizations located around the globe. More than 2000 documents per month, including emails, drawings, schedules, reports, notes, contracts and legal documents had to be shared, stored and managed. The project required strict management of deadlines in order to avoid contract penalties relating to work delays. It was also necessary to execute a smooth transition among all of the technologies in place at the different companies involved in the project. The project required access to data created by multiple programs, including AutoCAD, MicroStation, Microsoft Word, Microsoft Excel, Lotus, Primavera P3, and Adobe Acrobat.

Considering the above challenges, Odebrecht determined that the best solution would be to implement a web-based project collaboration system. The requirements of the system included the following: project team members should be able to view documents without requiring them to purchase the software applications with which the various documents were created; the system had to be easy to use, and should not require a support and maintenance team; the system had to have robust document and process management system for storing, viewing, tracking and routing of documents, requests for information and other project communications; and the system had to be accessible from any computer with Internet access anywhere in the world.

Odebrecht evaluated a number of project collaboration systems and selected Citadon's ProjectNet (Citadon, 2002) as it fully met the company's requirements. The use of ProjectNet made it possible to control the project from anywhere around the world, at any time. Specific capabilities that ProjectNet brought to the project team included:

- secure access control at the folder, document and form (construction administration forms) level ensuring that users could only view what they were given permission to view;
- Microsoft Outlook style interface that allowed users to utilize their existing knowledge of a simple and intuitive interface;
- organization of documents that matched the specific work processes and document naming conventions of the project;
- viewing, downloading, printing and plotting through the Internet of over 250 document types providing fast and easy access to project documents without the need for the applications in which the documents were created;
- a complete audit trail that captured the actions of users at every level in ProjectNet — file actions such as viewing and downloads were tracked, as well as when somebody responded to a Request for Information (RFI);
- management reports that allowed the project team to track use throughout the system, the number of submittals outstanding, document uploads and downloads, etc.

Project team members were able to find and access documents more quickly and to track the status of documents and communications from any location, 24 hours a day. They did not have to learn how to use the various software applications that the documents were created in as ProjectNet is able to view any kind of document. Odebrecht calculated that they saved over US$5000 per month in reduced document transmittal and printing costs alone. Other savings included reduced software acquisition costs to support viewing of the various document types used on the project. Delays typically associated with document access, review and dissemination were reduced dramatically. Since contractors on site had the most current and accurate information available to them, rework was kept to a minimum. The project is expected to complete in July 2002, six months ahead of schedule.

Author's commentary

The integration of disparate technologies has been a standard challenge associated with cooperative projects as more and more companies use multiple technologies and tools to assist in the ability to work on projects globally with geographically distributed teams. The use of web-based collaboration systems is becoming a common feature of such projects, with companies reporting major benefits in increased productivity, reduced administration costs and accelerated completion times, as demonstrated by Odebrecht in this case study. However, the challenge of developing structured information standards for exchanging schema level data between software applications remains to be fully addressed.

Summary

Good communications and associated interpersonal processes in organizations are important ingredients of organizational effectiveness. Without effective communication, even the most brilliant strategies and best-laid plans may not be successful. Communication is the transfer of messages or information from a sender to a receiver through an appropriate medium, with the message being understood by the receiver. The messages may be in verbal or non-verbal forms or a combination of both and the channels through which communication takes place may be formal or informal or a combination of both. The message may be distorted and affected by noise, which interferes with good communication. In the international context, differences in language and culture are sources of such interference and individuals who operate globally need to be aware and take necessary precautions to minimize such effects.

Traditional approaches to project management are inefficient in handling the dynamic and fluid nature of today's design and construction processes and their associated extended supply network environments, particularly in the international project environment. The growing potential of a variety of electronic media, in particular the Internet, for communications on international projects has been recognized by the global players and is already being exploited. By using the latest Internet-based technologies, companies can create an advanced, fully integrated, collaborative project management framework that provides a long-term solution for success well into the future.

Further reading

Buchanan W. (1997), *Advanced data communications and networks*, Chapman and Hall, London.

Citadon (2002), *Citadon, Inc.*, San Francisco, http//www.citadon.com.

Chu C. (1998). *The chinese mind games*, AMC Publishing, Beaverton, Oreg.

ebXML (2002), *Electronic business XML*, http//www.ebXML.org, accessed November 2002.

eConstruct (2002), *eConstruction European Commission funded project*, http//www.econstruct.org, accessed November 2002.

Kennedy J. and Everest A. (1991), *Put diversity in context*, Personnel Journal, pp. 50–54.

Kirpalani, V. H. (1985), *International marketing*, Chap 4, Random House, New York.

IAI (2002), *International Alliance for Interoperability*, http://cig.bre.co.uk/iai_uk.

IAI-NA (2002), *International alliance for interoperability — North America Chapter*, http://www.iai-na.org/aecxml/mission.php, accessed November 2002.

ISO (1992) ISO TC184: 'STEP Part 1: Overview and Fundamental Principles', *Industrial automation systems and integration product data representation and exchange*, ISO DIS 10303-1, International Standards Organisation (ISO), Geneva, Switzerland.

ISO (1997) *ISO TC184/SC4: 'STEP Part 11: The EXPRESS language reference manual'*, ISO 10303-11, International Standards Organisation (ISO), Geneva, Switzerland.

Pace R. W. (1983), *Organisational communication: foundations for human resource development*, pp. 56–57, Prentice-Hall, Englewood Cliffs, N.J.

Peters T. and Austin N. (1985), *A passion for excellence: the leadership difference*, Random House, New York.

Peters T. J. and Waterman Jr R. H. (1982), *In search of excellence*, Harper and Row, New York.

Stallworthy E. A. & Khardanda O. P. (1985), *International construction and the role of the project manager*, Gower, London.

Chapter 11

Project management

Introduction

The activities of international companies specializing in construction normally break down into those offering consultancy, specialist design services and expertise, and construction companies who specialize in managing the construction process and realizing built facilities or infrastructure projects. It is usual for larger organizations to offer the complete range of services and expertise. Hence, consultant services may be independent or integrated as part of a construction company. Other companies involved will be suppliers of materials and construction products, plant and equipment suppliers. Specialist subcontracting companies will form a major part of the construction supply chain and will involve electrical, mechanical and other engineering specialisms alongside other specialists, e.g. piling and groundwork, steel fabrication, rain-screen walling, finishings and equipment. Construction project management is specifically concerned with the management and control of all project activities from inception to the final completion. This will include design, procurement, mobilization and commissioning.

The main task of construction project management is to deliver the completed project in the most effective and efficient manner. The approach to be taken will depend on corporate strategy and the amount of business infrastructure that the firm has in place in the country where the project is to be undertaken. At one extreme will be a newly appointed project manager who will be expected to deliver the project using a combination of home, local and third country resources, together with support from head office located in the home country. At the other will be a well-established indigenous company, wholly or partly owned, which will provide the necessary logistics, infrastructure and support to run the entire project.

The procurement system and associated contractual arrangements adopted will also have a large influence on project strategy and the necessary actions to deliver the project.

This chapter is concerned with the necessary decisions, actions and arrangements that are required to be put in place and executed in the fulfilment of the project. Account will be taken of the location and environment within which the project will be completed.

Project management

Construction projects are temporary activities with a defined start and finish, normally with durations ranging from six months to five years. Each project will have its own unique circumstances brought about by the nature and location of the site, together with its type, complexity and size. These circumstances raise special problems since projects usually require to be mobilized as quickly as possible to perform the tasks involved, after which the temporary project infrastructure will need to be dismantled prior to withdrawal from the site. Although many construction companies have their own systems and procedures, these will very probably require adaptation to meet the special circumstances of individual projects. The learning curve for project managers is therefore steep and this places a great deal of emphasis on experience and 'know-how', since there is limited chance to recover if fundamental mistakes are made. A policy of 'right first time' coupled with tight monitoring and control are important prerequisites to a successful project outcome.

Normally, projects involve many different organizations covering design, management and logistics, specialist services, products, materials, plant and equipment. It is therefore likely that major projects will require complex management involving a high degree of coordination and dynamic decision-making to maintain adequate control. The systems and procedures selected must have the capacity to deal with a wide variety of situations as well as unexpected events that will require skilful improvization. This implies that there must be inherent flexibility without the loss of the form or structure necessary to facilitate effective decision-making and control. These dynamics may result in difficulties and shortcomings that are outside the boundary of the project and this places pressure on project management to mitigate adverse effects by timely and correct actions. Failings in project management often arise from lack of clarity and definition of project systems and organization structure compounded by inadequate planning and control. There may also be potential for interpersonal problems and conflicts where leadership is weak and a poor level of teamwork exists.

The criterion for project success depends mainly on satisfying well defined needs articulated by the client and the anticipation of associated desires and preferences that may not be formalized in the normal manner. Figure 10.1 illustrates the interaction between the client and the project management team, which should be adequate and continuous from start to finish of the project. The client has an important role to play in clearly stating requirements from the outset and then working closely with the project manager and the project team to accommodate necessary changes and problems as the project progresses to its ultimate conclusion.

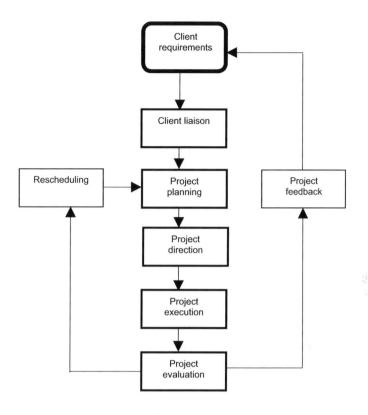

Figure 11.1: Client–project team interaction

Defining the project requirements

The process commences with the client's brief, which should be clear and concise. If this is not the case then steps should be taken to acquire missing information, decisions and directives. A complete and well-founded project brief will serve to reduce the number of costly changes which may be necessary later in the project to accommodate client needs that have been overlooked. The expert client will be used to briefing the construction team and will have the necessary expert staff to make this task relatively easy. Clients who seldom procure construction projects will not have the benefit of in-house experts and will either rely on the services of an independent client representative or will depend entirely on the project manager for advice, supported by the construction team. The selection and appointment of the design team can progress before or after the detailed brief is established. Much will depend on the procurement route selected by the client. It may be highly desirable that the principal designer is appointed before the brief is developed so that design expertise can be taken into account. Armed with this information, the process of feasibility can commence. Options possessing the capability to meet the needs of the client should be explored by identifying issues, constraints, opportunities and assumptions. These should be carefully evaluated to enable a preferred option to be selected. A concept design should then be prepared together with a project cost plan and budget. The concept design will provide the solution in terms of architecture and structure, together with internal design. At this stage, initial consideration should be given to the manufacturing and construction methods to be utilized. Value judgements should be made alongside risk assessment to ensure that the best options have been selected.

The client should then be asked to scrutinize and evaluate the proposal, which in turn will activate a series of iterations that should result in the adoption and approval of the concept design. This is essentially a cycling process as shown in Figure 11.2. The concept design will overlap with the remaining two design stages which in turn will overlap to a greater or lesser degree depending on the speed required of the design process and the ability of the design team to coordinate and control their activities in unison (Figure 11.3).

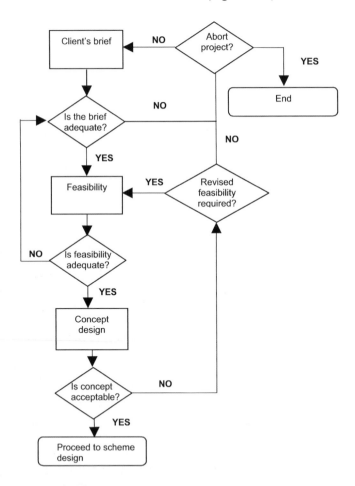

Figure 11.2: Feasibility and concept design cycling process

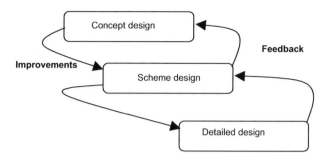

Figure 11.3: Design stage interaction

The scheme design

The scheme design involves developing the general arrangements to ensure good design coordination between the specialist members of the design team. Such matters as aesthetic appearance, cost, safety, quality, sustainability and life cycle performance should be considered. More detailed planning and integration regarding off-site manufacture, on-site construction and materials will be dealt with at this stage. The scheme design should also be accompanied by a project master plan, proposals for resource procurement, construction programme and method statement. The detailed design will involve the preparation of production information. Consultants, suppliers and contractors will become involved in design detailing of all the project's components and plans will be finalized for manufacture and assembly and the supply of materials. Figure 10.3 illustrates the overlap and interaction between the three stages of design outlined above.

Ongoing throughout the design process will be the preparation of specifications, schedules and other documentation required by the procurement route selected. The development of the design must be in accordance with client requirements and statutory approvals. The design should be harmoniously integrated with legal, cultural, social, political and environmental considerations. Local knowledge and expertise will play a large part in ensuring the appropriateness of the design and gaining the necessary approvals before physical construction work can commence. The largest and most successful global construction consultants have set up regional offices that employ competent local architects and engineers to provide a comprehensive and informed design service. They will have direct knowledge of local conditions and the availability of skills, manufacturing potential and suitable materials, which will be invaluable in the determination of the best solution for clients.

Selection of the preferred procurement route

Much will depend on whether the client chooses to opt for a consultant or a contractor-led solution. In the former case, the principal consultant will take charge of managing the development of the brief and the design. The principal consultant may act in the role of project manager who will be responsible for advising on the appointment of the design team and the procurement route to be selected. Alternatively, the consultant may be a global multidisciplinary practice that provides a fully integrated project management and design service. Where a contractor-led solution is preferred, then the contractor will be responsible for the total process involving design, procurement, construction and commissioning and in some cases post-occupation facility management.

In the event of extremely large and complex projects it is normal practice to set up a joint venture between consultants and contractors who agree to pool expertise and resources expressly for the purpose of designing and constructing the project. Great care will be necessary in establishing the joint venture agreement, which must set out clearly the demarcation of roles and responsibilities between the participants. The appointment of a capable project manager and support staff will be a prerequisite to a successful outcome.

Development of a project strategy and method of execution

A fundamental point of strategy concerns the extent to which operations will be directed from head office in the home country and the commensurate delegation of authority to the local project manager. Where a company is well established in the country concerned it is more likely that services and support will be available from a local office or from a joint venture partner. In the case of a single project, the only option will be to control operations directly from the site using services and support from head office. In this case, the appointment of a local agent and/or an adviser will also need careful consideration. Decisions will also need to be taken concerning the use of expatriate staff and the number of local and third country staff to be employed and at what level.

A key factor will be the strategy to be adopted in the appointment of the project supply chain and the extent to which it can be effectively integrated to provide harmonious and continuous production on site. A wholly local supply chain would be ideal, assuming that the required quality and range of goods and services are available and the price is competitive. Invariably, this will not be possible and consultants, contractors, component suppliers and equipment suppliers will need to be engaged from the home country and third countries as required. This is especially the case in LDCs where there may be limited local expertise and suitable resources. Under such circumstances, extra effort will be required to communicate effectively to overcome language barriers, cultural differences and work ethics, alongside variations in working practice and procedure. There is no substitute for experience and expertise across all of these areas, since additional pressure will be placed on the systems to be used and the organization structure selected to monitor and control the project.

Project mobilization

Project size and complexity and location will also have a fundamental influence on the procurement of resources and arrangements for timely delivery to site of the correct quantity and specification of resources. A full analysis and evaluation is required of the geographic location and the environment within which the project will be constructed. The outcome will need to be appraised and the logistics necessary to deliver a construction project effectively according to specified objectives and targets would need to be established. The peculiarities associated with legal, social, political and cultural requirements must be fully evaluated and taken into account.

Environment of the project

Projects located in an urban environment with ready access to good roads, services and adequate supplies of skilled labour, equipment, materials, components and communication systems are far easier to deal with than sites in remote areas with difficult access and no services. The logistics involved in setting up a self-sufficient site with the necessary infrastructure to support an adequate working environment and living accommodation for the workforce requires careful planning and organization, since enabling works are often extensive on large projects and are a prerequisite to work commencing on site.

Where materials, components, fabrications, plant and equipment need to be imported, then sufficient time will be necessary to procure, ship and import such items to arrive at the site in time to facilitate the construction programme. Shipping delays, bad weather and port congestion are just a few of the innumerable difficulties that can occur with the potential to disrupt the project.

Local weather conditions should be evaluated throughout the duration of the project. Note should be taken of special constraints imposed by seasonable factors such as monsoons, extremely hot weather and difficult sea conditions and, where necessary, allowances should be made in the master construction programme.

Local knowledge is also invaluable in the interpretation of legal requirements, custom and practice, which might be quite different to their initial appearences. Prior knowledge and experience of local cultural etiquette will also be helpful in smoothing the way for business decisions and the management of local employees. Where a local office does not exist, arrangements will need to be made with local suppliers and steps should be taken to make contact with local officials concerning statutory requirements and obligations.

Determination of site infrastructure

The provision of temporary site infrastructure is essential for construction projects and is normally referred to as enabling works that must be completed before construction can start. These works may be extensive and therefore should be commenced in sufficient time to facilitate the early completion of the project. Enabling works can be divided into the following categories:

- access roads, helicopter pad, landing strip, means of defining the site boundary internal working space and storage areas and parking areas for vehicles;
- provision of services including electricity, water, sewage disposal and communications equipment — each of these services will require temporary distribution systems around the site, which will vary as construction progresses;
- site accommodation in the form of offices, canteens, washrooms, lockers, toilets, first aid and welfare facilities, common rooms and living accommodation;
- site lighting and security systems;
- facilities for maintaining and servicing equipment;
- secure storage areas for materials, components and equipment.

Establishment of the systems and organization structure to be used

The key appointment will be that of the construction manager who will be based on the site and will be responsible for providing the direction and leadership necessary to physically complete the project successfully. The construction manager will undertake full responsibility for the mobilization of the project including the establishment of the systems and organization structure to ensure that the management control processes are appropriate to the needs of the project.

Construction staff appointments will need to be made in accordance with company policy, moreover it will necessary to undertake the early appointment of those site staff who will be responsible for the procurement of the necessary infrastructure and resources to mobilize the project and progress it through the initial stages of construction. According to company policy, some of this work will be undertaken by staff based at the head or local office, prior to the necessary site-based appointments. The employment of expatriate staff tends to be expensive and, where practical, steps should be taken to recruit local staff who have the necessary qualifications and experience, or who can be trained to undertake the tasks involved. Typically, appointments will include site managers and supervisors, procurement staff, site engineers, cost engineers, planning engineers, administrators and clerical staff.

Companies experienced in working overseas will be likely to have policies concerning staffing levels and these will need consideration and adaptation to the specific circumstances of the project. Policies relating to the establishment of systems and procedures that harmonize with corporate systems will make the task of establishing an efficient site office that much easier, given that some adjustment may be required to meet local needs. In the case of companies with little or no experience of working in foreign countries, this will be a process of breaking new ground and will require much more thought and effort. Under these circumstances, the tendency will therefore be to rely on experienced expatriate staff until more knowledge is gained about local conditions

Underlying these processes will be systematic planning and steps towards building an effective project team.

Increasing client requirements associated with project complexity and faster delivery times have emphasized the need for more formalized and better-organized project start-up activities. It is very important that a project commences on a sound basis, since mistakes made early in the project tend to be difficult to rectify and, as a consequence, the adverse effects are often not fully recovered by the time that the project reaches its conclusion.

Managing and controlling the project

During the mobilization period, consideration should be given to the control requirements of the project and the manner in which it is to be managed. To achieve project efficiency it will be necessary to accept and implement methods and concepts that have the potential to provide efficient working practices that eliminate duplication of effort and minimize waste. The following stem from corporate policy, but where they are effectively applied they will impact on the efficient delivery of projects.

- Total quality control (TQC) requires an approach to management that improves the effectiveness and flexibility of a business as a whole by ensuring that quality targets are attained and that waste or non-productive effort is eliminated. This requires an integrated approach that examines and evaluates the interactions and contributions made by all parts of the business. Those found to be effective would be retained and improved, while those considered to be less effective would be amended or eliminated altogether. The dynamic process of continual improvement aimed at meeting customer requirements and maintaining competitiveness is a powerful tool in the quest for improved quality and greater efficiency.
- The concept of 'right first time' aims to eliminate errors and misunderstanding that cause disruption and confusion leading to waste. At the heart of this philosophy is attention to planning and detail, such that potential problems are identified and removed from the system, to be followed by constant monitoring and, if necessary, actions to achieve the desired outcome. This approach is closely associated with the concept of zero defects where it is expected that the project will be delivered free of defects associated with the construction process.
- 'Just in time' (JIT) management principles are directed to ensuring that the right services, materials and components are procured to meet the planned and specified quality requirements of the project at the right time and without waste. JIT uses a variety of techniques including value analysis, flow processing, method study and process control.
- Cellular technology (CT) sometimes referred to as 'quality circles' concerns the implementation of the concept of self-directed teams. Under these circumstances the teams are set tasks by management;

however, it is left with the team to develop its own culture and working practices.

It is the role of the project manager to interpret the needs of the project in relation to the aims of the company and its corporate strategy and the needs of the client. These will be further modified by the environmental and cultural needs imposed by the disposition and international location of the project. It is therefore clear that the knowledge and experience of a project manager who is familiar with international construction practice will be a key element in the successful delivery of the project. The following sections are intended to provide more detail about the prime tasks and requirements involved.

Creation of the project team

The overall management of a major overseas construction project will be the responsibility of the project manager. A person with a variety of backgrounds can undertake this role. Moreover, the individual appointed should have adequate management skills and a dynamic attitude, together with a knowledge and experience of international construction in order to deliver the project effectively to the quality standard, on time and within budget. Leadership and the ability to command respect are the key requirements of the role and involve the creation of a sense of harmony and team spirit as people join the project team. The motivation of team members and a good sense of judgement and fairness in the resolution of conflicts will reinforce the need for the project team to work together towards common goals laid down by the project programme.

The maintenance of good communication between the design team and the construction team is essential and potential problems should be identified early and resolved before they have the chance to cause disruption to the progress of the project. It will therefore be an important part of the project manager's role to ensure that adequate communication is taking place between all members of the project team.

The project will have a control boundary within which the project manager's influence should be paramount. All projects, by definition, work as open systems that draw on knowledge, information and resources from home, host and third country sources. This will require a high level of planning and organization to increase the likelihood of obtaining relevant inputs to the project when required. Major projects normally require a broad range of input from the supply chain and, since it is seldom the case that matters go entirely to plan, it is essential that adequate monitoring and control should take place. Because of the dynamic nature of the project supply chain, the approach to monitoring should be one of checking and seeking out likely problems and then solving them before they have time to make an impact.

The role of the project manager is generally interpreted within this text as the delivery of the project according to the aims and objectives set by the client and covers the oversight of the total construction project process. The project manager may be employed by the client or by a construction company responsible for the total process. In both cases the contractor will appoint a construction manager who will directly control the construction process and will work in close liaison the project manager and the design team. The following sections cover the whole range of activities, but the reader will need to make allowance for the distinction between these roles.

Project planning and control

Planning and control represent the core functions necessary for successful project management and should be accompanied by well-formulated and adequate procedures installed at the inception of the project. The planning and control cycle shown in Figure 11.4 represents a dynamic process commencing with the creation of a project plan based on a methodology determined to deliver the project in an efficient and timely manner. Usually, the overall project programme consisting of major project activities will be broken down into a hierarchy of more detailed construction programmes that will provide time schedules for specific tasks. These will be periodically monitored to determine progress, and variations between planned and actual progress will be recorded. Progress gains and shortfalls will be analysed and reports will be prepared, together with forecasts and recommendations for remedial action as necessary. Ultimately, it will be the project manager's responsibility to institute the necessary management decisions and actions to ensure that the project will be completed within the scheduled time. This process will operate through the full time span of the project.

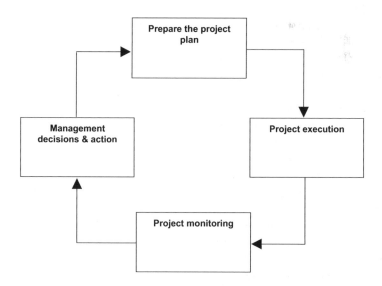

Figure 11.4: The project planning and monitoring cycle

The core control documents will be the master project schedule and its associated method statement. These provide the productivity benchmark and determine the construction method and sequence to be used set against a time-scale covering project commencement to handover. The master schedule will be broken down into a hierarchy of sub-programmes to provide for more detailed control of the project. These will have a progressively shorter time horizon and the work breakdown will consist of more detailed activities. Figure 11.5 shows three levels of breakdown, namely stage, monthly and weekly. Depending on the size of project it may not be necessary to use all levels.

The production of detailed work programmes will assist the following project objectives:
- execution of the work in an efficient and safe manner;
- achievement of quality standards;
- performance within budget;
- achievement of time targets; and
- coordination and effective utilization of resources.

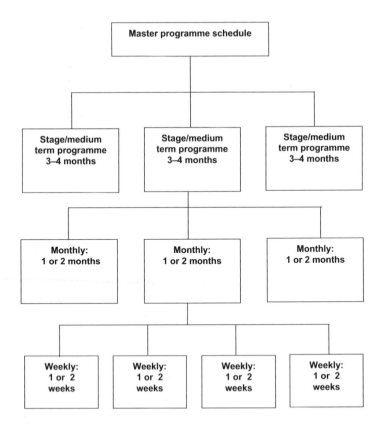

Figure 11.5: Project master programme and its hierarchy of short-term programmes for close project control

The project programme will be supplemented by detailed schedules that will be tied into the target dates specified for project activities. Design information, specifications, instructions and approvals will be required in advance of work commencing on site. Where long lead times exist, for example to enable the design and manufacture of specialist components, then sufficient time must be allowed in advance of work commencing on site. Failure to recognize such requirements may lead to unnecessary project delays and disruption to the natural working sequence of the project. Information requirement schedules will be necessary to determine the dates when drawings and specifications will be required by the site team. The schedules should also account for the need to manage and control the pre-delivery of materials and components, as well as the pre-site activities of subcontractors.

It is normal to use project management software to create project programmes and to produce associated control schedules. The majority of software is based on network analysis and will provide well designed schedules in time-scaled network (linked bar chart) or precedence network form. Programmes can be updated and reproduced for control and archive purposes. Some software provides resource scheduling and levelling, together with budgetary control reports and predictions using earned value analysis. More sophisticated packages will include risk and sensitivity analysis.

The prime benefits to be derived from effective project planning are:

- efficient working methods and construction sequences;
- the foundation for the determination of information requirements;
- a system of effective monitoring and control of resources;
- the facility to anticipate problems in advance and encourage early remedial actions, therefore avoiding unnecessary extra costs;
- effective budgeting and cost control;
- safe working methods and practices, and
- a framework for the assessment of risk.

Communication of project information between the design and construction teams and between contractors, suppliers and specialists can be effectively achieved using the Internet, and it is now common for project management software to incorporate facilities for email and transmitting project documentation. This aspect is especially important where members of the project supply chain will be based in the host, home and third countries.

Building the project supply chain

The creation of the project supply chain is one of the most important tasks concerning project management. The prime aim will be to appoint competent consultants, suppliers and contractors who understand the requirements of the project and can work in harmony with other members of the project team to deliver the completed project to the client satisfactorily. Prior knowledge and experience of working together is an important advantage. The growth in the use of partnering has brought about trust and non-adversarial management that encourages long-term teamwork and provides the potential for extension over multiple projects.

The execution of construction projects in foreign countries makes it much more difficult to build complete teams that can move from one project to another. The specific requirements of working in a particular country may require the appointment of new members of the supply chain who will need to be properly inducted into the working practices to be adopted by the project. Projects undertaken in certain regions of the world may preclude the involvement of a long-term supply chain partner and, as a consequence, the necessity to search for and appoint a suitable replacement. It is therefore important to construct the supply chain most carefully, and new appointments need to be thoroughly vetted to ensure that they can deliver the performance and quality required.

Procuring goods and services will normally be in accordance with procedures laid down by company strategy. Decentralization of the purchasing and procurement function from head office and the appointment of local staff with devolved responsibility may be a necessity. As a general rule, it will be an advantage to centralize procurement of resources obtained from third countries and where it is more likely that advantages can be accrued from on-going partnerships. In the event that it is necessary and desirable to acquire goods and services in the host country, then there may be a good argument for appointing a local procurement officer who would be responsible for advising on local appointments and for liaising with local suppliers. An alternative solution would be for more devolved responsibility to be given to an expatriate who would manage a locally appointed team of junior staff.

The price of goods and services should never be the only criterion for the placing of contracts and orders. Consideration should be given to design and product quality, performance, conformity to international standards and codes and workmanship. Where a supplier or contractor is new, then previous work should be subjected to close scrutiny and references should be taken up. Where necessary, manufacturing facilities should be visited and staff should be interviewed to establish their competence and their ability to work with the rest of the supply chain. It may be desirable to insist on performance bonds in case of default. Such requirements could be relaxed once a good working relationship has been established.

When suppliers and contractors are invited to provide quotations or to negotiate for work they should be provided with full information and documentation. This will avoid disputes and misunderstandings, which could prove to be detrimental. Any changes in requirements or specifications should be notified immediately to ensure that all factors are taken into account.

Organization of the site

Prior to taking possession of the site, it will be necessary to plan the site layout within the boundaries defined by the client. Reference should be made to the project method statement and the master schedule to establish the most economical working methods to be adopted as the work progresses. Where security is an issue or the public needs to be excluded from the site for safety reasons, then it will be essential to erect hoardings and fences with strategically located access gates and check-points. The objective should be to ensure continuity of the work and the effective coordination of activities. The site layout should provide the best possible working conditions and a safe working environment for all site personnel.

The physical nature of the site and the extent and nature of construction work will have the largest influence on the methods and work sequences to be adopted. Within the site boundary it will be necessary to create areas for the safe storage of materials and, where required, space for site fabrication of components and assemblies. The location of batching plants, cranes, hoists and forklift staging will need to be carefully considered in relation to working space and transportation routes within the site.

Site accommodation will provide for offices, canteens, rest rooms, first aid facilities, toilets and, where required, living accommodation. Space will also be necessary for subcontractors to establish their own compounds for offices and the storage of their own materials and components.

The solution to the site layout should be derived using all the information and facts available. Materials handling should be kept to a minimum by employing motion economy principles, such that materials should be delivered and stored in areas that allow for optimal movement economy to the point of fixture or installation. The use of method study techniques such as flow process diagrams, multiple activity charts and simulation software can be extremely helpful in establishing the most efficient layout. Comparative analysis of alternatives will also be helpful in deciding the final selection of layout.

Project management and communication

The project manager will be ultimately responsible for building an efficient and effective site management team, capable of integrating consultants, contractors and suppliers from different countries and cultures. It is therefore important that the project is well organized and planned from the outset and strong management practices should be adopted to deal with problems quickly. Management decisions and actions should be transparent and, in the main, they should be judged to be fair and even-handed by all concerned.

Communication will play a key part in the delivery of good project management and nothing should be left to chance. Perception and understanding should be continually checked to eliminate potentially detrimental and harmful effects leading to disruption and discontent. Language problems will need to be minimized by the use of competent translators and the use of universal communication through drawings, sketches and diagrams. Where the project manager and other senior staff have competent multiple language skills then this can be extremely beneficial.

Adequate liaison and communication must take place post-appointment of supply chain members and pre-commencement on site. The operation of JIT principles will depend heavily on sufficient liaison to ensure that contractors' and suppliers' commencement dates and deliveries conform to the requirements of the project programme. Facilities should be ready on site to enable contractors to immediately commence work and integrate with the work of other contractors.

A key feature of the project control process will be site production meetings. These may be stratified according to the needs of the whole project or its component parts. In this manner team meetings can be limited in size and have an objective agenda that can be more easily related to the physical construction of the project. The purpose of such meetings should be to examine performance and progress, to determine problems and shortfalls, and to seek agreed solutions regarding future actions. Project monitoring and rescheduling will provide a key element in the communication of instructions and the targets to be achieved. Short-term plans can be drawn up using layouts of the relevant parts of the site, which can be annotated, and colour coded to indicate the progress to be achieved by various contractors working in close proximity to each other.

It is important that the project manager maintains adequate discipline and control over the conduct of the project, and vital for site safety that breaches of the established rules should be quickly and effectively dealt with to avoid contempt. A major difficulty is that different cultures will have different values and attitudes towards the well-being of individuals and, in extreme cases, the value of life. Hence, safety standards applied on the project must be properly communicated from the outset and rigorously implemented. This may involve the imposition of fines and, for the worst breaches, dismissal from the site.

Project budgets and financial control

Formulation of the project budget

The preparation of a project budget derives from two principal sources, namely the project estimate and the project master schedule, which provides the work breakdown structure (WBS). Budgeted costs are allocated to project activities and the distribution of expenditure over the time-span of each activity is determined to provide weekly/monthly expenditure forecasts. The accumulation of activity expenditure occurring for each project time period will provide the budgeted expenditure forecast for the project. The accumulation of periodic expenditure normally produces an 's' curve against which income can be budgeted and the difference between the two represents the cash requirement to fund the project (see Figure 11.6).

Allocation of costs and cost coding

It is normal practice to group project activities to cost centres that represent major parts of the project, e.g. foundations, structural frame, Grid A1:B2, or they may be individual buildings or facilities, e.g. pump house, Building A. Each cost centre may be allocated a budget, which in turn will be broken down, as necessary, into component resources, e.g. labour, materials, plant. Costs will be recorded against each cost centre and in this manner periodic profitability reports can be generated for each cost centre to provide control information for the project management team.

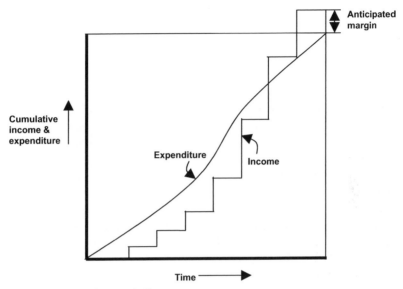

Figure 11.6: Project cash flow

Project cost control

The majority of project management software packages incorporate a cost control module that makes provision for preparing a budget based on cost centres and will incorporate the valuation of work completed which can be set against actual expenditure. In this manner, progress and profitability can be determined. Software will also accommodate omissions or additions to the project in the form of variations. Project management should be provided with periodic financial reports to assist with early remedial decision-making. The importance of adequate feedback systems for the estimation of future work should not be overlooked.

Cost optimization

Where the project programme requires to be compressed, it may be beneficial to examine the most economical way in which this can be achieved. The technique of cost optimization utilizes critical path analysis to determine those activities on the critical path that are cheapest to expedite. Time reduction along the critical path will eventually use all the spare time on non-critical paths and therefore they also become critical. Further time reduction will require buying time from more than one critical path. As this process continues, the time reduction becomes more expensive and activities will progressively reach their crash times where further time reduction becomes impossible. Eventually, the point is reached where no further time reduction is possible and the project is then at its ultimate crash time. A reduction in project time will save fixed overheads and in the early stages of the optimization process the cost to expedite may be less than the overhead saved. Hence, there will be an optimum time in which to complete the project (see Figure 11.7).

Earned value analysis

Earned value analysis (EVA) is a technique used for the evaluation and financial analysis of projects throughout their life cycle (Lockyer & Gordon, 1991). The first task is to create a planned budget known as the budgeted cost of work scheduled (BCWS). Essentially, this will normally take the form of an 's' curve derived from project activities. The work as it progresses is costed according to the original budget and at any point in time during the project the budgeted cost of work performed (BCWP) can be determined. The difference between BCWP and BCWS represents the schedule variance (SV) and the ratio created (BCWP/BCWS) provides the schedule performance index (SPI). A negative SV and an SPI ratio of less than 1, shows that the project is behind schedule, as defined by the budget. By dividing the original project duration by the SPI, an estimate of the revised project duration can be obtained (see Figure 11.8).

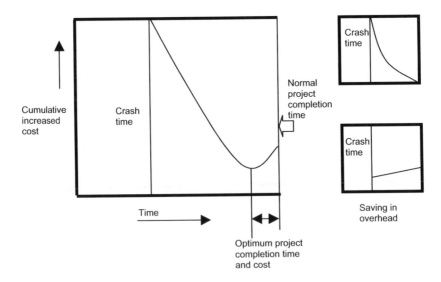

Figure 11.7: Project cost optimization

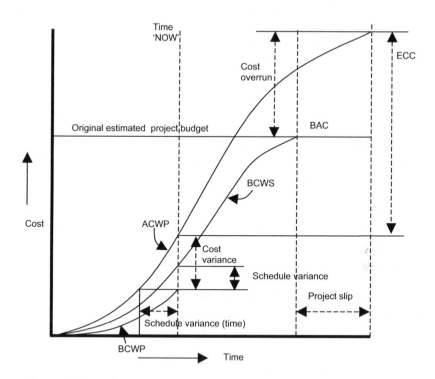

Figure 11.8: Project earned value analysis

The actual cost of work performed (ACWP) is derived at any point during the project scheduled time from the project accounting system. The cost variance (CV) can be determined by the difference between the BCWP and the ACWP. Further, the ratio analysis (BCWP/ACWP) provides the cost performance index (CPI). A negative CV and a CPI of less than 1 indicates that the project is subject to a cost overrun. Conversely, a positive CV and a CPI greater than 1 shows that the project cost performance is better than expected.

It is also possible to determine the estimated cost to completion (ECC) and by adding the ACWP the forecast of the project completion cost (FCC) is obtained. EVA is therefore a straightforward and consistent method for the evaluation of project performance and it allows for comparisons between projects utilizing the project indices SPI and CPI.

Safety, health and welfare

Construction is potentially a dangerous and risk-prone activity brought about by the need to transport and lift heavy loads and the need to work at height. The process itself is dynamic and involves continual physical change and movement. These are the circumstances under which the unforeseen occurs and the risk of accidents is high. The need to concentrate on achieving production targets often

247

means that workers fail to spot warning signs and potentially dangerous situations. A long track record exists throughout the world confirming construction as one of the most dangerous occupations, and global statistics point towards a high incidence of serious injury and death.

The employer has a duty to maintain a safe and healthy working environment, which should be built into the human resource management cycle. There will, of course, be legislation governing the implementation of safety policy and practice but this tends to vary considerably in comprehensiveness, quality, implementation and enforcement. In AICs, acceptable safety standards and enforcement are high compared with NICs and LDCs where standards are more likely to be flouted in the face of increased productivity and the payment of incentives.

The construction company must comply fully with local safety legislation; however, such requirements should be compared with the requirements of company safety and occupational health policies. If there is an apparent shortfall then action should be taken to comply with legislation and steps will be required to inform and train site staff in safe working practices and procedures.

Occupational health relates to illness which can be directly attributable to the environment of the workplace. Repetitive strain injury, job stress, sick building syndrome, asbestosis and back problems can all be attributed to health disorders created in the workplace. There may also be indirect consequences which result in alcoholism and drug abuse. The implementation of good working practice and the provision of employee counselling will considerably help in all of these cases. A multi-cultural and ethnic workforce will make this task especially difficult and considerable effort will be required to achieve acceptable and consistent standards of occupational health.

It is the responsibility of the project manager to adopt and implement safer systems of work. This effectively means that the construction methods to be adopted should not place workers in danger. Risk assessment should be undertaken to recognize potential dangers and steps should be taken to mitigate risk by the provision of guard rails, safety nets, fail-safe mechanisms, protective clothing, etc.

There should be a strong management commitment to the implementation of safe working practice through health and safety committees, regular inspection, comprehensive training and the imposition of fines and penalties for breaches of safety codes.

Successful implementation of health and safety policy will mean that the workforce will remain in good shape and costs associated with time off work will be largely avoided. A safe site will encourage good morale and a sense of well-being which should be reflected in increased productivity, which will more than offset the cost of health and safety provision.

Commissioning and handover

Commissioning

As the project nears completion, steps must be taken to benchmark and test the systems within the building. HVAC systems, transportation systems, water supply, power, lighting, sprinklers, alarms, lighting, communications equipment cleaning systems and welfare facilities will all need to be tested, adjusted and balanced to produce the desired specification performance. Operating manuals will need to be prepared for the client's facility manager and training must be conducted for personnel involved. Safety in the use of the building should be a major consideration in the preparation of documentation.

Incomplete items of construction work and finishings will need to be logically finalized prior to snagging inspections to ensure that the work is complete and accords to the drawings and specifications. The project will need to be cleared of debris and residue construction materials before being thoroughly and systematically cleaned.

Handover and withdrawal

Withdrawal from the site will require the removal of all plant and equipment, together with storage compounds, temporary roads, hoardings, gantries, staging and the like. Landscaping, walkways, roads, external lighting, security systems and fencing will be completed.

On final completion, the project should be handed over in its entirety to the client. In the case of PFI projects, then responsibility will be transferred to the part of the organization that will be responsible for the management and maintenance of the built facility over the agreed concessionary period. It may be the case that a project is handed over in phases, in which case, the above procedure should apply to each phase. There may be exceptions were agreement may be reached to complete certain parts of the project after handover due to unavoidable circumstances. These should be fully noted and agreed.

Following handover, defects will be rectified without cost for a period determined by the contract. In certain cases, a contractor may prefer to maintain a maintenance facility on site for the duration of this period.

Case study 11.1: Jamnagar refinery and petrochemicals complex, India, Bechtel

In 1995, an Alliance was created between Reliance Petroleum Limited, the largest private company in India, and Bechtel to undertake the engineering, procurement, project management and construction of its US$ 5.4 billion Jamnagar refinery.

Bechtel worked in close association with Reliance to produce the designs and procure steel and other relevant materials for the construction of the complex. By adopting this approach, Bechtel was able to award contracts to Indian contractors, thereby providing technological efficiency while taking advantage of the lower cost Indian labour force. As the project progressed, Bechtel substantially increased project management staff by the introduction of 30 senior personnel and set about transferring technology and expertise to Reliance engineers. This process increased Indian management expertise and eventually Bechtel was able to withdraw significant numbers of engineers and management staff. The increasing use of Indian staff on site resulted in lower costs, improved performance and a growing confidence that the joint team could build the world's largest refinery in 24 months with a capacity of 27 million metric tonnes per annum, one-third of India's refining needs. The project also included the world's largest paraxylene production facility, the largest captive power plant in India and the country's largest private sector port.

The scale of this project required that teams of engineers in London, Houston and New Delhi worked shifts around the clock to produce more than 80,000 engineering drawings that guided construction. The process was made more efficient by utilizing electronic communication via the Internet. Engineering drawings and documents could be transferred instantly between multiple offices and suppliers. Three-dimensional models were expeditiously reviewed and transmitted from London to Reliance HQ in Bombay and then to the site.

The multicultural site team had to cope with huge quantities of materials such as steel, concrete, fibre optic and material cable. Over 80 shiploads of refinery equipment were imported and cargo-handling facilities had to be constructed for this purpose. Temporary housing on site had to be provided for 60,000 construction workers and a training centre was constructed to increase the expertise of the local workforce and staff in accordance with the requirements of the project.

The project team was called upon to be innovative in finding solutions such as pouring the reinforced concrete pipe rack frames in situ rather than using precast concrete. This approach achieved considerable cost savings. Despite being disrupted by the biggest cyclone to hit the area for a century, the project began phasing operations in June 1999.

In the first half of the fiscal year 2001, the estimated downstream economic activity fed by the Jamnagar refinery complex was US$ 26 billion, more than 6% of India's GDP. In 2001, the refinery was expected to generate US$ 850 million in foreign exchange and it was also expected to save US$ 1.2 billion through import substitution.

On 26 January 2001, the Gujarat earthquake — whose epicenter was 110 km away — did very little damage to the refinery complex and within one week it was able to recommence full production.

Author's commentary

This huge project has a number of interesting and relevant features concerning the mobilization, infrastructure requirements and the decision to implement a localization policy to employ Indian site staff and contractors. Moreover, the most important aspect was the close alliance developed between Bechtel and the client Reliance Petroleum Limited who took an active and major part in delivering project success.

Bechtel were successful in transferring 'know how' to local engineers and contractors through staff development and training carried out on site in a dynamic manner to achieve the 24-month construction schedule. The vast infrastructure facilities required to handle imported equipment, together with temporary housing on site for 60,000 personnel and the provision of training and welfare facilities are a prime example of the enabling and mobilization work necessary for a project of this magnitude.

The control and transmission of drawings and other documents via the Internet, the building of multicultural teamwork and the generation of cost-saving innovative solutions are examples of best practice intended to benefit all concerned.

Case study 11.2: A new wharf for the Port of Monaco, Dragados S.A., Spain

At the end of the summer in 2002, Grupo Dragados completed the world's largest floating dock, intended to extend the Port of Condamine in Monaco. The total project will cost 150 million Euros and, when complete, will double Monaco's mooring space for boats and will provide parking for over 400 cars.

The 350 m long x 44 m wide and 28 m deep floating dock, covering 6 hectares and weighing 160,000 tonnes deadweight, will incorporate 43,000 m^3 of concrete and 13,500 tonnes of steel.

Port Condamine is Monaco's main port, which was completed in 1914. Today, the Port of Monaco attracts a large number of people and boats; however, it does not have facilities for cruise ships, hence visitors have to stop in Nice and travel to Monaco by road. The project has generated a great deal of local interest and expectation with embarkation space already booked for the 2004 Formula 1 Grand Prix.

Because of restricted site space in Port of Monaco, the prefabrication of the floating dock by Grupo Dragados, together with the Spanish Builder FCC and the French builder BEC, took place in the south basin of the Crinavis dockyard in the Port of Algeciras in Southern Spain, which has easy access to the open ocean.

On completion of the dock, Drace Grupo — Dragados' marine subsidiary — will flood the basin to float the dock and then make the dock ready for sea. The dock will be towed using powerful tugs from the Port of Algeciras to the Port of Monaco, a journey scheduled to take 12 days at 3 knots per hour.

On arrival in Monaco, the dock will be anchored to the ground through a 350 tonne metallic ball-and-socket joint manufactured in the facilities of the French Nuclear Company. The movement of the dock will be restricted by a series of metal chains tied to posts anchored in the seabed. The turns applied on the ball joint will minimize movement caused by the waves, hence the dock will remain stable.

The dock is expected to last for at least 100 years according to the design and the quality of the concrete and steel used for construction. It will be fully equipped to moor 200 m cruise ships and will have parking space for 400 vehicles and a store for sporting boats on four levels. The superstructure will comprise new offices for the port authority, shops, walkways and roads. The dock is expected to transform Monaco's leisure activities and it will have a lighthouse restaurant on the north side.

Author's commentary

Monaco's new floating dock is a good example of innovative civil and marine engineering to solve a difficult congestion problem in the Port of Monaco. The Crinvais dockyard provided the ideal location for Dragados and its partners to fabricate the dock and make it ready for transportation by sea. This solution means that the on-site construction time is considerably reduced, with minimum disruption to the busy and prosperous Port of Monaco.

Case study 11.3: Carquinez bridge, Crockett, California, USA, HBG

HBG Flatiron, Inc. is the managing partner in a joint venture including two sister companies, FCI Constructors, Inc. Northern Division and Interbeton, Inc., to construct a new suspension bridge across the Carquinez Strait navigation channels. The new bridge, costing US$ 189 million, will be the third bridge on the site replacing the existing bridge constructed in 1927 and will provide for westbound traffic on the Interstate 80. The bridge is scheduled for completion in mid-2003.The existing bridge carrying eastbound traffic will be seismically retrofitted.

The bridge has three spans comprising a total of 3465 feet and will be the first major suspension bridge in the USA for 35 years. The Carquinez bridge features two 400 ft high concrete towers founded on driven piles comprising 12 foundation piles, 3 m in diameter by 51 m long, with an additional 42 m rock socket.

The superstructure comprises a steel orthotropic deck section fabricated in Japan and shipped in three ocean-going barges. The bridge sections of up to 50 m long will be jacked into place off the bridge main suspension cables. The new 82 m wide deck will accommodate four vehicle lanes, a bicycle/pedestrian lane and wide shoulders.

The contracted time to complete the project is 1200 working days, with every day a working day, equating to 3 years and 15 weeks.

Author's commentary

HBG Flatiron won the high profile Carquinez Bridge project in the face of fierce international competition. The project schedule is tight and requires a high level of project management expertise to achieve the targets laid down.

Case study 11.4: Channel Tunnel rail link, United Kingdom, Bechtel

The project comprises the construction of a new high-speed rail line between London and the Channel Tunnel that links the UK with existing high-speed tracks in France and Belgium. The link is being constructed in two phases, primarily because of the high cost associated with acquiring land and the archaeologically and environmentally sensitive nature of the project, which passes through some of the most beautiful countryside in the UK and the densely populated suburbs of South-East London.

Bechtel is a joint-venture partner with Rail Link Engineering (RLE), responsible for design and construction of the link, and is also a shareholder in London and Continental Railways (LCR), the original owner. It therefore plays an integral role in the US$ 7.8 billion project, which is one of Europe's largest construction projects.

A major challenge has been the creation of a single identity for RLE, which was formed in 1996 and was staffed with more than 900 personnel from Bechtel and its three joint venture partners: Arup, Halcrow and Systra. The RLE management group had to work hard to create the necessary infrastructure to establish an effective collaborative team that could cope with the political and environmental sensitivities of the project as well as the technicalities.

The construction of Phase 1, which joins existing rail lines at Fawkham junction, is scheduled for completion in 2003. The link provides a route through the market town of Ashford and passes under Blue Bell Hill by a specially constructed tunnel before crossing the River Medway by means of a reinforced concrete multi-span bridge adjacent to the existing road bridge.

Phase 2 extends from North Kent under the River Thames and through Stratford in East London to St Pancras station in Kings Cross, Central London. New stations will be constructed at Ebbsfleet in North Kent and at Stratford, which is already an established transport hub for East London. St Pancras station, which features Victorian architecture, will be extensively rebuilt and enlarged into a new international rail terminal that is linked to London Underground and the UK's domestic rail network.

The introduction of the new link is expected to dramatically increase the number of international rail travellers and will provide fast commuter services from Kent into London.

Author's commentary

The cost of this project has been high due to the need to accommodate heritage, environmental and archaeological conservation. The rail route largely avoids sensitive habitat by following the existing transport corridors created by the M20 and M2/A2 motorways. However, it has been necessary to clear woodland and grassland along the 109 km route.

The project's environmental programme is a great credit to RLE and LCR compensated with new woodland and grassland. In addition, special attention has been paid to acoustic and visual barriers as well as accommodating the needs of flora and fauna, which will ultimately also benefit from the project.

Summary

Project management strategy applied to international construction implies a close relationship with the client who should be fully engaged throughout the process. The unique nature of projects and the integration of the construction supply chain means that professional management and treatment of people are key factors that identify project management as a dynamic function demanding an innate ability to cope with change. Construction project managers must be highly skilled and motivated and their contribution is crucial to successful project outcomes. It is therefore essential to attract and recruit adequately qualified and experienced project managers, or those individuals with the ability to develop in the role given training and experience.

The autonomy and degree of responsibility of the project manager will depend on corporate policy and the extent to which support is provided from available corporate infrastructure, either provided locally or on an international scale. Managers of larger projects are more likely to have greater responsibility and this will certainly be the case in joint venture projects. Joint venture project managers have the added responsibility of coordinating and controlling inputs from stakeholder partners and, in certain situations, acting as a mediator.

The relationship between corporate systems and systems developed specifically for the control of the project will need to be harmoniously integrated to ensure seamless control without the generation of gaps in responsibility. Further, the adoption of a project matrix structure implies the necessity for leadership, teamwork and communication between all concerned with the delivery of the project.

Effective project mobilization is highly dependent on the performance of the design team and the provision of drawings, specifications and schedules on which the procurement of the necessary resources can be based. There will also need to be close liaison between the design and construction teams and the supply chain.

The case studies demonstrate the importance of effective control systems utilizing project management software and the communication of information by means of the Internet. Technology has facilitated much improved communication, both corporately and between the members of the project team but there is considerable scope for further development. Other management techniques with potential to further improve efficiency and productivity of construction projects include cellular technology, total quality management, JIT and zero defects.

Safety is a major priority for international construction companies who seek to ensure the well-being of all those working on projects and the security of the general public. Construction is inherently dangerous and therefore requires constant effort, monitoring and action to reduce accidents. Clients also expect to be provided with safe buildings which, in addition, provide for healthy and comfortable living and working environments.

The twenty-first century will see the continuing need for major worldwide infrastructure and building projects that are sympathetic to sustainability and conservation issues. The emphasis will be on ongoing development in the construction project management process brought about by continuing advances in global networks, alliances and advances in construction technology. The final chapter attempts to explore future horizons for the global construction industry.

Further reading

Akintola A. (2001), 'Just-in-time application and implementation for building material management', *Construction Management and Economics*, **13**, Issue 2, E & F. N. Spon.

Bechtel home page (on-line www.bechtel.com).

Bennett J. (1995), *International construction project management: general theory and practice*, Butterworth/Heinemann.

Codling S. (1998), *Benchmarking,* Gower, Aldershot.

Cornick T. and Mather J. (1999), *Construction project teams: making them work properly*, Thomas Telford, London.

Grupo Dragados SA home page (on-line www.dragados.com).

Halman J. I. M.and Burger G. T. N. (2002), 'Evaluating the effectiveness of project start ups: an explanatory study', *Int. J. Project Management*, **20**, Issue 1, 81–89.

HBG home page (on-line www.hbg.nl).

Lampel J. (2001), *Towards a holistic approach to strategic project management*, **19**, Issue 8, 433–435.

Lockyer K. & Gordon J. (1991), *Critical path analysis*, 5th edition, Pitman, London.

Neale R. H. (1995), *Managing international construction projects: an overview*, ILO.

Van Der Merwe (2002), 'Project management and business development: integrating structure process and products', *Int. J. Project Management*, **20**, Issue 5, 401–411.

White D. and Fortune J. (2002), 'Current practice in project management', *Int. J. Project Management*, **20**, Issue 1, 1–11.

Chapter 12

Future horizons

Introduction

The physical dimension of the business world, and particularly that applicable to construction, has been made much smaller by two major developments over the past twenty-five years. The first has been the development of the Internet, which has transformed global communication concerning all aspects of life and business. The Internet is arguably the single most important technological development that has and will continue to influence the social, economic, political and cultural nature of the world. The second development concerns the rapid expansion of air travel and the dramatic reduction of the cost in real terms, which enables businessmen to travel to anywhere in the world using regular scheduled services at short notice.

The advent of containerization and the development of port facilities, together with more efficient ships and the introduction of integrated transport systems have increased the feasibility and mobility of materials and products, thus increasing choice available to customers. These developments have manifested themselves in the global construction industry by providing clients and construction teams with the option of importing the best and most suitable materials, components and fabrications from anywhere in the world. The extra cost of transportation may be justified by long-term life cycle advantages, or simply by the value attached to reputation and aesthetics.

The political and economic map of the world has also changed. The collapse of the USSR and the emancipation of the former communist block countries marked the end of the 'cold war'. This has led to the commencement of a process to integrate these countries into the free world economy and commercial markets. The consolidation of the European Union (EU) and the introduction of the Euro have been major developments in the unification of Europe, which are continuing with expansion to include many of the former communist countries such as Hungary, Poland and the Czech Republic. The emergence of Asia as a regional force and the potential of the Chinese market are examples of the development and change that has taken place and will continue to occur in future. The growing influence of the Association of South-East Asian nations

(ASEAN) represents another important regional trading block in Asia. The introduction of the North Atlantic Free Trade Area (NAFTA) involving USA, Canada and Mexico is a further example of a major trading block. The so-called 'triad' represented by the EU, NAFTA and the Asian countries including Japan and China is set to dominate world trade in the foreseeable future. However, this presents a problem that must be addressed regarding those continents and sub-continents outside of these trading blocks. Africa, the Indian sub-continent and South America present special problems associated with economic robustness, poverty and their ability to keep up with development. Although China is one of the world's largest economies, it is weighed down by its huge population of 1.25 billion people, which manifests itself in widespread poverty, especially among its rural population.

World governments have become increasingly aware of scientific evidence regarding the depletion of natural resources such as oil, fossil fuels, timber, ores and aggregates. The reduction in forests brought about by urban and agricultural development and the emission of greenhouse gases, it is argued, will cause global warming resulting in dramatic climate changes, the melting of the polar ice caps, increased levels of ultraviolet radiation and a long-term increase in sea levels. Awareness has also increased of the amount of natural resources that are wasted and consigned to landfill. A unified 'world order' concerning conservation and the protection of the world's environment is still to be agreed, although there are tentative, but promising developments such as the system of carbon credits.

Within the context of this introduction, the final chapter attempts to address the prime movers for change and tries to make some prognostication about the future shape and development of the global construction industry.

Extrapolation of global construction business strategies and concepts

The ability to compete with the best will, arguably, continue to be the most important strategic aim for global construction companies. This will necessitate being at the centre of key markets and will require continuing improvements in client service, product quality and prices. Market intelligence to establish change and developments in customer needs, alongside perceptive anticipation of market trends, and the creation of new demand for products and services will continue to be one of the cornerstones of success.

The case studies cited in previous chapters have demonstrated the importance of developing centres of excellence strategically located around the world according to the proximity of markets and the availability of resources and expertise. These may be geared to a worldwide market, or they may be restricted in scope to cater specifically for regional tastes and requirements. There is also a perceptible trend in the development of closer relationships and strategic alliances upstream with clients, on the same level as partners and downstream with the supply chain.

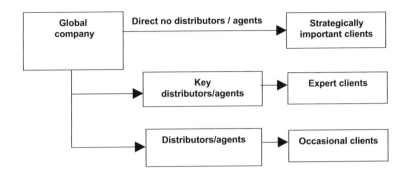

Figure 12.1: Developing client–customer relationships

Important clients are singled out for special treatment geared to winning repeat business. It is worth noting that organizations such as Bovis Lend Lease, Skanska and AMEC openly state that their aim is to exceed client expectations and emphasize tangible and recognizable value added to a client's business by the supply of built facilities, infrastructure and services.

The prime aim in all cases is to win repeat business and to develop closer relationships and understanding with clients to help to sustain and develop competitive advantage that is difficult for the competition to break down. Where distributors and agents are concerned, who are more likely to be involved with material, product and equipment suppliers, there is also some evidence of differentiating between key distributors and those that may have multi-distributorships (Figure 12.1).

The development of global business networks will continue to be an important aspect of strategic business development. With the global spread of major construction companies brought about by expansion, merger and acquisition, greater emphasis will be placed on ensuring the efficiency of corporate intranets and their role in accurately and instantly communicating relevant information throughout organizations. Evidence from the case studies indicates that most global construction companies wish to provide their subsidiaries with as much autonomy and empowerment as possible to deal effectively with local conditions and circumstances. However, it is important that adequate corporate control is maintained to protect the shape of the organization and its chosen strategic direction. There is also the issue of brand image and the importance of identifying the values of the corporation. Lafarge (case study 4.2) provided an example in the 'Lafarge Way' together with its set of cross-cutting 'Principle Actions'.

Network arrangements and strategic alliances between international partners by means of joint ventures, technology transfers and market-sharing arrangements are in a continual state of development and the global construction industry will continue to add levels of sophistication to the adoption of such approaches. There will also be the potential to develop interesting future relationships with national, provincial and local governments who are becoming more interested in private financing of public facilities and services. Scope will also exist to develop closer associations with bodies that can contribute to competitive advantage through their activities, e.g. trade unions, universities, research institutes and trade associations.

Political and economic influences comprise a significant part of coping with the changing global business environment. There is major concern about protectionism and trade restrictions that prevent the development of free trade. This is dealt with in Chapter three where attention in the WTO case study (3.1) has centred on the plight of LDCs and their future ability to attract adequate direct foreign investment to underwrite the effort to reduce poverty and improve living conditions.

Global construction companies continue to play an important part in the delivery of infrastructure projects in LDCs, funded through the World Bank and other development agencies. Nevertheless, the only major solution to the creation of real long-term prosperity is by means of direct foreign investment. Key to this is political and social stability linked to education that will encourage investment in manufacturing facilities to take advantage of potentially lower labour costs.

The growing global trend towards privatization will continue to offer new opportunities to global construction companies. There will be a trend towards providing new facilities and services, resulting from the growing awareness of the need to protect the Earth's environment and to reduce waste and conserve finite natural resources used in the construction of buildings and infrastructure. Growing competitiveness by the adoption new technologies and the continuing viable development of existing technologies will be important to the long-term success and ultimate survival of existing global construction businesses. Not least in this process will be the role that the Internet will play in the development of global competition and the commercial and economic advantages that it presents by its ability to provide instant information, communication and dynamic business interaction.

Human resource considerations in the twenty-first century

During the twentieth century there were major changes in the way that people were valued and treated. At the start of the century, people were considered as a resource to be hired, controlled and fired according to overriding and paramount business needs. In the first half of the century, the authoritarian approach to management was dominant and employees were given orders, which were expected to be obeyed without question or comment. As the twentieth century progressed, this paradigm was increasingly subjected to questioning, especially in AICs where better levels of education and advances in technology provided individuals with the expertise and 'know-how' to challenge convention. Moreover, developments in society and social policy increasingly recognized the importance and rights of the individual. The result is now a more widely accepted socially responsible approach to management and leadership that accommodates the requirements of business, but at the same time supports the development of the individual and recognizes civil rights issues. This, of course, does not apply universally throughout the world and there is still a significant proportion of the world's population that do not enjoy the same working conditions, civil rights, freedom of speech and social welfare as those that exist in free western societies. It is encouraging that some progress is being made and the expectation is that this will continue throughout the twenty-first century. The role of strategic leadership encapsulates the following leadership practices:

- focus should be on the process leading to the outcome;
- confidence should be measured and expressed in objective terms;
- knowledge should be acquired and leveraged;
- the enthusiasm, innovation and creativity of individuals should be nurtured;
- work flows should be influenced by value and relationships;
- the importance of integrity is demonstrated by actions;
- respect should be earned and not demanded;
- diversity of action and function should be sought;
- emphasis should be on the leadership and achievement of the group, rather than the individual;
- employees should be viewed as organizational citizens who comprise a critical resource that requires significant investment, and
- operation should be primarily through a global mindset.

During the twenty-first century it is expected that there will be significant demographic changes and trends that will affect the nature and composition of the global workforce. AICs have the lowest workforce growth rates, that are in danger of falling to zero growth, or into decline as is the case in Germany. This situation will encourage the importation of immigrant expertise to make up the shortfall and the development of mechanization to reduce the need for unskilled and semi-skilled labour. NICs will continue to experience higher workforce growth rates, with China, Turkey and Mexico leading the pack. In general, women will continue to join the workforce in increasing numbers. This is a significant phenomena, in that it has been argued that women will not be giving birth to so many babies with consequential long-term demographic effects. Because of developments in medical science the world's average human longevity is increasing and it is suggested that people will live significantly longer and will have longer working lives. Therefore, in AICs the combination of a falling birth rate and greater longevity will mean that the average age of the workforce will increase.

Virtually all governments throughout the world have recognized the importance of good primary and secondary education, followed by a robust tertiary education system that is capable of producing graduates with the necessary knowledge and skills to take up roles as professional engineers, scientists, economists, accountants and managers. AICs and NICs have taken positive steps to increase participation in higher education and to promote courses that support technological, scientific and commercial advancement in pursuit of increased prosperity and living standards. Similarly, LDCs have increased the number of indigenous universities geared to producing graduates.

Cultural differences and their effect on business strategies are important to global success and it should be appreciated that what might work in a local or regional market does not necessarily translate elsewhere. Therefore it will be necessary for a number of steps to be taken to modify strategies, or to abandon them completely in favour of new approaches that fully address cultural needs. It should also be appreciated that cultures are not static, since they are in a constant state of change and development, especially in aspects related to social trends and the nature of work ethics and values.

The assignment of company employees to global roles is an important consideration. Case study 7.1 illustrates the significance that Skanska attaches to proper training and preparing its personnel to undertake overseas project assignments. This can also be enhanced by the adoption of valid and reliable screening methods to ensure that the right personnel are selected for individual assignments at any level within an organization.

Sustainability and conservation

There is a growing awareness that projected increasing rates of consumption of the Earth's non-replaceable resources will eventually cause them to run out one by one with potentially disastrous consequences. Hence, sustainability and conservation are crucial factors that will influence all businesses, and especially that of construction, in the twenty-first century. Sustainability is more than simply making energy savings; it also includes reducing environmental pollution and the conservation of natural resources. Currently, there is room for considerable improvement and the 'circle of blame' shown in Figure 12.2. illustrates the difficulties that conservationists are currently facing.

Significant gains can be made to improve sustainable lifetime performance of new buildings by utilizing effective designs consisting of appropriate materials. There is evidence to support this case by citing the achievement of high added value for relatively little additional effort.

Construction has a considerable appetite for the consumption of non-replaceable natural resources. It consumes 40% of the total world usage of sand, aggregate, clay and iron ore, 25% of virgin wood use, and 40% of energy use and water withdrawals. Construction also contributes significantly to the total amount of waste generated, typically in the region of 15–20%.

Construction is also a great consumer of rural land caused by the need to expand urban areas to meet the demand for economic growth. The consumption of the countryside and the destruction of trees that consume carbon and generate oxygen must be checked. One way of achieving this is by clearing derelict urban sites and making better use of brownfield sites for new development. Improvements in the efficiency of resource utilization have a direct bearing on slowing the degradation of the landscape, toxic run-off, loss of biodiversity, global warming and improving air pollution.

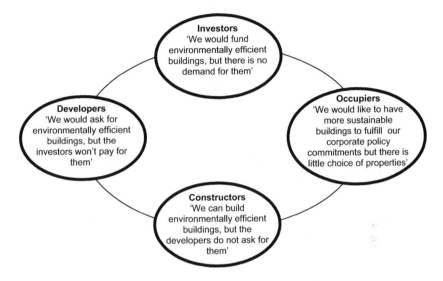

Figure 12.2: The circle of blame
Source: *Towards sustainability — a strategy for the construction industry*

There are indications that the amount of waste being consigned to landfill is getting out of hand and this is a major symptom of waste generated by a throw-away culture. More attention is required in the design of products and fabrications to allow for the economic recovery and recycling of waste.

The International Panel on Climate Change has shown that the twentieth century was the warmest since records began and the 1990s was the warmest decade. It is also significant that 1998 had the warmest average annual temperature. Carbon dioxide in the atmosphere is 51% higher than in 1750 and average global temperatures are expected to increase by 1.4–5.8°C in the next century. The Kyoto Protocol targeted a reduction in greenhouse gases by 12.5% against 1990 levels by 2008–2012. It is predicted that emissions will need to be reduced by over 60% before 2050 if climate change is to be controlled. Of course, evidence of this sort cannot be conclusive, since opponents will argue that the Earth's climate has always been subject to variation as a natural phenomena. However, the collective weight of scientific evidence suggests that global warming is taking place and that prevention is better than cure. The climate change levy introduced in April 2001 places a tax on carbon emissions and this is expected to increase energy bills by 10–15%, but these are avoidable if precautionary measures are taken. Hence, clients will be interested in solutions and new building designs that have low energy consumption and contribute to the sustainability of non-replaceable resources. Buildings using energy generated from renewable sources will be exempt from tax. In this regard, the two solutions given most publicity are wind power and the use of photovoltaic cells. However, there are other promising developments, i.e. hydrogen, advanced electric batteries. There are, of course, other traditional methods such as hydroelectric power and secondary energy generation from power stations and the incineration of non-reusable waste. The EU is planning to improve energy efficiency of new buildings by 22% by 2010.

If climate change occurs as predicted, this will bring higher UV levels, hotter summers and the likelihood of climatic disruption in the form of storms and high winds. Buildings will require the ability to withstand damage caused by extreme conditions and there are fears regarding dry summers causing subsidence in clay soils and damage caused by UV to plastic windows and cladding. Hence, part of the sustainability argument relates to safe, robust buildings that can provide a quality internal environment that does not foster disease and promotes healthy living.

It may, therefore, be concluded that there are benefits to be derived from adopting a sustainable approach. The strategic benefits relate to positioning a company to cope with sustainability issues by incorporating principles within products and services to reduce risk. The operational benefits concern increased efficiency and cost reduction and the revenue benefits derived from being more attractive to clients by helping them to achieve their good environmental management policies and practices.

Emerging issues

The events of 11 September 2001 have had a profound effect on raising perception concerning the vulnerability of infrastructure. This includes whole cities as well as airports, dams, power stations, reservoirs, public buildings, roads, railways and waterways. The attacks on the World Trade Centre in New York graphically illustrated to the public that the unthinkable is not the fictional subject depicted by Hollywood movies; it can actually happen. The terrorist attacks, combined with the growing awareness of global warming and the apparent increasing regularity of natural disasters such as earthquakes, flooding, tornados and storm damage have made the world's population uneasy and less secure in their living environment.

Issues and concerns relate to how the owners of infrastructure can best make investments to reduce infrastructure vulnerability to natural hazards, climatic change and terrorist attacks. In the case of new facilities, this will principally concern design issues, but in the case of existing buildings what retrofitting will be necessary?

Initial consideration has revealed that there must be a holistic and integrated approach, since cities act as systems where one part directly impacts on another and therefore 'cause and effect' is a paramount factor. This raises the need for new concepts in areas such as systems analysis, intelligent infrastructure and specific technologies such as strengthening foundations, building envelopes, improved fire resistance and barriers to contain damage. This, in turn, will impact on thinking throughout the global construction industry.

The twenty-first century will present unprecedented change and challenge for the global construction industry. There are emerging key issues, together with those that are already in a state of development. These will need to be addressed in terms of how they impact on the role of the global construction industry and the service that it provides to its clients and national societies and economies.

Some of the key issues are identified below:

- climate change and global warning;
- sustainability and waste reduction;
- security and safety;
- integrated transport systems and reductions in traffic congestion;
- impact of new developments in communication and information technology;
- demands created by cultural and demographic changes;
- the need to reduce poverty and improve living standards in LDCs.

The twenty-first century will present greater business opportunities, but these are likely to involve more complex and all-embracing solutions to more difficult problems. This implies the need for greater expertise and further technological development if real progress is to be made. It is therefore likely that solutions will be found in technology and science, customer-centric thinking, e-commerce and aspects related to integrated supply chains. There will also need to be a shift in practices and attitude and constant re-appraisal of improving delivery quality standards. The outcome will be assessed in terms of value added to better working conditions, improved living standards, lower construction costs and more effective sustainability. Achievement of these ideals will require an integrated approach that is based on joined up thinking relating to:

- promotion of new technologies to provide intelligent monitoring and control systems for buildings;
- efficiency and competitiveness;
- adoption of sustainable solutions based on whole life cycle principles;
- maintenance of built facilities by retrofitting, conserving heritage and replacement;
- investment in people, including personal development, better management and attention to safety, health and welfare;
- progressive introduction of automation, especially for heavy workloads and hazardous situations;
- improved project management and risk assessment;
- long-term strategic thinking and planning and
- improved return of investment.

Figure 12.3 provides an illustration of the scope for improved futures performance.

Future developments will be mainly technology-driven through creative thought and innovation requiring investment in research knowledge generation, linked closely to research and development.

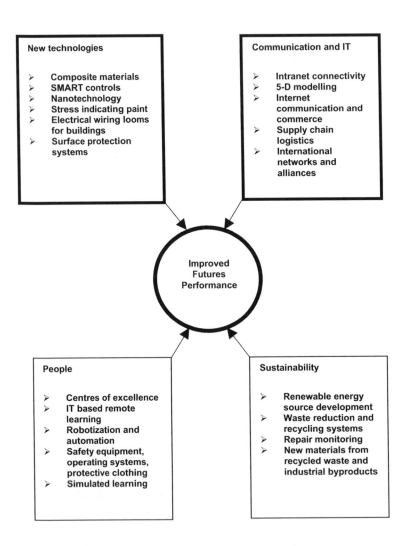

Figure 12.3: Improved futures performance

Developments in innovation and research

Because of the diverse nature of the global construction industry and the fact that it involves many interrelated areas and disciplines it is important to understand the applicability and relevance of innovation and research. It is also essential to understand the relationship and difference between innovation and research.

Innovation is about the creation of new ideas and thinking that can be applied in one form or another to provide a solution to a problem. It may be the direct result of creativity or it could be developed from the outcome of a defined programme of research. Hence, there is not necessarily an intrinsic link between innovation and research in the sense that one must always lead from the other. Relevant research and development (R&D) applicable to the global construction industry can be classically divided into two main categories as shown in Figure 12.4.

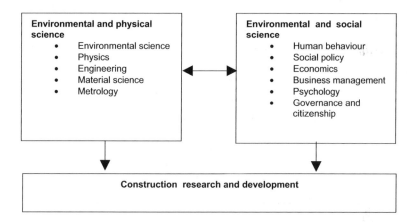

Figure 12.4: Categories of construction research and development

On one hand are the hard sciences typified by physics and engineering and on the other are the soft sciences concerned with human behaviour. The difficulty for construction R&D is that in many instances both areas will need to be addressed to provide a feasible solution.

The applicability of innovation and research and its importance depends on individual construction disciplines and the contribution that they make to the creation of the built environment. Figure 12.5 shows the relevant areas of research interest for each of the major construction disciplines and indicates the relative importance to competitive advantage. Clearly, those disciplines with design and product development responsibility must attach greater importance to innovation, research and development in order to maintain market position by differentiating their product or service from competitors. It may also be stated that construction is not at the forefront of global research but it quickly becomes a beneficiary of R&D from other areas such as information and computer technology.

To meet the needs of global clients and governments it is important to identify themes and key drivers that provide direction and prioritization of innovation and research.

From evidence collected it is postulated that the following broad themes, suitably broken down into elements, will provide the direction of R&D for at least the first ten years of the twenty-first century:

- sustainability and conservation of the environment;
- environmental protection and safety;
- development of new technology;
- people;
- communication and interconnectivity.

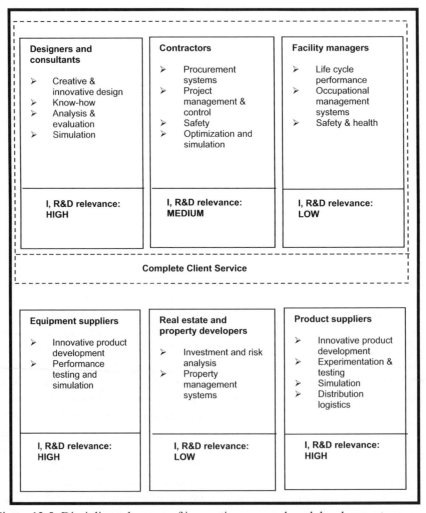

Figure 12.5: Discipline relevance of innovation, research and development

The SWOT analysis shown in Figure 12.6 provides an assessment of the potential and actions that need to be addressed by the global construction industry in order to address the above themes.

Strengths	Weaknesses
➢ Necessity ➢ Establish global industry ➢ Strong consultancy base ➢ Areas of strength	➢ Diverse research base which is broad but not deep ➢ Low connectivity ➢ R&D budget relatively small ➢ Lacks multidisciplinary research ➢ Life cycle efficiency and sustainability requires improvement
Opportunities	**Threats**
➢ International political harmony ➢ Development of private–public partnerships ➢ Growing environment sector & climate change ➢ Sustainability ➢ Increased connectivity, networking and alliancing	➢ Economic cycles ➢ Inadequate knowledge base and a lack of skilled personnel ➢ High risk and change ➢ Low profitability

Figure 12.6: SWOT analysis of global innovation and research and development

To deliver relevant innovation and research it will be important to maintain a robust framework that is capable of identifying the practical areas where research should be applied and who is going to carry it out. Research providers include universities, research agencies, trade associations and professional bodies. Normally, universities and research agencies will be funded by means of a combination of government and private funding. Public funds will be allocated in accordance with identified priority areas and calls for bids from applicants. Applications will be judged on merit and track record. Private funds will usually be on a consultancy basis, or by means of public sector initiatives involving matched funding. It is anticipated that, broadly speaking, these arrangements will continue for the foreseeable future.

There is a need to improve the communication and connectivity between industry and universities to increase the relevance and value added contributed by innovation and research to meet future needs of clients and society at large (Fairclough, 2002). By involving industry in research from the start it is more likely that the effort and cost of development will be forthcoming to bring initial research to the reality of useful practical application.

Infrastructure & the environment	Transport	Airports Rail Roads Freight logistics
	Energy	Electricity Oil Gas
	Environment	Climate change Urban & rural land use Multidisciplinary challenges
Construction & the environment	Construction	Procurement Design, quality & safety Construction management
	Water	Water supply Sewerage & treatment Coastal defences & waterways
	Environment	Waste management Contaminated land Remediation Air pollution
Manufacturing	Process	Product design & materials development Methods, automation & robotics Technology transfer

CROSS-CUTTING EXPERTISE
Architecture, interior design and landscape architecture Engineering: Civil & structural, geotechnical, mechanical, electrical and production Information Management & Technology Physical and Environmental Science Economic, Social Science, Management and Finance

Figure 12.7: Global construction industry innovation, research and development framework

Research undertaken by trade associations and professional bodies will be supported by members. In the latter case the amount of funding is likely to be low; however, the potential exists for pump priming valuable initiatives.

To provide a basis for funding construction research, there should be in place an accepted and recognized framework, which relates to the research themes and priorities adopted. Figure 12.7 provides an illustration of such a framework that provides the basis for managing the allocation of funds and the monitoring of progress. Typically, on completion a research project should be evaluated in terms of stated research objectives and the quality of the outcome.

The intellectual ownership of research is a vital and sometimes contentious issue. Where collaboration occurs between different parties it is important to establish a written and legally binding agreement about intellectual property rights (IPR), irrespective of who is providing the funds. Therefore, it is advisable to employ the services of reputable legal experts, especially where the research is likely to result in major commercial advantage and wealth creation. It may also be advisable to register new developments, inventions and innovations that have the potential to be developed into an international patent using the services of a patent attorney. As the global construction industry becomes more competitive and the quest for competitive advantage becomes more important, it will be commensurately vital to seek out new ideas and knowledge capable of being developed to provide real value added for clients and the efficiency of the construction process. Those organizations that invest in innovation and research will be at an advantage if they are able to exploit it in the advancement of business interests. However, this implies that there will be no dissemination for the benefit of society at large, other than brief details being made available for publicity and promotional purposes.

Academics are judged individually by their respective universities on the quality of publication and review by peers. This raises a potential conflict of interest where a collaborating industrial partner might ask for research findings not to be placed in the public domain for commercial reasons, hence there must be a clear understanding and agreement from the outset. There is also the general expectation that where public funds are made available for research, then as a rule results will be published for the benefit of all concerned.

In the foreseeable future it is anticipated that the governments of economically strong nations will continue to fund research through universities and national research institutes and agencies. A prerequisite for the approval of such funding will be that it is in the public interest. There is also growing popularity for matched funding where a government will fund industrially based research provided that a competent research team with a proven track record is involved and industrial parties put up 50% of the necessary funding. This type of research is intended to improve efficiency and promote competitive advantage, especially in the international market-place. In future, most governments will expect industry to increasingly support industrially based research from profits or borrowing. Under these circumstances, companies will need to be convinced of favourable chances of return given the level of risk involved.

Summary

Competitiveness among the leading players in the global construction industry is set to increase. The organizations featured in the case studies, together with others not included, are already operating global strategies, geared to expansion of core business and the acquisition of subsidiary companies to increase diversity and provide a broader business base.

In addition to operating globally, businesses are also being developed regionally to meet local needs and to take advantage of local strengths such as the cost of labour and the availability of raw materials. Mergers and joint ventures feature strongly in expansion into new markets. They also provide opportunities for the provision of expertise and financial strength to take on large projects that would otherwise be out of range. There is a growing trend in global alliances and the acquisition of successful national and regional companies to strengthen the global company's operating portfolio. Indications are that global business is becoming more connected and interactive in meeting corporate goals, which in turn are becoming more demanding. The growing awareness of the importance of sustainability and the conservation of the environment and protection of the world's climate will require an increasingly sophisticated technological approach. Those organizations that are willing and able to invest in and developing their knowledge, expertise and capacity will be most likely to succeed. This does raise the problem of the large number of smaller construction organizations throughout the world that have low profits and limited capacity to invest. This is a serious issue, especially for those construction based organizations that operate in NICs and LDCs.

Given the importance of the built and natural environment to all nations within the world, there does need to be a concerted effort on the part of national governments to encourage the broader development of the global construction industry to improve performance so that the challenges of the twenty-first century may be fulfilled.

Further reading

Building Centre Trust (2001), *Annual review*, Building Centre Trust, London.
Corso M. (2002), 'From product development to continuous product innovation: mapping routes and knowledge', *Int. J. Technology Management*, **23**, No. 4.
Executive Program (2001), *Designing and managing vulnerability*, CERF/IIEC, Washington, DC.
Fairclough J. (2002), *Rethinking construction research and innovation*, DTI, London.
Foresight (2001), *Constructing the future*, Department of Trade and Industry, UK.
IMF (2002), *International monetary fund world economic outlook* (on-line www.imf.org).
Sustainable Construction Task Group (2001), *Reputation risk and reward*, Centre for Sustainable Construction, BRE Watford, UK.

Index

Note: Page numbers in *italics* refer to figures

Index compiled by Indexing Specialists (UK) Ltd: www.indexing.co.uk